SHIFTING GEARS

SHIFTING GEARS

THRIVING IN THE NEW ECONOMY

Nuala Beck

HarperCollins*PublishersLtd*

The author wishes to gratefully acknowledge the assistance of Brian Milner in the writing of this book.

First Edition

Canadian Cataloguing in Publication Data

Beck, Nuala, 1951-
    Shifting gears : thriving in the new economy

ISBN 0-00-215785-3

1. Corporate planning. 2. Technological forecasting. I. Title.

HD30.28.B43 1992   658.4'012   C92-093931-7

---

93 94 95 96 97 98 99 ❖ RRD 10 9 8 7 6 5

To Frank, whom I had the good sense to fall in love with and marry eighteen years ago, and to my mother and father who gave me so much — including the courage to question.

CONTENTS

TABLES AND CHARTS

ACKNOWLEDGMENTS

Writing this book has evoked many fond memories — and created many new ones, chief among them the long hours that I spent with Brian Milner, without whose exceptional talent (and perennial good humor) this book would not have been possible. Through Brian, I have gained an awesome respect for the craft of writing. In addition to my gratitude, he also has my promise that I will never abuse subordinate clauses again so long as I live. I also wish to thank Brian's wife, Sylvie, and baby Katrina for their generous donation of Brian's time.

The early research for this book goes back many years to a research project entitled "Sunrise Statistics," which my consulting firm undertook for M. K. Wong & Associates Inc. of Vancouver. To Milt Wong, a dear friend and mentor, I owe my deepest debt of gratitude. His boundless enthusiasm, his vision and his integrity have been important beacons that have guided me, personally and professionally, through my career.

I also owe my thanks to Tony Boeckh at the Bank Credit Analyst who gave me my first job as a young and incredibly naive economist. His brilliance has inspired me to this day. Victor

SHIFTING
GEARS

THRIVING
IN THE
NEW
ECONOMY

Koloshuk and John Bennett, who hired me at McLeod Young Weir, taught me that the harder I worked, the luckier I would get. I will forever be grateful for their guidance and friendship. I also have a special place in my heart for Frank Ricciuti, the best research manager and boss an economist could ever have. His integrity in research and superb management skills, and above all his kindness, will always be remembered.

Since founding Nuala Beck & Associates Inc. in 1984 I have learned many things. No consulting firm can attain success and recognition without the dedication of a talented team. Barbara Jones and Anne-Marie Richter have been the embodiment of dedication, loyalty and friendship. It remains one of my life's greatest pleasures to work with them. I also have special memories of the early years of this research working with Jay Myers, whose keen intellect and many kindnesses will be remembered always.

As the publishing deadline for this book drew near, Anne-Marie's incredible organizational and research skills were once again displayed as she marshalled her worthy team — Joe Connolly, Margaret Moores and Derrick Reisky — into action, updating every number in this book. My sincere thanks to Stan MacLellan for his vast experience and wisdom and for making invaluable suggestions every step of the way. My thanks as well to Rosemary Serel for her characteristic efficiency in assisting me with the sundry tasks that this project has entailed.

Catherine Dowling receives my warm thanks, not only for her research and fact-checking skills, but for her tireless efforts until just hours before her son was born.

Many thanks also to Bruce Little at *The Globe and Mail* who, in the summer of 1991, officially "unveiled" my firm's research on "The New Economy" in a full-page feature article. Twelve months later we are still receiving telephone calls concerning his article.

One of the earliest calls I received from Iris Skeoch at Harper-Collins will forever stand out in my memory. Sometimes first impressions are the most accurate, and her genuine warmth and unparalleled professionalism aptly describe the corporate culture at HarperCollins. A special thanks as well to Tom Best, Gary Weigl and Judy Brunsek for their constant good humor and enthusiastic support for this book.

And finally, I owe thanks to my husband Frank, who has suffered through countless cold dinners with characteristic good humor. His support, encouragement and sense of perspective have meant more to me than words can ever say.

And to my family, whom I have neglected — especially my mother and father and dearest Aunt Frances, who went for weeks on end without so much as a phone call — I dedicate Chapter Nine of this book with profound gratitude for a lifetime of common sense so generously shared.

The final chapter of this book is dedicated with love to Liam, Chris, Ellen, Carrie, Tim, Lisa, and Jamie. Set out in hope to climb the highest peaks and fortune will smile on all you mean to do — the future belongs to you.

Nuala Beck
Toronto, Canada
September 1992

INTRODUCTION

With the century drawing to a close, apocalyptic visions are again dancing in people's heads. You hear it on the street and read it in the news headlines and best-selling economic scare books: "The economy is doomed. This recession will never end. It's a depression that will make the Dirty Thirties seem like good times by comparison. Millions of people will never work again!"

Instead of religious leaders warning us to prepare to meet our fate, we have economists, columnists and talk-show hosts using these difficult times to preach a message of doom and despair. These seekers after darkness show up in every period of great change, but historically they have found their best audiences at the turn of the centuries, when people expected — and most feared the consequences of — tumultuous upheaval. Are we going to be like the superstitious people of bygone eras and make the silly presumption that the world ends here? Or is something else — something much better — just beginning?

Just look outside your window and you can see that the world is changing. But what is it changing into, and what do these changes mean, in *practical terms*, for the decisions that individuals,

SHIFTING
GEARS
─────────
THRIVING
IN THE
NEW
ECONOMY

companies and governments have to make in their day-to-day lives?

What has been making the headlines and the nighttime newscasts is the bad news — the inevitable turmoil and pain that march in lockstep with each and every transformation — presented as if it were the result of political incompetence, plain bad luck or some international conspiracy (usually a version of the Japanese-are-out-to-destroy-us approach to economic analysis). But what we're not being told is that there is a genuine silver lining underneath the grim layoffs, the plant closings and the bankruptcies. Mighty new industries are rising up to replace the tired old ones.

The problem is that the experts charged with explaining our future are still being guided by the beacons of the old economy, which is why their forecasts appear a lot gloomier than they should be. The plain truth is that things change, and always have. In *Shifting Gears*, what I have set out to do is identify what the North American economy has changed into and design a clear road map to the future.

The exhilarating task began more than four years ago with one simple question: What's growing and what's not? After examining in detail hundreds of industries through my consulting firm, Nuala Beck & Associates Inc., it became clear that many of the industries long considered the powerhouses of the economy had actually been in decline for much longer than most people realized. Meanwhile, scores of other industries that were being described as "emerging" and "still too small to really matter" were in fact simply huge.

Once it became clear that these new industries were now North America's mighty engines of growth, the challenge became one of how to measure their strength and influence.

Most of us are much more comfortable in the world we have always known; we are so busy taking care of our day-to-day concerns that we often fail to see change until it has overwhelmed us. Economists are no different. For all their skills at peering ahead, they much prefer spending their time looking back. Change slinks like an unwelcome visitor into their intricately designed computer models, ripping apart comfortable assumptions and carefully crafted sermons.

But change doesn't strike like a bolt of lightning out of the blue. If you know where to look, you can see it coming for miles. One hundred and sixty new economic indicators later, I was elated to find that charting the new economy was more than a vague exercise in guesswork. Instead, it could be nailed down to hard numbers on a timely, accurate and, for the most part, monthly basis.

Just as it was strikingly obvious that new economic indicators were vital, it was also apparent that the problem of measuring the strength of the new economy wasn't simply a matter of economics. I could see that the nature of value had changed, and that you couldn't measure new wealth with the old tools. Twenty-five new financial ratios showed that accounting and financial analysis weren't really doomed, they were just out of date, and that the new nature of value could also be measured with blinding precision.

But this book is not merely about numbers and trends. Nor is it an academic treatment that describes the theories and relationships at work in the new economy. That will come later. For now, my goal is to lay out a road map that can be read and followed by anyone eager to make sense of the changes affecting all of us, whether we hold in our hands the fate of a giant corporation or simply our own economic futures.

Since I first started talking about my findings about eighteen months ago, the response from business and government at every level has been overwhelming. But it is the response of people whose lives have been so affected by change that has touched me the most. Through them, I've learned that economics is about the real world.

THE TRIP TO MECCA

DEAD PLANTS AND A GOLD EARRING

To every young economist, the fount of all knowledge is the U.S. Department of Commerce in Washington — or, more specifically, its revered Bureau of Economic Analysis. Textbooks are filled with references to this powerful bureau, whose experts crunch the numbers that pour into the department's computers from every nook and cranny of the world's mightiest economy and then provide a reading of its health. These are the people who decide if a recession has begun and when it is officially over — the ones who ring the bell that calls us to prayer for better times or to rejoice in our salvation from despair. Canadians listen for these bells too, because their own well-being is so unavoidably tied to that of their largest trading partner.

So, when I arranged a visit to the Bureau of Economic Analysis one December day a few years ago, I felt sure that I was on the road to Mecca, where the secrets of a changing universe would be unveiled.

As the taxi wended its way through heavy traffic that afternoon, my heart was thumping. When the driver came to a stop in front of a McDonald's restaurant, I was sure there must be some mistake, but the cabbie assured me that we were in the right place. The Bureau of Economic Analysis was located above a hamburger joint in a part of town that had seen better days. I looked up and down the mean-looking street and wondered if I could make it to the lobby without losing my handbag to a mugger. Finally, after paying the cab driver, I took a deep breath and dashed inside.

From the lobby, I was ushered into the offices of a senior economist, one of the hundreds of people charged with analyzing the American economy. As I stood in the doorway, I stared at the forest of large, gangling rubber plants — all limp and lifeless — that blocked out the light from the window behind him. To this day, I don't know whether the plants suffered in sympathy with the recession or whether they were just never watered. Maybe they looked that way when the economist moved in. In any case, it wasn't a promising first impression.

I can still see the rickety wooden chair in which I tried to sit. It was one of those old things that graced government offices in the 1940s that you could wheel across a room. But not this particular one — not if you wanted to avoid a lifetime of chiropractors' bills. If the Addams family had had a corporate office, this would have been it.

The economist, who spoke in a slow, southern drawl, seemed to fit perfectly in this unexpected tableau. His graying hair fell past his shoulders, and he wore a large gold earring in his left ear. A Commerce Department ID tag dangled from a gold chain, and a V-neck sweater draped over a casual shirt completed the picture. I felt distinctly overdressed in my Saks Fifth Avenue business suit and fashionable navy pumps.

I explained that I was anxious to learn what ground-breaking research the bureau had undertaken in light of the stunning changes that had been occurring in the global economy. What numbers could I take back to my clients that would help them make intelligent decisions?

The economist reached over to his right to an ancient bookcase. A sign on the wall above read: "If you want to soar with eagles, don't fly with turkeys." He sifted through reports until he fished out a large one labelled "Input-Output Accounts." It was dated 1978.

"That's the structure," he drawled.

"No, no, no. I'm here about the future, not the past. What I'm interested in is what's happening today and what the bureau thinks might happen tomorrow."

He looked at me the way a parent might eye an errant child, and he gave me an answer I will never forget: "It may not be timely, ma'am, but it's accurate."

It suddenly hit me that the economic old guard was hopelessly out of touch. Any lingering nostalgia I might have harbored for the traditional approaches to economic analysis was forever swept away. I would have to find the answers on my own.

A New Beginning

Imagine that you're standing in an elevator going down the outside of a tall building, looking at the street below. The people and cars loom ever larger. Traffic is moving constantly; absolutely no one is standing still.

That's how the real world works, but it's not the way most economists see it at all. For them, the world consists of elaborate theories, complex computer models and mathematical formulas only they and a handful of worshipful graduate students can decipher. The absolute worst thing that can happen is change. Unless conditions can be counted on to remain the same, the math just doesn't work, and their tidy twenty-year projections become not just irrelevant but *dead wrong*.

When I set out to identify how and why the world was changing and what it was changing into, I wrongly assumed that such work was already being done elsewhere. Lord knows, there is no shortage of learned institutes in North America and abroad whose job it is to keep on top of economic developments. At the very least, I thought, someone, somewhere, if only as a purely academic exercise, would have done the necessary digging and research. I could simply take those findings and interpret them for clients managing businesses and pension funds and government departments in the real world. I had no intention of reinventing the wheel.

That's why it was such a shock to discover that the Mecca of knowledge I had been seeking simply didn't exist. Even Japan, which is supposed to be trailblazing the way into the new economy, is just as wedded to the old numbers as everyone else. Statistics Canada, widely regarded as the best such agency in the world, has only now begun to look at the problem. *The whole world has changed before their eyes and economic researchers have been asleep at the switch.*

My experience in Washington was truly an epiphany. It was at that point that I gave up trying to cling to the old religion and started developing a new approach that would make some sense of what was happening all around me.

THE NEWS ISN'T NEW

The next time you watch a business news program, take a close look at all the useless information that flashes on the screen. Someone once said that gold prices were important, so the TV people dutifully provide them night after night, even though it doesn't make a bit of difference whether the price of the shiny metal went up or down a dollar in the past day. Then, the on-camera announcer, with a wide smile or worried frown, reports the latest rise or fall in the stock market index, which for the most part consists of companies operating in the old economy.

Once a month the newscaster will tell us what 1,400 fewer homes built in January or what a 0.1 percent increase in machine-tool orders really means for the economy. And the expert can really trowel on the gloom if a plant has closed or a couple of companies have gone out of business.

It should come as no surprise that the picture invariably will be bleak. Many of us are left debating whether it's even worth getting up

SHIFTING
GEARS

THRIVING
IN THE
NEW
ECONOMY

the next day. But the truth is that we learn very little from the so-called information that bombards us daily. Almost all of what is churned out by the media relates to an economy that no longer exists. Gold prices and housing starts once mattered a great deal, and they are still useful indicators in their own way. But they are no longer crucial pieces of the economic puzzle — and the parts that *are* key aren't being measured. The companies included in the stock indexes in New York, London or Toronto, for example, have been around for decades and have reached a sufficient size to attract huge amounts of trading in their shares. High-growth companies driving the new economy tend to be less widely held or private.

TV viewers and newspaper readers aren't the only ones being misinformed about the true state of the economy. Take a look at *Business Week*, the respected voice of corporate America. This magazine feeds its vast readership with economic statistics that meant a great deal when most of us were still learning nursery rhymes. Today, an executive could learn more from Mother Goose than from the magazine's measurement of the economy through its production index.

How could such a supposedly tuned-in publication put Microsoft's Bill Gates, a leading emblem of the new economy (and, not coincidentally, the richest man in America, with an estimated worth of $6.4 billion), on its cover and then proceed to list such useless items of information as coal production, rail freight, the amount of crude oil refined and the number of trucks manufactured in the latest ten-day period? Does Bill Gates know or care about any of these? More important, should we?

The U.S. Commerce Department finally revamped its flagship publication, *Survey of Current Business*, in April 1990. The bureaucrats promised an exciting 28-page section of data and charts that "are widely used in analyzing current cyclical developments." The makeover cost millions, but what did the public really get for its tax dollars? Cotton-spindle activity, sheep and lambs and textile output were all dutifully recorded. But semiconductors, the most crucial of all products in the new economy, didn't rate a single mention. Economists always seem to be measuring yesterday's economy when today's is staring them in the face.

WHY GOVERNMENTS GET IT WRONG

Where did the media and their soothsayers start going wrong? George Bernard Shaw is remembered, at least among economists, for having said that if you laid all of them end to end they would not reach a conclusion. Time and again, it's not just the media but politicians who are drawn to this or that flavor-of-the-month theorist — sometimes, a whole school of them. And if the President of the United States or the Prime Minister of Canada is relying on outdated numbers about industries that are no longer central to the economy, it shouldn't be surprising if his government reaches entirely wrongheaded conclusions and makes seemingly stupid policy decisions.

Picture the scene some seventy years ago, when the auto industry took off. Car-manufacturing plants were stretched beyond their capacity and companies were expanding like crazy to meet what appeared to be endless demand. Retail sales soared, road and housing construction boomed, all thanks to this relative newcomer to the industrial scene.

But the economy-watchers were probably too glum to notice. After all, their major gauges of economic health had never looked worse. Pig-iron production had been falling, railway operating income was flat, the coal mines were being hit by strikes, and textile production was tailing off. The only verdict possible for anyone still focusing on these statistics was that the economy was in dire straits. But then, they were evaluating the wrong information — just as they are today.

Now let's jump to a hypothetical crisis meeting in the Oval Office, circa mid-1992. President George Bush looks worried. His election chances hinge on the state of the economy, and his top advisers tell him that the situation is particularly bleak. The auto industry, the lifeblood of the nation, is in grave peril, and in the immortal words of Charles Wilson, president of General Motors in 1953, what's good for GM is good for the country, and vice versa. Housing is also depressed, and the U.S. banking system is on the verge of going down the drain. If a real old-timer is in attendance, he will probably add that production of pig iron, coal and textiles is in its eighty-fifth consecutive year of decline. Now, that's a troubled economy!

But what would the reaction be if someone in the room was able to show conclusively that, far from being at death's door, the U.S. economy was back from the brink, that it was surging spectacularly toward new heights, with dramatic growth driven by all of the main engines and a huge increase in the country's high-tech trade surplus? Imagine the renewed public confidence, the revival of consumer spending, the end to unnecessary Japan-bashing. The entire mood of the nation would be dramatically different, not to mention President Bush's fortunes and those of his good buddy, Prime Minister Mulroney.

In the parts of the economy that really matter, the slump has ended. So why isn't anyone aware of it? The governing parties have been hammered in the polls over their management of the economy. They have no vested interest in keeping us miserable (or themselves unpopular), so at least part of the blame has to be laid on the economists who set the current mood of doom and gloom some time ago with their dark and entirely erroneous predictions.

Who's to Blame?

Academic economists aren't the real problem here. My sense is that the academic world is far more aware of what's going on out there than most professors let on. Their response to my own work has been far more positive than I had expected. They stay with the old, it seems, because there is nothing sensible to replace it. As soon as a more useful explanation of the universe does come along, they seem genuinely receptive. It's the ones like me who are real-world economists, out there advising government and industry on a daily basis, who are causing all the trouble — people who make their living from tracking numbers that have lost their big meaning.

I can clearly recall a conversation with one economist employed by a manufacturing association firmly rooted in the old economy. Most of his members were slashing jobs and closing factories. Many had gone out of business. Yet he wouldn't budge from his roost. "Don't tell me, little lady, that the world is changing," he said. "I've got ten thousand members. That should prove something."

"Yes, it proves that your membership has dropped by more than 50 percent in a decade and that you probably won't have enough left for a decent bridge tournament by the end of the century."

Imagine a convention of buggy-whip makers gathering around the turn of the century. Their highly paid economist (if indeed such an animal existed at the time) is asked about the threat posed by those newfangled horseless carriages. "Just a passing fad," he answers confidently. "Nothing will ever replace the horse-drawn conveyance." But he has spent his entire working life tracking buggy-whip sales. For him, and for the people he works for, the buggy-whip is at the center of the universe, and he cannot accept that things could possibly be any other way.

Today's economists are no different from our mythical adviser to a dying industry in a bygone era. The first crime they commit is in insisting that we can hold the world constant and sidestep the reality that economies constantly evolve. They and their textbooks (a lucrative sideline for many) still tell us that technology and innovation are "exogenous variables." That's a jargon lover's way of saying that change doesn't matter in the grand scheme of things, even now, near the end of the twentieth century! Are we economists really the last to know?

Economists have drummed it into everyone's heads that the world is static. No other science works this way. It would be like teaching physics students that the sun revolves around the earth,

SHIFTING
GEARS

THRIVING
IN THE
NEW
ECONOMY

and then wondering why none of the kids can figure out which end is up. With such a totally unrealistic basis for research, who could possibly explain something like gravity? When the apple hit us on the head, we would have no framework, no context, no rhyme or reason for what happened. Just a mystifying bump on the noggin!

Dr. Despair and the Flat World

Let me tell you about my favorite dinosaur from the Pleistocene era of economic thinking. "Dr. Despair" is the kind of person who would have told Columbus that the world was flat — even after his safe return from the New World. Nothing, in his view, has changed since he was a kid in graduate school worshipping at the feet of the old economic gods. Dr. Despair would be aghast at the suggestion, but he would fit perfectly in any society that clings to the old orthodoxies the way Linus does to his blanket.

He could never have been a Nikolai Kondratieff, the brilliant Russian economist who devised a new way of explaining the economic universe nearly seventy years ago, only to pay dearly for his ideas because they clashed with the Communists' unchallengeable view that central planning was the only correct way to run an economy. The Stalinists accused him of "rightist deviation" in 1930 and he disappeared soon after — a lesson to all that some people in power would rather believe that the earth is flat than jump into the risky business of change.

For all his education and research credits, Dr. Despair is no less narrow-minded in his refusal to acknowledge that there might be another way of looking at the economic universe. He takes great issue with any suggestion that the North American economy is moving in directions that he hadn't foreseen. Nothing can persuade him that he is living with the ghosts of economic theories past. The world is going to end and that is that. Some economists seem fated to wander through life — and the classroom — with those signs proclaiming: "Repent! The end is nigh."

The "Class-Ridden" Years

I didn't know it at the time, but my own search for Mecca took a wrong turn years before my fateful trip to Washington. Just about anybody who has ever sat through an economics lecture wonders at some point how what they're hearing could possibly relate to the real world. It took me a lot longer than most to realize that it simply doesn't.

I lost more friends in university by urging them to take an economics class. After sitting in for a couple of weeks, they would invariably act as if I had completely lost my mind. "This stuff is your idea of fun? It's so *boooooring!*" They could hardly wait to get back to something useful, like medieval English.

Keith Acheson, an economics professor at Carleton University in Ottawa, is a cut above the rest. He taught me all I needed to know about macroeconomics (the big picture), but I had to admit that, much as I loved the work, it would never be anyone's idea of fun on a Friday night. I so clearly recall a gray November day, sitting in class reading my textbook and thinking to myself: It's just not possible for something this interesting and exciting to be presented in such a tedious way.

It must be engraved on the first page of every teacher's manual: "To be taken seriously, economics must put at least 62.5 percent of all students to sleep." You would need to be an ancient Greek to make sense of some of the equations, and what do dead Greeks understand about a modern economy anyway? In one class, the professor (who will remain nameless but never forgotten) constructed an unbelievably complex diagram, only to announce just before time ran out that he had made an error in his calculations; he erased the whole thing. I had taken careful notes for forty-five minutes, and all of them were useless. No wonder so many of my friends thought I was crazy to stick it out!

I remember being scared out of my wits by the very first chapter in my textbook. That's the one that argues impressively that everything

SHIFTING
GEARS

THRIVING
IN THE
NEW
ECONOMY

in economics is governed by the theory (not a *notion*, mind you, but a full-blown *theory*) of *scarcity*. That means that all things are in short supply, and we, as future economists, would be charged with the awesome task of allocating these scarce resources. They drum it into your head again and again that there will never, ever be enough to go around — and that might help explain why economists are so prone to Hamlet-like fits of despair from time to time!

There is only one tiny problem with the sacrosanct theory of scarcity — it doesn't work in the real world. Each great era of growth in history has been based not on scarcity at all but on *abundance*. The great economic expansion of the nineteenth and early twentieth centuries was fueled by cheap steel that was readily available at ever-declining real prices. In the next great period of growth, the entire basis of our incredible postwar expansion was the widespread availability of cheap energy, particularly oil, without which mass manufacturing would not have thrived. In my book, that's scarcely scarcity.

In the new economy — the one most economists are just beginning to realize is upon us — vast supplies of microchips at ever lower prices have sparked an industrial revolution.

All of this flies in the face of everything that we've ever been taught about economics. Dr. Despair and others like him may be the last to know, but economics is definitely not about managing scarcity. It's about the exact opposite. Does General Motors mention scarcity when it talks about its woes? Certainly not. GM talks about excess capacity, excess competition and excess product. It's in trouble at least partly because it has the factories to make far more cars than people are willing to buy.

Now, if students have not been thoroughly depressed by the time they have finished Chapter One of the economic bible, along comes Chapter Two, a downer if ever there was one. Here, we come across another of the economists' mantras — the *law of diminishing returns*. This isn't a notion, or even a theory. It's an inviolate law, stating flatly that you will make less and less profit until the economics eventually drive you straight into the ground. And yet, in the real world, what we actually see is the *law of accelerating returns*, where technology and innovation can enable profits to keep rising.

Economists who insist, however, that these two factors are superfluous to the grand econometric model they have designed will never be able to understand why the old laws no longer apply. They would have no rational basis to explain the phenomenal success of Microsoft Inc. or Dell Computer.

LEARNING THE ROPES

Perhaps my luckiest break was deciding not to pursue a doctorate. It probably would have ruined me. In my very first job — as a research assistant with Bank Credit Analyst, a highly respected Montreal-based firm of consulting economists — it took me all of ten days to realize that while I called myself an economist I knew absolutely nothing about the way economies actually worked. With the help of a brilliant (and very patient) mentor, I realized that a lot of people weren't getting the economics they needed to make intelligent decisions.

Take the typical treasurer of a mid- to large-sized company. This person has to know — preferably before it's too late — about the major financial trends that might blow his or her company clear out of the water. And yet, the in-basket is almost certain to be stacked high with useless blurbs that drone on and on about economic output going up, down or sideways. What earthly good does it do to know what the world looked like three months ago, especially when it wasn't even your world?

In my next job, with a major investment dealer, I once had trouble finding a client behind the mountain of research reports on his desk.

"That's a lot of research material for just one week," I remember saying.

"That's my in-basket for one day," replied the portfolio manager, who made it clear that he had no intention of wading through even a fraction of the reports on his cluttered desk.

15

**SHIFTING
GEARS**

THRIVING
IN THE
NEW
ECONOMY

How, I began to wonder, could I possibly justify taking up an hour of a harried executive's time merely to tell him or her why my economic forecast was 0.1 percent higher or lower than that of everyone else in the investment community? They couldn't have cared less, and if they did, they were crazy. From that moment on, my real passion for economics became making it useful in the real world. There's a sense of wonder when you see a whole new picture that actually makes sense. The apple had hit me squarely on the head and cleared my economics-fogged brain. The puzzle finally came together for me with three simple circles.

THE THIRD CIRCLE

I was attending a conference one day when my thoughts drifted out of the overheated room and wandered back to all the changes that had been occurring around me and why no one else seemed to be noticing. A lifelong doodler, I picked up a pencil and began idly drawing on the notepad in front of me, ignoring the fourth speaker in a row to drone on and on about how fate had teamed up with the state to make his industry's life miserable in these hard times.

When I looked down, I had sketched a bunch of overlapping circles, and suddenly things that simply did not add up using conventional economic theory started taking logical shape.

If the otherwise unmemorable meeting had gone on as long as it seemed, I could have traced circles by the thousands, right back to ancient times and the rise of the first organized national economies. Egypt, Persia, Greece and Rome, the master of harnessing global trade and production to the service of empire, could all be defined through their own circles of growth — natural economic progressions (though in those days stemming from religious, political or military motives) with common characteristics. But as interesting as such a trip back in time might be, we really

SHIFTING
GEARS
THRIVING
IN THE
NEW
ECONOMY

only need to turn the clock back about 150 years to see how we got where we are today.

By identifying three circles, each representing an economic movement that shaped the period from 1850 to the present, I had stumbled on a key to understanding the forward movement of our economy today. I've called these models the *commodity-processing*, or C Circle; the *mass-manufacturing*, or M Circle; and the *technology*, or T Circle. Each circle contains certain key, common elements; each makes sense of vast economic changes that otherwise don't fit into a sensible pattern; each is the natural extension of the one preceding. Specific industries, even the economies of entire nations, can be defined by their place inside these circles. And once that's determined, their future — and yours — can be foretold with a remarkable degree of precision.

After running my original musings through the gauntlet of hard economic analysis, it became clear that the key to each circle is a single, crucial ingredient whose abundant supply, at steadily falling prices, acts as a springboard, or catalyst, to levels of growth never before witnessed. In the commodity-processing era (the C Circle), it was cheap steel. In the succeeding mass-manufacturing era (M Circle) it was energy, specifically oil, whose discovery in vast quantities around the turn of the century fuelled the consumer-driven manufacturing boom that shifted the center of economic power to the United States from Britain.

Today, in the T (technology) Circle, the world is being driven by huge supplies of another product that was unknown outside the closely guarded doors of Texas Instruments and one or two other research laboratories thirty years ago — semiconductors, or microchips, so cheap and plentiful they can be stuck in watches to tell you when it's time to wake up at your next board meeting. The technological leader in this circle is Japan, but America isn't nearly so far back as its internal and external critics like to think. Which only goes to show how uninformed the experts can be when they have no clue how things work any more!

Economic Evolution

TM

COMMODITY DRIVEN

Pig-Iron Production
Railroad Operating Income
Inner Tube Production
Coal and Coke Production
Textile Mill Production
Cotton Consumption

MANUFACTURING DRIVEN

Industrial Production
Capacity Utilization
Machine Tool Orders
Retail Sales
Housing Starts
Auto Sales

TECHNOLOGY DRIVEN

Computer Production
Semiconductor Production
Instrumentation Sales
High Tech Trade Balance
Knowledge Intensive Employment Growth
Medical Starts

**SHIFTING
GEARS**

THRIVING
IN THE
NEW
ECONOMY

Besides those single, vital building blocks, each circle has other identifying traits.

- Every era has its *engines* — a handful of strategic industries that drive the entire economy and typically have risen rapidly out of humble origins. The roaring engines of the C Circle were steel, railways, textiles and coal. These were superseded in the mass-manufacturing era by autos, housing, machine tools and retailing. The T Circle, as you might guess, has been turbo-driven by computers and semiconductors, as well as telecommunications, instrumentation and the health and medical industry.

- Every era has its *virtuosos* — the innovative entrepreneurs, scientists and engineers who use existing technology merely as a stepping stone to new methods, processes and products, rather than endlessly reinventing the wheel.

- Every era can be defined by the *technology* these innovators develop. They spend their working lives looking for that better mousetrap, whether it's Henry Ford and his sturdy Model-T car or Jack Kilby and his microchips. (Ironically, Kilby, the Texas Instruments scientist who invented the first integrated circuit the size of a matchhead, never stopped using the slide rule that his pocket calculator made obsolete in 1971.) When they find it, the stage is set for the next explosive round of growth.

- Every era has its *technological pacesetters*, from Britain in the commodity-processing circle, to the United States and Germany in the manufacturing era, to Japan and the U.S. today. The key is the financial might needed to develop the better mousetraps.

- Every era has its own *management practices*. The C Circle, for example, saw the appearance of the first truly giant firms, cartels and trusts that weren't dependent on the whims of royalty or the vagaries of the trade winds. It was here that the foundation was laid for the first great industrial fortunes — a departure from the land- or merchant-based wealth of old.

- Every era has its *philosophers*, the gurus who spend most of their time formulating theories about an economy that no longer exists and may never have — except in their ideal universe.
- Every era has its *fast track* — the jobs that lead somewhere and provide the best chance of hitching dreams to reality in the workplace. In the M Circle, blue-collar workers achieved a level of prosperity beyond the wildest imaginings of previous generations. For the first time, factory laborers had the American dream within their grasp. Many acquired homes of their own, annual vacations, private transportation and other advantages that had long been the sole preserve of the rich.

Today, it's the workers in the new economy who have the best hope for a secure future. Individual computer or communications companies may come and go, but the worker with T Circle skills will still be better off than those being kicked off the assembly lines of the incredible shrinking auto industry and other outdated sectors. Seniority doesn't matter much when the company has sunk to the bottom of the lake. Everybody drowns, no matter what position they had in the boat!

- Every era has its *losers* — industries that were once a major economic force but are now more or less in permanent decline. Just ask the rail manufacturers or pig-iron producers.
- Every era has its *emerging industries* — fledgling sectors destined to carry the world into the next great period of growth, but still seeking a firm foothold. Once it was automobile manufacturing. Today it's genetic engineering and artificial intelligence.
- Every era has its *roadblocks*, easily identifiable barriers that have to be overcome before the transition can be completed.

A natural limitation on the growth of the commodity-processing circle was the lack of standards — in everything from education and electricity to railroad tracks. In the manufacturing era, assembly-line technology overcame the severe restrictions on capacity

**SHIFTING
GEARS**

THRIVING
IN THE
NEW
ECONOMY

caused by the old batch, or piecemeal, system of production, while rapid transportation removed the major roadblock to market access, and integration of design, production and marketing shunted aside idea-strangling bureaucracies. The current technology-driven circle has developed through the application of electronics and miniaturization to largely remove the limitations of existing energy and materials. Without the magic of integrated circuits, computers would be way too unwieldy and far too expensive for ordinary mortals like you and me ever to make use of them.

• Every era *organizes work* in a particular way, linked to the needs and goals of society at the time, which is why change is doubly painful. Not only does the nature of the work change, so does the social structure that underpins it. The abolition of child labor and other worker reforms in the C Circle (when some industries were known as "slaughterhouses" for the high death rate of employees, some barely out of diapers) was, in its own time, as revolutionary a move as the organization of work along assembly lines in the M Circle and the later rise of middle management and the development of a professional class.

What doesn't (and can never) work is the grafting of old approaches and structures onto the new economy. That's why companies that have failed to make the successful leap from one circle to the next seem so unbelievably incompetent. Giants like General Motors once represented all the strengths and glories of the mass-manufacturing era. Yet today they are described in unflattering terms — "bloated," "groping," "slow" and "sloppy" — prisoners caged in their own past.

The Future Is Now

The transformation from one circle to the next can — and usually does — occur before we realize it. Many people are still waiting for the great age of technology, convinced that the future lies in computers and telecommunications and robotics. But that future has been the present for at least a decade. We're already moving toward the next great circle of growth, led by rapid advances in biotechnology, and we haven't yet caught up to the changes that carried us out of the mass-manufacturing era in the 1970s.

One morning you wake up, trip over the cat, stumble into the kitchen, pour yourself some coffee and sit down to read last year's newspaper. It isn't really last year's, but it might as well be, because the emerging industries have already emerged, the statistics were outdated long before they got to your table, and the economy has already moved far beyond the point described in your *Wall Street Journal* or *Financial Times*.

There is nothing terribly complicated about how economies have been evolving for the past century and a half, leaving some industries better equipped than others to survive and thrive. It doesn't take a rocket scientist or even a trained economist to figure it out, but it does require coming down to earth and looking at the real world once in a while.

THE C CIRCLE: 1850-1918

In the mid-nineteenth century, economic life revolved around commodities, shipped in massive quantities by the new steamship lines and railways to feed the hungry mills and belching smokestacks of Manchester, Birmingham and the other great centers of the new industrial age. By 1850, the new manufacturing processes had combined with free trade to usher in a period of unprecedented prosperity, with Britain at the top of the world. When Queen Victoria and Prince Albert presided over the first international trade fair, the Great Exhibition of 1851 at London's Hyde Park, the royals and other visitors were astonished at the industrial might on display in some fourteen thousand exhibits.

"We are living at a period of most wonderful transition, which tends rapidly to accomplish that great end to which indeed all history points — the realization of the unity of mankind," an obviously

SHIFTING
GEARS
THRIVING
IN THE
NEW
ECONOMY

impressed Prince Albert gushed. He had reason to be optimistic. Trade in such key products as cotton, iron and steel had soared to undreamed-of heights. The working class never had it so good. The British dominated world trade and finance, and the pound sterling had become the strongest currency on earth.

A look at the major economic indicators of the day reveals how that commodity-based world worked and how well it was charted. Just as markets wait breathlessly today for the latest word on retail sales or housing numbers to flash onto their computer screens, economy watchers sat around their cramped London offices waiting for the dispatches bringing vital news of pig iron, cotton, textile mills and coke (for blast furnaces, not designer drugs). Pig iron had a particularly avid following, because it was the key ingredient in steel, whose abundance and low cost made all else possible. The U.S. Department of Commerce's *Survey of Current Business* still tracks pig-iron production, while *Business Week*, an otherwise up-to-date publication, continues to track rail freight and coal production, as if they portend something today. In the C Circle, they really did.

Similarly, in days gone by, the *Financial Times* and other journals kept close track of rail and steamship activity, because it was essential for their business readers to know when those cotton, tin and rubber shipments were arriving from the colonies. Look today, and you will still see shipping schedules dutifully printed in some periodicals, although they mean little to anyone apart from the owners of the vessels, the insurance brokers and the relatives of the crews.

In their day, though, these were among the gauges that accurately recorded the performance and movement of the chief industries — steel, textiles, railroads and coal — on which the entire economy revolved. And they had as powerful a psychological impact on the public as housing starts or car sales statistics do today. Companies made life-or-death decisions based on such vital and timely barometers as railroad operating income and cotton consumption.

In those days, there was considerably more time to consider your actions because of the extraordinary length of the average business

COMMODITY ECONOMY

•**ERA:** Industrial Revolution to circa 1918

•**KEY FACTOR:** cheap steel

•**FOUR ENGINES:** Textiles, Coal, Steel and Railroads

•**INFRASTRUCTURE:** Railroads, Shipping, Telegraph

•**LEADING ECONOMIC INDICATORS:**
   Pig-Iron Production
   Railroad Operating Income
   Inner Tube Production
   Coal and Coke Production
   Textile Mill Production
   Cotton Consumption

SHIFTING
GEARS

THRIVING
IN THE
NEW
ECONOMY

cycle in the commodity-processing world. It took as long as six months just to get raw materials like cotton over to the English factories. This was definitely not your "just-in-time manufacturing." And God help the textile mills in Birmingham if the cotton crop turned out to be rotten or the American Civil War shredded shipments. They felt the impact until new supplies could be brought in. The Civil War cut British cotton supplies by nearly two-thirds, from a high of 1.08 billion pounds in 1860. Try to imagine a computer manufacturer coping with the loss of two-thirds of its microchip supply virtually overnight!

The understanding of business cycles in those days merely reflected these harsh realities. A slowdown in the economy wasn't worth mentioning until there had been at least nineteen consecutive months of falling production. Now that's a hard landing by anyone's standards! (Compare that with the rule of thumb of the last few decades, which says that six months of decline equals recession!) One depression lasted for sixty-five months — almost five and a half years of continuous decline!

Like earlier and later eras, the commodity-processing circle was destined for transformation. The British stayed on top as long as they remained the principal processors of the world's raw materials, but eventually they ran into foreign competitors who could run textile machines and turn out pig iron with the best of them, cutting into the old players' monopolistic control of the market and forcing prices down. Trade fairs like the one in 1851 speeded up the technological transfers, prompting nationalists of the day to wonder if they should be revealing their production secrets to the rest of the world. Others observed that the British got back at least as much through firsthand glimpses of German, Belgian, French and American inventions.

About the same time, new technologies were changing industrial processes, as well as the design and construction of the factories built to house them. The British, with fortunes invested in outmoded buildings, techniques and equipment, stood by helplessly as others undercut them on costs and bettered their quality, waving a sad farewell to their huge trade and financial advantage. The age of processing was coming to an end, and its masters were not up to the challenges posed by the new age of machines.

The M Circle: 1918-1981

When Henry Ford was starting out on his remarkable career in Detroit, a bustling town that gave full vent to the creative energies of some amazing innovators, the economy of the first circle was showing enormous cracks. But at the time, even the most prescient of fortune-tellers would have had trouble forecasting what was about to happen. Carriage and buggy-whip makers were still turning handsome profits in a growing market, and the few cars on the dusty, unpaved roads were little more than fanciful toys for the adventurous rich. Some of the communications technologies pioneered toward the end of the nineteenth century must have seemed just as esoteric to the leading financiers and industrialists of the day, who were doing fine bankrolling the traditional industries they knew so well. Yet, within a few short years, Ford and others would shape consumer products out of the new technologies that would set in motion an awesome economic transformation.

By the time Ford's vast Rouge River assembly plant west of Detroit had roared into life in 1918, his manufacturing genius had already carried capitalism onto a higher road. Like the modern-day computer whiz kids who often start by experimenting in their basements or garages, Ford had begun modestly in the new high-tech business of car-making. And like many innovators today, he was a failure at first, an obsessed (and more than a little eccentric) creator. No one could have guessed that within a few short years, Ford's idea of bringing affordable automotive technology to the masses would turn him into America's richest man, transform the very nature of the economy and ignite the greatest period of industrial expansion the world had ever seen.

SHIFTING
GEARS

THRIVING
IN THE
NEW
ECONOMY

The tinkering technologist of his day did it by making an ultra-modern product everyone had to have; and he did it better, faster and cheaper than any of his competitors. As Ford perfected his manufacturing techniques and boosted production to unbelievable levels, costs steadily declined. His company needed fewer workers to make more cars, which were sold at ever-decreasing prices. By the start of the First World War, Ford was churning out nearly 250,000 vehicles a year. That was almost as many as were produced by the rest of the nascent industry combined (some 300 companies, most of which live on today only in the memories of the most dedicated car history buffs). The price of a Model-T fell from $950 in 1909 to $360 in 1917.

Although the market was flooded with the popular cars, the public's appetite seemed insatiable. Henry Ford set out to fill the demand he'd created by building the gigantic Rouge River plant, the manufacturing marvel of its day. Ford, with his drive and vision and mastery of the latest in technology, played a key role in ushering in what I have identified as the M (for mass-manufacturing) Circle of growth, the second great wave of expansion after the Industrial Revolution.

During the long period of decline, those who had bet even modest sums on the new industries were in a position to reap huge rewards. When Ford bought out his minority shareholders in 1919, a schoolteacher who had gambled $100 on this unlikely car venture in 1903 received $262,000 for her tiny stake, on top of earlier dividends of $95,000.

The same thing has been happening, almost unnoticed, in our own time. It's no accident that just as Henry Ford, a source and product of the new economy circa 1919, was America's wealthiest person, today it's Bill Gates, the thirty-six-year-old founder of Microsoft Inc., the booming software company that's emblematic of the current T Circle.

Ford's legacy itself might soon be little more than a marketing and financing company, its manufacturing farmed out to others in Japan

MASS-MANUFACTURING ECONOMY

•**ERA:** 1918 to circa 1981

•**KEY FACTOR:** cheap energy, especially oil

•**FOUR ENGINES:** Autos, Machine Tools, Housing, Retailing

•**INFRASTRUCTURE:** Highways, Airports, Telephone

•**LEADING ECONOMIC INDICATORS:**
Industrial Production
Capacity Utilization
Machine Tool Orders
Retail Sales
Housing Starts
Auto Sales

SHIFTING
GEARS
===
THRIVING
IN THE
NEW
ECONOMY

and elsewhere who do it better, faster and cheaper. Such shifts are inevitable. By the 1890s, Britain was already losing its edge as high-tech industries like car and telephone manufacturing were taking root in rich American soil. Within a matter of years the consumer would be king, and aggressive American companies were poised to take advantage of the enormous shift in markets. It was the age of mass production to feed mass demand. Voracious consumer appetites had always existed, but innovative manufacturers and seemingly inexhaustible supplies of cheap energy now combined to create the conditions by which they could be satisfied. Filling these new needs and wants led to others that no one had predicted, and no country's manufacturers were better placed to meet the challenge.

The United States quickly took over the game from the battered and soon-to-be war-shattered economies of Europe. The Americans came to dominate international trade, and the dollar naturally replaced the British pound as the world's most important currency.

That doesn't mean commodity-processing industries ceased to exist. The railroads still run, though not as often or as profitably. Somebody still grows cotton, and you can still buy shirts and sheets made from the fluffy stuff, though they are more likely to come from low-cost Third World countries like Mauritius and the Philippines than from one of the great industrial economies. Their source is irrelevant to us, because the old industries don't drive anything but themselves.

The smartest industries adapt once it becomes clear that their old markets are doomed. Carriage-makers, for instance, gained a new lease on life by making bodies for the auto industry. Once seen as a minor, eccentric sideline, the new business ended up saving them from extinction. Pig-iron producers and other processors similarly invested in new technology and products (usually alloys) to meet the changing demand. The markets for most commodities grew bigger, not smaller. Detroit, after all, needed tons more metal and rubber than Manchester ever did. Suppliers of raw commodities, like coal, flourished by redirecting their shipments to different destinations.

The old firms that remained rigid in their ways went down like the dodo birds they had allowed themselves to become.

The mass-producers took over as the main turbines of the economy, led by autos, first through Henry Ford's wizardry, and then, from the 1920s on, under the helmsmanship of mighty General Motors, the rising colossus against which all manufacturing enterprises the world over came to be measured. It is no accident that GM's steady decline coincided with the waning of the M Circle, beginning with the massive oil price shocks of the 1970s and the rise of smarter foreign (read Japanese) competitors making better (read quality) products at lower prices.

A Time of Turmoil

As the news headlines make plain, the shift from one circle to another is always marked by turmoil and hard times in the declining economy. In the past, shifting gears was accompanied by severe depressions, at least partly because the rising new industries typically were unable to make enough of an impact right away to compensate for the rapid decline in the old economy.

Business cycles shortened drastically in the mass-manufacturing era. Recessions hit faster than ever before, leaving economists groping for numbers that would somehow explain what was happening. The old rules didn't seem to apply, but no one could quite figure out why not. No matter how hard they looked, they couldn't find the answers in the traditional statistics, the ones that had always proved so reliable!

As industries sprang up from virtually nowhere, it became imperative to measure their ultimate impact on the economy. Pig-iron and textile stats wouldn't reveal a thing about the burgeoning auto, housing, machine-tool or aircraft industries, none of which had even existed scant years earlier.

Picture the top economists of the day trying to figure out the new economic universe in, say, the 1920s, when none of their numbers made sense any more.

SHIFTING
GEARS
═══════
THRIVING
IN THE
NEW
ECONOMY

First expert: "Gee, things must be bad. Pig iron has been falling for twelve years. Cotton looks terrible, and the railways haven't been this awful since the crash of '93. But the numbers don't add up to a recession."

Second expert: "I know what you mean. I keep waiting for those nineteen consecutive months of total economic decline, but things just get better. And everyone's walking around smiling. I've never seen so many people with so much money to spend. But they sure aren't spending it on pig iron. I need a ride home. Did you bring that new Ford of yours to work?"

Even in the depths of the Great Depression, the economists could not ring the bell and shout, "Aha, the recession has commenced. We told you it was coming." (That's the way literate economists would phrase it. The rest might have said something like: "Holy #$?@! What do you mean I'm dehired?") The fact is that at no time in the mass-manufacturing era did the world ever come close to meeting the old economists' criteria for misery. By historical standards, in fact, the Crash of '29 was quite short and mild — a milquetoast among downturns.

NIGHTMARE ON MAIN STREET

Like those hopelessly equipped economists, most of us are addicted to bad news. Take what I call the "Great Scare" books, like Ravi Batra's *Surviving the Great Depression of 1990*. Or the latest in an ignoble tradition of frightening the bejeezus out of ordinary folk: *The Great Reckoning* by James Dale Davidson and William Rees-Mogg. These dismal tomes, which come out with monotonous regularity, can do serious damage to the psyche. If we had listened to them, we would all be hunkering down in cement bunkers in the wilderness living off dried vegetables.

Film fans love horror, but when the popcorn's finished and Freddie ("I'm baaaack") Krueger, the slasher, leaves the screen and the lights come on, no one but the certifiably insane imagines we're really living out a Nightmare on Elm Street. And as far as I'm concerned, the only difference between Freddie and the theorists of gloom is that Freddie's a lot more entertaining.

Reading one of these blasted books on "the coming end to life as we know it" somehow convinces us that the monsters are going to come leaping off the page to ruin our lives. I know, because as a young economist I once let one of those fearmongers scare the hell out of me.

The first "Great Scare" book I read, in 1975, convinced me that I needed to hoard as much gold as I could get my hands on, stuff it all into a Swiss account and stock my kitchen to the rafters with dried peas. If I had believed that Freddie actually existed, I would probably still be eating those damned peas. And I would have been stuck with an awful lot of gold — at $900 an ounce — going steadily down in value.

The key to why we buy what the doomsters tell us is the feeling that somehow the authors of these potboilers know more than mere mortals do about the future. Why would someone believe a horror story packaged as truth? Because the writers, like those slick TV evangelists, are saying: "Believe me, for I have seen the true light! And I am an *expert.*"

My first scare came right after starting my first job in August 1974, at the Bank Credit Analyst. The German Herstatt Bank had just collapsed. This was supposed to be the bolt of lightning that signalled the failure of the whole international financial system as we had grown to know and love it — the bolt of lightning that so many had been waiting for. Yet here we are eighteen years later and I don't even recall why the German bank went under.

The only people affected were the doom-and-gloomers and those who were on the wrong side of an exchange contract. My first scare book actually provided a list of provisions to stock up on to survive the coming crash. My newlywed dream was to one day own a house and, if our careers really took off, maybe a pool in the backyard far enough away from the apple tree to avoid the falling

SHIFTING
GEARS
———
THRIVING
IN THE
NEW
ECONOMY

leaves. Instead, I was told I should be worrying about buying a survival farm far enough away from the city to escape the rising tide of violence brought on by mass deprivation. And what really frightens me is that I did start worrying about these things.

Well, as you probably know, the world continued. People went on lining up to get into Disneyland. Lovers still got cards and flowers and candy on Valentine's Day. And the scaremongers sat down to plot out more science fiction dressed up as fact, all the while adding up the royalties from their lucrative fright stories.

But apart from the damage they can do to your stomach, what really ticks me off about the "Great Scare" books and their pervasive popularity is that they can siphon off some of the energy, the creativity and the drive that we can and should be directing toward the tomorrows of our lives. What if Bill Gates had spent the best years of his life stocking up on dehydrated food and waiting for the world to end? He would never have had the temerity to build a giant company from scratch, employing thousands. There should be a public warning on the covers of every one of these books: "Entertainment only. Not to be taken seriously. Do not throw yourself off the nearest bridge."

A friend of mine, an expert in fixed-income investments who I'll call Sam, has spent most of his working life preparing for the coming depression. He lives in someone else's house because he's absolutely convinced that when the crash comes it will wipe out the value of all property. Over lunch one day, I explained to him how the nature of depressions had changed and about how we had already been through the collapse of the old economy in the 1980s. I told him that the new economy had already taken hold and, to use Sam's own jargon, the next long wave was already under way.

Sam turned very quiet and stared into his coffee cup for a while. Then, in a soft but firm tone, he said: "Don't try and change my mind. This is *my* religion."

I reached for my glass of white wine and thought again about the truth of an old piece of advice: You can change a lot in this world, but never try to change someone's politics or religion.

So, if you share my friend Sam's ideology of fear, please don't read what comes next. Because I'm going to tell you things that would have me branded me as a heretic and burned at the stake by the gloom-and-doom brigade.

THE NEW WAVE DEPRESSION

A chapter in the bible of modern-day economics is the Gospel according to St. Kondratieff. Nikolai Dmitryevitch Kondratieff, whom I've mentioned before in connection with the dangers of free-thinking, was a brilliant Russian economist who, in the early 1920s, identified repetitive patterns of prosperity and depression and estimated that the average duration of each long wave between really bad times was fifty-four years. The depression of 1874 was almost on target, occurring fifty-five years after the collapse of 1819 (but what's twelve months between a couple of dismal scientists?). From 1874, using Kondratieff's theories, it would have been possible to forecast that 1928 or 1929 was going to be a very bad year.

Speaking of the Great Depression, my handy *Encyclopedia of Economics* (McGraw-Hill, 1982) states:

"One of the things that inhibited government actions in the early years of the Great Depression was the absence of useful suggestions by economists. Contemporary economic doctrines in 1929 insisted that the market was self-correcting, but as the economic situation continued to worsen without signs of recovery, economists began to question their theories."

Notice that they were only questioning. The world was going to hell in a handcart, and the experts were starting to ask questions.

The encyclopedia continues this entirely unintentional humor by noting that by 1939 — ten miserable years later — "a growing number of American economists ... were espousing a new approach to economic policy." Not all, not even necessarily a majority. Just a "growing number," and most of these worked for the Roosevelt administration, which meant that it was their job to find a way out of

35

SHIFTING
GEARS
—————
THRIVING
IN THE
NEW
ECONOMY

the mess. Forgive me for ranting, but it happens every time I think of how dismal this dismal science can really be.

It was government intervention, starting in the 1930s and based on the model provided by the brilliant English economist John Maynard Keynes, that provided the safety nets that changed not the fact of depression but the way they would unfold in the future. Because depressions can unfold in different ways, there is still a ready market for "Great Scare" books today. People are still waiting for a depression that has almost ended.

But back to the future according to Kondratieff. The next very bad year should have been 1983. And in all the ways that really count, Nikolai the Great was once again dead on the mark. The mining industry fell into a deep slump in the mid-1980s, while the oil market only collapsed in the latter part of the decade. Every old industry peaked at a different time and then sank into its own depression. Kondratieff never carved in stone that a depression had to take place in every industry at the same time. It's only his disciples who assumed that a depression had to take everything over the cliff at once.

Imagine if Moses had come down from the mountain and people said: "It can't be Moses. He was supposed to wear white. And this guy's robes are blue. The book says white!" Well, that's what happened in the 1980s. The depression came and went, but everybody is still waiting for the great single crash, missing what actually occurred: *a multiplicity of interconnected events.*

Out of the ashes of that new wave depression a whole new economy has risen, and the timing is exactly as the old Russian predicted. The old economy peaked in 1981-82, and we moved into the next great era of growth.

The T Circle: 1981–

Somewhere along the line, economists missed the boat again. A new, technology-driven circle of growth has replaced the aging

TECHNOLOGY ECONOMY

•**ERA:** 1981 to ???

•**KEY FACTOR:** cheap chips (microchips)

•**FOUR ENGINES:** Computers and Semiconductors, Health and Medical, Com and Tel, Instrumentation

•**INFRASTRUCTURE:** Telecommunications Satellites, Fiber Optics, LANs and WANs, Radio Frequencies

•**LEADING ECONOMIC INDICATORS:**
  Computer Production
  Electronic Components Production
  Instrumentation Sales
  High Tech Trade Balance
  Knowledge Intensive Employment Growth
  Medical Starts

**SHIFTING
GEARS**

THRIVING
IN THE
NEW
ECONOMY

manufacturing ring, and scarcely anyone noticed. The statistics that told us so much about the economy's health during the second phase (the M Circle) are still treated with a reverence they no longer deserve. No self-respecting economist would argue today that pig-iron output could reveal much beyond how those hardy pig-iron producers are faring. Yet they persist in telling us that housing construction, which accounts for just over 3.5 percent of the U.S. economy, actually means as much as it did in 1950 when it made up 7.2 percent of all economic activity.

That's why the experts have so much trouble explaining what's going on now. The prophets mumble about the severity of the current economic slowdown; the crisis in industry; rising unemployment; a weakening currency. But they do it after examining yesterday's numbers, or the detritus left by the debt-laden merger mania that gripped North America in the '80s.

Now, statistics can be massaged to produce all sorts of results. But no matter how you shake or stir them, the numbers show plainly that a new economy, embodied in the third circle of growth and driven by technology, information and innovation, has emerged, with little fanfare, in the past decade. And though it would be impossible to tell from the general statistics, this new economy is absolutely booming, with no peak in sight.

No Pain — No Gain

Now, you're going to ask: What about all those layoffs? The wrenching factory closings? The soaring bankruptcies? The collapsing house prices? The gloom and doom that drips gleefully from the lips of the soothsayers, frightening us out of our wits and leaving us wondering if there will be any future to worry about?

These things happen, but I can say unequivocally that if you operate in the third circle, your chances of surviving and growing, of rising up the industrial ladder, are significantly better than if you're stuck in the old economy.

I'm often asked where individual industries — and even entire countries — fit into the different circles. Well, some industries — and countries — adjust far better than others. Telecommunications, a particular Canadian strength, has always been at the cutting edge, employing new technologies to make the successful leap from one circle to the next. No one happily taking advantage of the speed of the new telegraph wire in the mid-1800s could have foreseen that it would one day be supplanted — first by the telephone and then, in the T Circle, by the miracle of satellite communications, cellular technology and electronic data transmitted through fiber optics and laser technology.

The passing of the baton from one group of runners to the next always involves a measure of uncertainty and pain. The main difference in the most recent shifting of gears is that it hasn't been accompanied by a cataclysmic event like a world war or a full-scale depression or an asteroid crashing to earth. Instead of a single big bang, the transformation into the T Circle of growth has occurred almost in slow motion, starting with the oil shocks of the 1970s, when the price of that key ingredient behind the remarkable expansion of the entire mass-manufacturing circle quadrupled almost overnight. Faced with a huge hike in costs for its basic building block and unprecedented global competition — after formerly proprietary U.S. secrets of effective mass production had been spread around the world by its highly skilled proselytizers — one old industry after another wandered to the edge of the cliff in the fog and fell into the abyss.

Apart from a handful of notable exceptions involving utter incompetence or the obvious fallout from the enormous debts piled up in the merger-madness, the problems have been largely confined to the old economy — the sectors that led the way throughout the mass-manufacturing phase but are no longer the driving engines they once were.

Certainly, companies planted firmly in the new economy have gone out of business and more will follow, collapsing like cheap suitcases. Inferior management or products or marketing or financing can

39

SHIFTING
GEARS
___
THRIVING
IN THE
NEW
ECONOMY

sink anybody, no matter how hot the industry. And who can protect themselves against the day the genius in the laboratory walks out with the company's biggest asset — his brain? Or a dozen other life-threatening reasons? But the collapses will not stem from being badly positioned, from failing to jump into the high-growth part of the economy. And if you're employed in this segment, you are far more likely to keep those paychecks and promotions coming than if you toil in the old economy, no matter how much union protection or seniority you may have on your side.

Some countries haven't yet made the leap into the technology era, and, unlike Canada, perhaps never will. But, they can thrive by meeting the needs of the new circle, just as Canada supplied the M Circle and is once again emerging as a major supplier to the T Circle.

Countries can be as stupid as individual industries or companies in adjusting to new economic realities, but, despite the wealth of evidence provided by politicians of every stripe, Canada has not traditionally travelled in dumb company. Would it help to shake off that chronic pessimism if you knew that Canadian profit margins have tended to be almost double those in the United States, and that we're not nearly as ignorant as some of our editorial writers keep telling us?

We never could cut it in the world of mass manufacturing, but why should we have to? We did far better by supplying the Americans than by trying to compete head-to-head with them. And it's a cinch we're better off supplying the Japanese than hitting our heads against a ceramic wall. Why would anyone in their right mind trade away from a commodity business that has a terrific profit to become manufacturers in a viciously competitive arena with lower gains? So we've stuck with the good stuff and cleaned up. And then, being Canadians, instead of patting ourselves on the back for being smart, we lay a national guilt trip on ourselves for not giving up all that hewing and drawing years ago!

The startling fact of life in Canada is that 70 percent of Canadians are already employed in the new economy, which shows just how well we have adjusted.

It pays to be a supplier of the right materials, and although many Canadians don't realize it, their country is emerging as the principal provider of many of the commodities needed by the technology-driven economy. We are so wrapped up in our wintry view of our future that we don't realize how incredibly lucky — and smart — we've been over the years. It's no secret, for example, that nickel is *the* metal of the new economy, while copper is the dark horse, and Canada happens to be one of the world's principal sources of both.

As supreme hewers of wood, miners of metals and drawers of water, Canadians have been uniquely well-placed to serve both the commodity-processing centers of mother Britain and the manufacturing dynamos of the neighboring giant to the south. In return, Canada has had one of the world's fastest-growing economies for decades. The bumpy ride that we're experiencing right now is caused simply by the shifting of gears as we move from supplying the stuff to the declining old economy. For people who aren't used to driving at high speeds, that's always a challenge. The best thing to do is follow Bette Davis's advice in the film *All About Eve* and fasten your seatbelts for the ride of your lives!

THINGS CHANGE

WHEN HARRY MET LARRY

L arry had been looking forward to his high-school class reunion for some time. It would be a chance to see old friends again, particularly Harry, his best buddy from their days on the football team in their small home town. Larry hadn't seen him for years and wanted to compare notes on their lives.

Harry did come to the reunion, but not with any great joy in his heart. People who think they're failures aren't exactly eager to show their faces at such gatherings, particularly when their own expectations of success had once run so high. And that was exactly how Harry saw himself: a dismal failure unable to live up to the ambitious goals he had confidently set for himself when he finished school. Only because his wife wanted to see old friends did he reluctantly agree to make an appearance.

When Larry finally met up again with Harry in the school gym and heard how badly his friend had fared over the years, he was shaken to the core. The Harry he grew up with was always exuberant, a person whose easy smile masked a solid drive to succeed. The Harry who stood beside him in early middle age was almost like a stranger, and looked far older than his years.

He had lost one job after another, an experience that shattered his confidence and destroyed his dreams. The boyish grin was gone, and he spoke so quietly Larry had to lean over to hear what he was saying. It was as if all his energy had been drained out of him. That night, as he listened and shook his head, Larry discarded forever his smug views about why some people make it in this world and others don't.

Harry and Larry both started out with boundless energy, enthusiasm and eagerness to "make it." Harry took technical training after high school and went to work as a draftsman for a machine-tool manufacturer. Larry started out as a quality-control technician with a small company that produced medical instruments. He was making less money than Harry but liked the lack of formality in the small firm, his high degree of independence and the profit-sharing plan, which he figured would come in handy one day. Larry stayed with the medical company as it grew, accumulating regular promotions, pay increases and, eventually, his share of rapidly expanding profits. Without realizing it, he had become a full-fledged participant in a booming segment of the new economy.

Harry's story was drastically different — and, tragically, much more typical of what has been happening to thousands upon thousands of skilled, industrious people, believers in the American Dream who never imagined for a moment that it would mutate into a terrible nightmare.

Like Larry, Harry had no intention of job-hopping, but fate had other ideas. Though he worked for several different firms over the years, through it all he stayed anchored in machine tools, the very bedrock of American industry — or so it seemed. Had Harry been aware of the economic sea-change occurring right outside his window, he never would have made the career decisions he did.

Although he was blissfully unaware of it at the time, Harry's troubles really started back in 1973, shortly after he took his first job. The industrial world was in the grip of the first "oil shock," triggered when the major petroleum-producing countries flexed

SHIFTING
GEARS
━━━━
THRIVING
IN THE
NEW
ECONOMY

their new-found muscles for political and economic gain. The age of cheap energy that had fueled a mighty manufacturing era and turned the United States into the world's unchallenged economic power for a half-century was coming to an end.

Through no fault of their own, Harry and many others like him were about to find their lives turned inside-out. Eventually, there would be pain and despair and suffering on a scale not seen since the Great Depression, catching almost everyone completely unprepared. What was to have been the best of times turned almost overnight into the worst of times.

Things were great in the early days. Harry and his wife, Joanne, a nurse who was staying at home with their first child, gathered enough money for the down payment on an attractive bungalow, and through careful budgeting they managed to meet their monthly mortgage payments without adding to their debts.

Then, unexpectedly, after five years in his first job, Harry was told to put down his drafting tools and go home. Nothing like it had ever happened to him before, and for the first-time self-doubt began to edge into his conversations. Before long, it would burrow into his very being. No matter how hard he worked, Harry just couldn't seem to do anything right once his world began coming apart at the foundations.

After five months without a paycheck, the young couple left town with only half of their original down payment. They were lucky to salvage that much; property prices subsequently plunged in the wake of a wave of plant closings in the area. Some coworkers were forced to walk away from their homes with nothing to show for years of work.

Harry had no trouble finding a job in another community, and without an understanding of the powerful economic forces that were beginning to swirl like a tornado above his head, it was easy for him to put it all down to personal mistakes or plain bad luck. Joanne returned to full-time nursing, and they bought another home. Harry decided to return to school for a university degree in business management. His new employer, a giant machine-tool manufacturer with plants all over the map, offered to pay his tuition, telling him that there was always a demand for bright young people with strong technical skills.

As ambitious as ever, Harry attended classes part of each day in a special work-study program that allowed him to speed up his schooling. Spurring him on was Joanne's announcement that another baby was on the way. Nine months after his wife gave birth to twins, disaster struck again. With six months to go before his graduation, the corporation sold off the division where Harry was employed. The work-study program was abruptly cancelled. Eight months later, Harry was on the street after the new owners decided to "streamline" operations to cut costs. No job, no university degree, three preschool children and nowhere to go.

It would be wonderful to report that things got better for Harry and Joanne after that, but they actually got worse. Harry fell into a pit of doubt and defeat and despair, convinced he was responsible for all of his own troubles, that he had somehow lost his way because he didn't have "the right stuff." Now, while Larry and his family live a life of relative comfort and security, scarcely noticing the impact of the latest recession, Harry and Joanne are unable to make long-range plans because the future is so uncertain.

Of course there are people out there who are incompetent or lazy or both. But there are far more like Harry, who had always assumed that plenty of hard work would provide all the security his family would ever need. They do the right things and still watch their life's hopes go up in smoke.

Harry may be trapped by changes he doesn't understand, but he's hardly alone. It could be the person wheeling a child through the shopping mall on a Saturday; the woman in the pharmacy reading the label on a vitamin bottle; your next-door neighbor; your friend; your brother or sister — you.

What really saddens me is that the heartache of lost dreams is not the inevitable fallout of the current economic changes, despite what

**SHIFTING
GEARS**

THRIVING
IN THE
NEW
ECONOMY

some experts say. True, what we have come through is no minor blip on the economic radar screen. It has been nothing less than a revolution, but it could be — and should be — virtually a bloodless one. There's more than enough room in the new economy to accommodate everyone. But first they need a proper road map to find their way.

The world of mass-manufacturing in which we all grew up has been displaced by the world of technology; industries, workers, communities, entire national economies that can't — or won't — adjust to the new realities are doomed. It's no understatement to say that, without the map, without some intelligent leadership providing clear directions out of this wilderness, we could be looking at another "lost generation" — millions of unemployed and unemployables hanging like a dark cloud over an otherwise bright future.

Harry's a survivor, and he's still relatively young. Knowing him as well as I do, I have high hopes that he'll ultimately pull the threads of his life together again. He'll get back on track by setting out a personal survival strategy, as millions of others should be doing right now.

The steps are simple, and the first is the most critical: *take stock of exactly what's growing and what's not*. Make sure — make darn sure — that the industry you hitch your hopes and dreams to is an industry with a future. Too many people make the mistake of taking the job that offers the highest starting salary, or the best-sounding title or the biggest perks. But all the bells and whistles in the world won't cushion you from disaster if you find yourself, as Harry did, trapped in the old economy.

The harsh reality is that if you are employed in the old economy, you have a better than 50 percent chance of losing your job. Russian roulette gives players better odds than that. No one can afford such a gamble, and it simply isn't necessary — not when the road map to the new economy can be so clear and easy to follow.

THE AGE OF CERTAINTY

As we move through the transition from the old economy into the new one that is rapidly displacing it, anyone who continues working in certain industries is assured a life of turmoil, if not actual unemployment. In other words, although employees in the new economy won't necessarily be working any harder or more diligently, there will be regular raises, bonuses, promotions — in short, a future. And it doesn't matter a whit how big or powerful the employer seems to be, or how many plants or divisions it operates around the world. If it's entrenched in the old economy, every one of its workers, from the highest-paid executive to the lowest-paid clerk, has a big question mark hanging over his or her future.

The key, as Larry unwittingly discovered, is to ride with the changes. It would have been fatal had he switched jobs to move into a segment of the economy that was slowly dying. That doesn't mean everyone has to become a computer whiz or obtain a degree in higher mathematics to prosper. Larry found a home in medical instruments, and plenty of other people are happily ensconced in the accounting, distribution, production, marketing and human resources departments of growth industries — food-processing, education, entertainment, even bicycles come to mind — that have seemingly little to do with the higher-tech aspects of business.

THE WILDERNESS GUIDES

The intolerably high unemployment rates that bedevil our politicians and economic planners show with vicious clarity just how many walking wounded have been left in the wake of the enormous upheaval. None of us can afford to wait for government to heal the wounds of change. By the time governments devise — let alone implement — the policies that are truly needed to bridge the gulf between the old economy and the new, it will probably be too

Twenty Fastest Growing Industries

INDUSTRY	SHIPMENTS 1992 TO DATE (1987$: billions)	ANNUAL GROWTH RATE 1992/1987	RANK
Electromedical Equipment	5.73	9.9%	1
Surgical & Medical Instruments	11.53	8.2%	2
Medicinals & Botanicals	4.93	8.0%	3
Semiconductors	28.84	7.8%	4
X-Ray Apparatus	2.26	7.8%	5
Motorcycles, Bicycles & Parts	1.54	7.7%	6
Farm Machinery & Equipment	9.98	7.7%	7
Oil & Gas Field Machinery	3.83	7.0%	8
Household Audio & Video Equipment	8.21	6.8%	9
Poultry Slaughtering	20.54	6.6%	10
Surgical Appliances & Supplies	11.58	6.3%	11
Household Appliances	3.19	5.9%	12
Plastics Plumbing Fixtures	0.94	5.8%	13
Biological Products	2.11	5.5%	14
Frozen Foods	15.64	5.0%	15
Sporting & Athletic Goods	6.36	4.4%	16
Agricultural Chemicals	7.8	4.4%	17
Measuring & Controlling Instruments	9.63	4.3%	18
Ice Cream & Frozen Desserts	4.8	4.2%	19
Pharmaceuticals	38.96	4.0%	20

late for people like Harry to get his life heading in the right direction, let alone make up for all of the lost years.

But sooner or later, because their survival depends on it, governments will have to alter the policies designed for a long-gone era and bring in measures that might actually accomplish something. What has encouraged me from my own conversations with senior officials is their genuine openness to new ideas. Like everyone else, they are well aware that what they have tried in the past simply isn't working in the present and certainly won't work in the future.

My main message for governments at every level is that they can do a great deal without spending more of what they don't have. It's not what you spend, but how wisely you spend it. Smarter policies could actually reduce our tax burden and the terrible waste of resources, both human and financial. The key is to stop pouring good money after bad — into training that will never produce a job and into industries that will never again rise to their former glory.

Here's a checklist of what every government can and should be doing instead.

1. **Marking the right trail.** Give people a road map they can actually read, with directions they can follow to the jobs in the new economy. Think of it as a wilderness training course, designed to point the way to people lost in the woods of the old economy. What they need is a good compass, a strong pair of hiking boots, protective programs to shelter them from the elements of change and a thoroughly detailed topographical map of the economic landscape, showing all the hills and valleys, the rocks and the quicksand along the route.

Maps of the new economy would be prepared on a citywide or regional basis, but for the truly adventurous, there would be a world atlas. Government officials might be amazed at how valuable — and inexpensive — this simplest of services can be. With proper directions and clear landmarks, refugees from the old economy could quickly locate where the industries, the jobs and their

SHIFTING
GEARS

THRIVING
IN THE
NEW
ECONOMY

futures lie, instead of wandering lost for the rest of their working lives. But governments will have to be more than wilderness guides for the trek to be a success.

2. **Training for real jobs**. Governments already spend billions every year preparing people for jobs that either no longer exist or soon won't. It wouldn't cost a dime more to shift gears and provide skills-training that might actually lead to a career with a future. Spending the money on three simple skills would give the unemployed or underemployed an enormous headstart and go a long way to bringing jobless rates down to politically tolerable levels.

First and foremost, computer literacy must be a national goal. While modern computer instructions in the form of symbols can be interpreted by people who can't read or write, it is crucial that everyone be able to read software manuals and other instructions.

The second priority is to teach people how to send and receive basic information via modern communications equipment like fax machines and modems, and to retrieve information from databases. This is only logical in what many correctly label "the information age."

Third, people must be given basic numerical skills. Math teachers have it all wrong when they rush students through grade school arithmetic so they can get on with the trigonometry and calculus that mean so much to the future engineers, scientists, professional mathematicians and baseball and hockey statistics nuts of this world. The rest of us mortals could do with a lot more sessions on how to use a calculator — or even a pencil — to figure out such basics as a percentage change. In a world of change, it's mighty useful to be able to measure it.

3. **Cushioning the blows**. The message here is that governments don't have to do it all alone. They should bring in the insurance industry as a partner prepared to offer added and extended coverage to the growing numbers likely to find

themselves out of a job. Governments need help with the soaring public costs of unemployment.

4. **Buying used homes**. It would be a farsighted government indeed that guaranteed people could move in search of work without losing whatever money they'd sunk into their own homes. Such a program would make it easier, at least economically, to leave a hard-hit community, where selling a home for anything resembling its original value would be next to impossible. It makes a lot more sense to get into the housing business than to continue to subsidize people who don't have a hope in hell of improving their lot in life because they can't afford to move to where the jobs are. Private insurance again might provide the answer. Mortgage insurance is already available to home buyers. Why not economic relocation insurance?

5. **Keeping kids in class**. Every government pays lip service to this goal, but when it comes to policies designed to achieve it, they come up terribly short. I'm talking not only of encouraging teens to complete their schooling but of keeping all students in school longer hours and more days every single year.

In a world where most households require two incomes to survive, it doesn't make sense to have children leaving school at three o'clock in the afternoon or spending entire summers on their own, often without a parent in sight. Some school boards have experimented with longer school terms, more hours and year-round semesters. The existing structure was based on a farm culture that required children for chores like planting, feeding and harvesting. It wasn't designed to provide lengthy vacations between all-too-brief periods of learning.

I can practically hear the anguished objections of teachers and cash-starved school boards. Few people readily embrace change, at least not before change completely passes them by. And this has already happened in education, where North Americans are falling further and further behind in the delivery of the knowledge and

SHIFTING
GEARS
━━━
THRIVING
IN THE
NEW
ECONOMY

skills necessary to find a niche in the new economy. If that's not a key purpose of our school systems, we really have to wonder what the heck is.

Even at the university level, it burns me up every time I hear academics debate the purpose of an education. Too large a camp still clings to the tired notion that universities must retain the high walls and deep moats that protect them from the real world. These preservers of the ancient order put up fierce resistance to the notion that students might be educated for an actual job market. Now, I have nothing against a classical education. It can be extremely fulfilling. But in these perilous times, such programs drain precious education dollars from the practical training desperately needed by the vast majority of future workers who wouldn't know Plato from Pluto. This "ivory tower syndrome" has become considerably less pronounced as universities have had to tighten their purse strings and come up with inventive ways of raising money — mainly by tapping into the private sector, which, business being business, tends to confine its Latin to "*quid pro quo*" — or, you do my R&D and I'll buy you a new laboratory. But for academics, old ideas die hard, especially the ones handed down from the late Middle Ages.

The second bone I have to pick with universities — and I could drag out a whole skeleton on this subject — is that their equipment and programs are often terribly out of date. Like the rest of us, universities have no choice but to meet change head on, by presenting processes, products and markets that actually resemble what's happening in real life. We need programs that are tied specifically to work in the real world. If students spend four years studying archaeology, they should be able to count on chipping away in the field once they leave school. Co-op programs that combine work and study are the answer.

6. **Making something of welfare**. Not everyone on welfare can be expected to become part of the labor force. Health or emotional problems, for example, leave some people ill-equipped for any economy — new or old. But it's only reasonable to expect that welfare be treated as a temporary bandage applied

on the economic battlefield. Most of the wounded would like to get back in the fight, but don't know how.

The tangle of programs available in most Western countries simply doesn't work. But they might if they were linked directly to real-life skills-training and community service that would restore people's dignity and give them a fighting chance. Only the infirm should be excused automatically.

7. **Making sense of economic development**. It has always seemed ludicrous to me to throw money into hard-pressed regions and municipalities without any coherent plan for what they should be doing in the future. In today's rapidly changing, debt-laden world, it is more than ludicrous — it's downright dangerous, and it's one of the reasons why so many people are so cynical about politics. Newfoundlanders know that the few hundred million dollars tossed at them won't give them back meaningful work to replace the jobs lost in the moribund fishery. What they need is aid that will assist in the shift to the new economy, where the real jobs and the only real future lie.

No community can be expected to change its economic base if it hasn't been given a clear sense of what exactly it should be changing into or the goals it has to achieve. If governments want a knowledge-based economy, they had better set specific targets against which the success or failure of their grants and other assistance can be measured. Otherwise, buckets of money will be going down very deep wells, to no productive purpose. There's no point keeping the old mines or mills or plants open for a few more years on government handouts when the same dollars could be used to nurture industries with genuine potential for growth in the new economy.

8. **Learning how and whom to tax**. Government tax policies are long overdue for an overhaul, as more than one critic has observed. If governments took a hard look at their policies,

SHIFTING
GEARS
THRIVING
IN THE
NEW
ECONOMY

they might be surprised to learn that effective tax rates on industries that are part of the new economy are typically higher than those applied to the teetering giants of the old economy.

The old manufacturing industries have been around so long that they have accumulated an impressive array of write-offs and tax concessions, mainly thanks to decades of dedicated lobbying. Newer industries, especially those like computer software that are knowledge-based, face unintentional penalties for not having old assets like big assembly plants that allow for large write-offs or generous depreciations.

Discouraging the growth of new industries through unfair taxation should not be the implied goal of any national government, not if it is serious about fostering a higher standard of living.

KEEPING THE BABY

The long and the short of it is that the new economy opens tremendous opportunities for government to be a participant in the process of change, instead of acting as a major roadblock to what, in the end, is inevitable.

Governments can do a great deal to bridge the gap between the old and the new. Some critics of public intervention advocate a free rein for the private sector to make its own adjustments to economic change. But just because government hasn't quite got it right yet, why throw out the baby with the bath water?

There's certainly no evidence to indicate that companies rooted in the old economy can shift gears on their own. Governments have a job to do that's every bit as crucial as the one they played in setting up the essential safety nets that underpinned the recovery from the Great Depression and paved the way for the long postwar expansion. It's high time that these social and industrial programs, so carefully crafted for an economy that's now outdated, be revamped to meet the needs of the new economy. It's fine to tell governments to mind their own business, but in the real world it doesn't work that way. No one can go it alone — and only a fool would try.

The adjustments we all have to make require plenty of teamwork. One look at the shell-shocked victims of change delineates in clear and unmistakable terms what awaits us as a nation if we don't work together.

The Wounds of Change

I received a telephone call recently from a fifty-five-year-old engineer who had spent his entire career with a global giant in the forest products industry. He wanted to talk about a television interview I had given on these very themes. As he continued speaking softly of his life and times, it became clear that he had given up trying to reverse his own unhappy fortunes, though he decided that my advice might prove useful to others and wanted me to know that.

The engineer's pain was clear in his voice. His career was over, his marriage had ended, his life's savings were used up. A highly educated man with two university degrees, he had toiled seventeen years in a high-paying job. As his employer's sales lagged farther and farther behind their own targets, and as smarter competitors with the right environmental solutions and better technology developed the new processes and new products that the marketplace was demanding, the engineer lost his job. He was stunned. Nothing like that had ever happened to him before.

"I'm from the old school, where the only people who lose their jobs are the people who deserved to be fired. I kept asking myself: What did I do wrong? And it nearly drove me crazy trying to find the answer."

The engineer, like many of us, was simply unprepared for change. If you're thinking of getting another job — or if the decision has been forced on you by circumstances far beyond your control — what do you do? The natural instinct is to do what Harry and the engineer did and stay with the industry that you know best, where your skills and background and contacts mean something. But what might seem like a logical solution can be the kiss of death.

The last thing anyone really wants to do is jump from the frying pan into the fire — from one job in the old economy to another — or, perhaps worse, to waste valuable time and energy, to say nothing of dwindling life's savings, waiting in futile hope for the world to revert to what it used to be. Things change, and none of us can afford to take it as a personal affront, as some kind of sign that we've done something terribly wrong, or that the changes are somehow our fault.

Why Fish Can't Fly

Look around your place of work the next time you have a chance. You will be amazed at all the clues lying around that point to whether your employer will live or die. And remember that size and history don't count for much. Your employer might have been a trailblazer thirty years ago, staking out plants and offices around the world, but if it hasn't figured out how to become an integral player in the new economy, its future — and yours, if you linger too long — will come nowhere near to matching its golden past.

It doesn't matter what fading industry you have devoted your life's work to — whether it be the fishery in Newfoundland, or financial services in New York, or the oil patch in Texas, or urban transit just about anywhere. Basic skills in the new economy are just plain different from the ones that were essential in the old economy.

In the old economy that has seen its day, you couldn't get ahead if you couldn't use a telephone, tell time, give the correct change, write your own name. The lack of these simple skills would have doomed you to a life of back-breaking work at low wages, with few prospects of getting ahead.

We all know and admire people who have achieved success against all odds, who, through no fault of their own, had to quit school at a tender age to help support their family during the dark days of the 1930s, or in the 1940s when so many breadwinners lost their lives in the war or were wounded and unable to work. Whether they were born in North America or landed on these shores in search of a better life, these successful people came equipped with an instinctive survival plan. Through sheer determination they pulled themselves up by their bootstraps, acquiring whatever skills they needed to better their lives and the lives of their children. They were willing to take chances because they knew in their hearts that the new had to be better than the old.

The same principles apply today to the millions whose lives have been turned upside-down by economic forces they don't understand and that no one has been able to explain to them. Certain basic life skills are just as vital today — the skills to function in the new economy.

The inability to drive a car in the old economy cut people off from a host of job opportunities. It's the same today with computers. People who don't know how to use them are reduced to scanning two pages of help-wanted ads instead of six. No one said car drivers had to know how to design a vehicle or even to keep it running; mechanics were available to do all of those things for us. It sufficed to be able to fit the key into the ignition and to learn how to drive the darn thing without wrapping yourself around a telephone pole. The same notion applies to computers today. You don't need to know how to program them or why they work, but you do need to know how to turn them on and off and how to load the software you need without crashing your machine.

When Alexander Graham Bell came up with the idea for the telephone more than a century ago, his business backers thought the invention was a waste of their time. Now it's impossible to imagine business life without a telephone. Within a few decades, not knowing how to make a telephone call became a real drawback when applying for a job. And an even bigger drawback was not knowing what to do when the black thing on your desk or on the shop floor started to ring. In the 1990s, it's equally vital to be comfortable with a fax machine or the voice-mail system that will probably be attached to your computer phone.

**SHIFTING
GEARS**

THRIVING
IN THE
NEW
ECONOMY

In the old economy, everyone had to know how to tell time. How else could they get to work in the morning? But in the global '90s, you had better be able to tell what time it is in Korea, or in Germany, or in Brazil.

No one would deny that reading and writing are important skills. Now the tools used for writing have changed — electronic pencils are rapidly replacing the old lead — and what we have to read to get on with the task at hand is more likely to be a software manual than a study on the finer points of typewriter maintenance. Similarly, the need to count change using arithmetic has given way to the convenience of the calculator. For many people, it's a frightening prospect that their jobs now require them to use the calculator function built into software programs such as Microsoft's *Windows*.

Such changes are sweeping through every industry, from the most complex to the most mundane. A real estate agent I know has just started using an electronic device that he wears attached to his belt. With a quick push of a button, he can find out instantly when another house has gone on the market and what it's selling for. The agent then picks up his cellular phone and makes appointments with prospective customers.

Being an old-fashioned sort, he wasn't sure he needed the new gadgetry (he wasn't even particularly thrilled when his office installed computers and started giving him printouts of the house sales in his district, going back as far he wanted). But then one day, in trying to close a complicated deal, he found himself stymied because the agent for the other side possessed none of the new tools. The result was a delay of only a few hours, but the cost in time — in a business where time is money — was far more than he was willing to pay.

The Seventy-Six-Dollar Solution

As the real estate agent now realizes, life without computers and modern communication devices is unthinkable. In setting out your personal survival plan, it's just plain common sense to take advantage of company-sponsored education programs in computers and other new tools of your trade. Change is inevitable, and you need to be a part of the process. Team management skills, communication skills (including effective speaking and writing) and numeric skills can mean the difference between success and failure. Don't be embarrassed about asking your children to teach you how to use a computer. It's the least they could do in exchange for all the money you laid out for their latest Nintendo game. Learning the major software programs, like WordPerfect, Lotus 123 or Excel, DBase and Microsoft *Windows*, should be a basic minimum for all of us. And it's a fact of life that, in the information age, you have to be able to send and receive information — in other words, to communicate — or you'll be left behind. In an industrial setting, it's vital to know the difference between CAD and CAM and why computer-assisted design goes hand in hand with computer-assisted manufacturing.

If you're out of work now, one obvious way to upgrade your skills is to volunteer like mad. Exchange your time and effort for whatever new skills you need. You might offer to work for a computer manufacturer or a medical diagnostics firm or an environmental consulting company for a month. Tell them you want to improve your know-how, and if they won't charge you for the training, you won't charge them for your time. Meanwhile, courses of all kinds from colleges, correspondence programs and local school boards are plentiful, cheap and short. You don't have to take a year-long class in English literature to master effective writing. Many courses are available at nights and on weekends. For seventy-six dollars or less — sometimes for free — you too can have a future in the new economy!

Only the Lonely

One last point for the people left behind in the old economy: There *can* be an up-side. You could, for example, find yourself rising rapidly to the top, albeit temporarily, as others see the writing on

**SHIFTING
GEARS**

THRIVING
IN THE
NEW
ECONOMY

the wall and bail out before they go down with the ship. In this kind of company, when the chief executive says that it's lonely at the top, he's not kidding!

But being trapped in the old economy really isn't a laughing matter for people like Harry. Their lives are being ruined, and their hurt, as Larry quickly realized at that eye-opening class reunion, is very, very real.

THE NEW REALITIES

At a time when we are awash in economic information from every conceivable medium, I am constantly amazed at how little of it has any relevance to the way the economy actually works and what our role is in it. The economy has undergone a vast sea-change in the past decade; entire industries have risen from modest origins to become mighty engines of growth. Yet their impact on all of us remains a remarkably well-kept secret.

The experts are taking the pulse of the economy in the wrong places and then providing a misleading prognosis based on outdated information and faulty assumptions. The new economy is much more than a batch of numbers on a printout. It's real, it's all around us, and it's constantly evolving. Where is it written that a particular company, industry or economic structure will last forever? Like a biological organism, each lives out its time on this earth, to be replaced by something else.

Children are born, and then one day their parents wake up and find themselves staring at teenagers asking for the keys to the family car. Then, in the blink of an eye, the kids are holding babies of their own. And then Grandpa and Grandma reach old age and

**SHIFTING
GEARS**

THRIVING
IN THE
NEW
ECONOMY

their health begins to fail. Would we be shocked if someone told us that kids eventually grow up, leave home and set up households of their own? Well, segments of the economy have been going through the same evolutionary process. Babies have grown up and turned into robust adults, while everyone has been busy worrying about the declining health of the grandparents. The hard times, which clearly have caused a great deal of pain and misery for those whose livelihoods depend on the old economic engines, need to be put in the context of this evolutionary shift.

What I call *the new realities* contradicts the conventional wisdom about how the economy works and what our place in it should be. Discovering that the gloom-and-doomers are looking at the wrong picture was like finding gold in a salt mine!

WHAT'S GROWING AND WHAT'S NOT?

Some of the biggest discoveries result from the simplest questions: Why is the sky blue? Why did the apple fall from the tree and hit me on the head? Where do babies come from? Why are wheels round? Why does the level of water rise when you get into the tub? Why do they call wrestlers "Tiny" when they weigh three hundred pounds?

The question I asked one sunny spring day in 1988 was this: What's growing and what's not? The search for an answer would take me off the conventional roadways mapped out by other economists and into uncharted territory full of unexpected twists, turns and hazards.

As I began poking through a hundred or so industries, I was surprised to find that the ones I was sure our future depended on, like autos and steel, were nowhere near as big as they had once been. Others, like semiconductors and communications, which I had not even thought of as major industries before beginning my quest, turned out to be huge.

To make some sense of the stunning changes, I pulled out a scratch pad and started ranking industries by their size and comparing them with where they stood back in 1972. The table on the following page is an updated and tidier version (no one could have read my original scribblings) of that first effort to figure out what was important to the economy and what was not.

I then decided to trace the growth and decline of 207 industries. There was nothing scientific about this number. It happened to be all the U.S. industries whose data I could readily get my hands on from the Bureau of the Census in Washington. When you're starting from scratch, you go with what you have access to.

It didn't take long to realize that dozens of industries had been in decline for a dog's age. Sixty-two of them had compound annual growth rates that were negative — in other words, they were shrinking year by year. Forty industries had passed their peak by 1975, and 118 that had been growing marginally were heading for big trouble by 1988. It wasn't difficult to figure out that an industry in decline for more than fifteen years was not going to be a big engine to anything.

What really caught my eye, though, was what was occurring at the other end of the spectrum, where forty-eight industries — in spite of the ups and downs of recessions, good and bad years, high and low dollars — had recorded compound real growth rates of 3.5 percent or better each and every year. The cream of the crop, nineteen industries, had long-term real growth of 5 percent or more, which would bring joy to the heart of any chief executive, shareholder or employee looking for security. When I examined these under the microscope, it was easy to spot the fascinating common threads connecting the various industries.

What's an "Engine"?

Not every industry that's growing is strategic. Some expand rapidly but lack the ability to pull others along with them. Figuring out why some industries turn into engines (industries that push forward the economy as a whole) while others don't led to months of

THE CHANGING STRUCTURE OF U.S. INDUSTRY

LARGEST MANUFACTURING INDUSTRIES IN 1972

1. MOTOR VEHICLES & PARTS
2. MEAT PRODUCTS
3. STEEL MILL PRODUCTS
4. TEXTILES
5. CLOTHING MANUFACTURING
6. PETROLEUM REFINING
7. DAIRY PRODUCTS
8. AIRCRAFT & PARTS
9. BEVERAGES
10. GRAIN MILL PRODUCTS
11. INDUSTRIAL ORGANIC CHEMICALS
12. SOAP & CLEANERS
13. PLASTICS
14. COMMERCIAL PRINTING
15. NEWSPAPERS
16. PHARMACEUTICALS
17. BAKERY PRODUCTS
18. HOUSEHOLD FURNITURE
19. INDUSTRIAL INORGANIC CHEMICALS
20. TIRES

LARGEST MANUFACTURING INDUSTRIES IN 1992

1. MOTOR VEHICLES & PARTS
2. PETROLEUM REFINING
3. AEROSPACE
4. COMPUTERS & SEMICONDUCTORS
5. MEAT PRODUCTS
6. DAIRY PRODUCTS
7. PLASTICS
8. INSTRUMENTATION
9. INDUSTRIAL ORGANIC CHEMICALS
10. RADIO & TV EQUIPMENT
11. STEEL MILL PRODUCTS
12. COMMERCIAL PRINTING
13. PHARMACEUTICALS
14. PAPERMILLS
15. ELECTRONIC PARTS
16. CANNED FOOD
17. NEWSPAPERS
18. PACKAGING
19. TELEPHONE EQUIPMENT
20. FROZEN FOOD

intensive research. But in the first few weeks, it was already becoming clear that

1. A strategic industry could not be in decline. How could an engine be going backwards and forwards at the same time?
2. Not every growing industry was an engine. Some were certainly expanding at an incredible pace, but they were still much too small to have an impact on the rest of the economy.

For example, the space commerce industry barely existed in 1987. By the next year, it was already a $1.8-billion-a-year business. By the end of 1991, it was poised to exceed $4 billion.

Research and development in space would seem an unlikely candidate for a major new industry. How could the manufacture of protein crystals in outer space possibly be worth much? And yet this year, NASA will begin leasing space-based R&D facilities on a regularly scheduled basis. (If your lab used to be in Milwaukee, Mars could have a certain cachet in the marketplace!) What was once the daydreaming of science fiction writers has indeed turned into a serious — and rapidly expanding — industry. But is it an engine? No. Just an interesting growth industry that one day might develop into a mighty economic force, possibly in our grandchildren's day.

Among other examples are artificial intelligence, or "expert systems," as the computer scientists call the development of "thinking" machines. This industry jumped 50 percent between 1987 and 1988 in the United States, but revenue was still a tiny $2 million. By the end of 1991, it had reached $140 million annually, which is not too shabby for life in a recession. But let's be practical. In an economy worth $5.7 trillion, $140 million a year isn't even a drop in a very deep well.

There's a fundamental difference between a growth industry and one that's also strategic. To be strategic, it has to pass the growth test, which eliminates car manufacturing and a surprising number of other businesses that still occupy lots of space in the economy and lots of ink (usually red and dreary) in the press.

**SHIFTING
GEARS**
─────
THRIVING
IN THE
NEW
ECONOMY

And to be strategic, it also has to have become powerful enough to make growth happen elsewhere in the economy. This criterion knocked a lot of industries off my list. The ones that were left stood out like a lighthouse on a rocky shore.

The high-growth strategic businesses — the engines — fell into four categories:

- Computers and semiconductors (including software and information services)
- Health and medical care (including drugs, biomedicine, surgical and medical equipment and supplies)
- Communications and telecommunications (including rockets and space equipment, radio and microwave communications and entertainment)
- Instrumentation (process controls, environmental equipment and consulting, optical instruments and lenses, engineering and scientific gear)

Industries like cars, steel, petroleum and housing, which were once the driving forces of the economy, still dominate the headlines with their continuing troubles, but they are simply no longer as important as they once were. They have been knocked out of the center-stage spotlight by a bunch of brash newcomers, some of which did not even exist as industries fifteen years ago but are certainly making their presence felt today.

Among the New Realities:

- The U.S. health and medical industry has become larger than oil refining, aircraft, autos, auto parts, textiles, steel and mining put together, and will employ one in ten Americans by the end of this decade. Any industry that accounts for 13 percent of the U.S. economy certainly qualifies as a major engine of growth.

In contrast, housing, which we have all grown up accepting as one of the key measures of economic well-being, accounts for only 3.9

THE FOUR ENGINES™

COMPUTERS & SEMICONDUCTORS

- Computer Equipment
- Semiconductors
- Software
- Information Services

HEALTH & MEDICAL

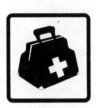

- Medical Care & Diagnostics
- Pharmaceuticals
- Surgical & Medical Instruments
- Surgical & Medical Supplies

COMMUNICATIONS & TELECOMMUNICATIONS

- Telecommunications Services
- Guided Missiles & Space Equipment
- Radio & Microwave Communications
- Entertainment

INSTRUMENTATION

- Optical Instruments & Lenses
- Engineering & Scientific Equipment
- Process Controls
- Environmental Consulting & Equipment

SHIFTING
GEARS

THRIVING
IN THE
NEW
ECONOMY

percent of the U.S. economy. It's not that housing no longer matters, it's just that other industries, like health care, now matter a great deal more.

- The aerospace industry employs more people than the auto and auto-parts industries combined. Think of it. The car-manufacturing giants and their huge network of suppliers are no longer as significant as the companies that make the satellites, space stations, rockets and other paraphernalia of the burgeoning space business. "Star Wars" and other enormously costly pie-in-the-sky projects may never get off the ground, but the industry was already booming without them.

- For those who think all the high-tech hardware comes from Taiwan, a fact of life today is that more Americans make computers than cars. More people work in the computer industry as a whole (equipment, semiconductors and computer services) than in the auto, auto parts, steel, mining and petroleum-refining industries combined.

- The software industry, which was barely a dot on the economic map before the 1980s, has been growing at the astounding rate of almost 25 percent a year to $42 billion annually.

- The electronics industry paid little attention to the terrible recession that has dominated the thinking of government leaders, central bankers and their critics for the past couple of years. American electronics employment alone has risen 18 percent in the past four years to 2.0 million people. In Canada, which is supposedly stuck in the woods and the mines and the oil fields, more people work in the sophisticated electronics industry than in pulp and paper — even in forest-rich British Columbia.

- More Americans make semiconductors than construction machinery, and more of them work in data-processing than in petroleum refining.

- Information and communications accounts for 8.5 percent of the U.S. Gross Domestic Product.

- More Americans work in accounting firms than in the whole energy industry. The number crunchers employ three times more people than the entire mining industry.
- More Americans work in biotechnology than in the entire machine-tool industry.
- The movie industry employs more people than all the auto industry.
- The equipment-leasing business barely existed fifteen years ago, but it is now almost as large as the whole petrochemical industry.
- Retailing employs more than five times as many Americans as the entire chemical sector.
- Compact discs have been around for only a few years, but the fledgling industry already takes in $4 billion in revenue a year.
- Computer consulting is even bigger — a $49-billion-a-year industry — while data-processing revenues in the United States exceed $35 billion a year.
- The travel-service industry is bigger than the petroleum refining and steel industries combined.
- Twice as many Americans make surgical and medical instruments as make plumbing and heating products.
- Canada is still labeled a hewer of wood and drawer of water, but more people in the forested province of British Columbia work in telecommunications and communications than in forestry.
- More Québécois have jobs in health and medical care than in the traditional sectors of construction, textiles, clothing, furniture, autos, forestry and mining combined.
- Ontario employs almost as many people in hydroelectricity as in the automotive industry, on which it long depended for its industrial success.
- More Nova Scotians work as teachers and university professors than in fish processing, forestry and construction put together. In fact, the East Coast province has the largest number of universities per capita of any province, making it one of the most knowledge-intensive regions in the country.

**SHIFTING
GEARS**

THRIVING
IN THE
NEW
ECONOMY

In no way, shape or form are these developments unique to North America. The same patterns show up in every major industrial economy. The trends sweeping through North America are also transforming the economies of Japan and Western Europe.

Four major engines are driving the new global economy, and it is the strength of these that is the true barometer of each country's current state and prospects. An analysis of these engines results in a far different outlook to one based on the traditional industries that dominated the old economy but can no longer pull the economic train to the top of the mountain. Both the United States and Canada have been expanding in the areas that count most, but we don't hear much about it, because most experts are busily watching the wrong locomotives.

The big surprise is that the new economy is real ... and that the future is a lot brighter than most people think.

THE U.S. RECOVERY
IS STRONGER THAN YOU THINK

- U.S. Medical Starts:
    up 19.1% on the year in July 1992
    from 12.8% in June

- U.S. Pharmaceutical Production:
    up 10.2% on the year in June 1992
    from 9.6% in May

- U.S. Computers & Office Machines Production:
    up 14.1% on the year in July 1992
    from 13.0% in June

- U.S. New Orders for Communications &
  Telecommunications Equipment:
    up 32.6% on the year in July 1992
    from 19.7% in June

- U.S. Consumer Electronics Production:
    up 9.1% on the year in June 1992
    from 9.0% in May

- U.S. Knowledge Intensive Employment:
    up 2.6% on the year in August 1992
    from 1.8% in July

- U.S. Real Technology Spending:
    up 16.4% on the year in the second quarter
    of 1992 from 13.8% in the first quarter of
    1992

- U.S. High Technology Trade Surplus:
    reached $2.9 billion to date in 1992, still
    one of its highest surpluses in history

THE LITTLE ENGINES THAT COULD

THE BAROMETERS OF GROWTH

The North American economy has been driven by big industrial engines since the end of the First World War. Until about ten years ago, one of those engines was automobile manufacturing and parts. But in the new economy, this engine has been replaced by computers and semiconductors. Health and medical care has supplanted housing; communications and telecommunications has taken the spot long occupied by transportation. Similarly, machine tools, a major force in the old economy, has given way to instrumentation, a category that includes numerically controlled machines, robotics, environmental controls and scientific instruments among its varied parts.

Each of the four new engines has had its good and bad years. And it's a fact of life that some companies, no matter how strong their growth, couldn't manage their way out of a paper bag, let alone stay at the forefront of a fast-paced, high-flying industry. But unlike the warhorses of the old economy, these new engines are at least producing goods and services that people want and are willing to pay for today.

Engine No. 1: Computers and Semiconductors

Microsoft, the U.S. software giant, was not even a gleam in its youthful founder's eyes until seventeen years ago. A decade ago, its annual revenue was a respectable but scarcely eye-popping $34 million. But by last year, the number had climbed to $1.8 billion, and the company is still expanding by leaps and bounds. At about $22 billion, it has a higher market value than mighty General Motors, the foremost manufacturer in the old economy. While GM has been closing plants and laying off thousands of workers, the software maker is adding some six dozen new bodies a week to its staff of about ten thousand. Not only is Bill Gates the richest man in America, but two other top executives have also become billionaires, several others are multimillionaires, and a couple of thousand employees have made it into the ranks of the millionaires. Call it the revenge of the computer nerds!

Not all manufacturers are in Microsoft's enviable position at the top of the computer roost. Many have gone under, and others have endured painful layoffs and cutbacks, proof (if any were needed) that being in the right industry at the right time is no guarantee of continuing success. Hard times take their toll on the new as well as the old, the big as well as the small. Giant IBM, a company that has made more than its share of mistakes, took a hit to the tune of nearly $3 billion in 1991. But my research results make it crystal clear that software and the other pieces that make up the computer world constitute a roaring engine that dwarfs the once all-powerful automotive industry.

More North Americans work in the manufacture of computers today than cars. And in the crucial domain of global trade, this new engine more than pulls its weight. Computers now account for an astounding 20 percent of all U.S. nonagricultural trade — one dollar in every five, or $26 billion in 1991. Add to that the $21.9 billion earned by U.S. software makers in foreign markets, and you're talking huge numbers — enough to make Americans think twice about the supposed disadvantage they face in the global arena.

SHIFTING
GEARS

THRIVING
IN THE
NEW
ECONOMY

Compare this with the figures for the automotive industry. American exports of all vehicles and parts combined last year was $22 billion, less than half the total of computer-related shipments; and even this number is skewed by the fact that much of the auto trade is "captive" — flowing between the U.S. parents and their branch plants in Canada as part of the automotive trade pact between the two countries.

In fact, the United States has a healthy and widening trade surplus in computers and the stuff that makes them work, something the Japan bashers should note. How much does it matter if the Japanese have a big edge in a fading industry like autos? Far more worrisome would be an assault on software makers and other American companies posting spectacular growth.

As the cost of energy, the key ingredient behind the growth of the car industry and other segments of the old mass-manufacturing economy, soared in the 1970s, it was inevitable that the major engines that depended on it would slip into decline. It was a normal, and predictable, part of the aging process. Less predictable was what would rise up to take its spot as an essential engine of the economy. But if we stop to think about it, computers are the logical next step in the transportation chain — the chassis that carries information, instead of people and goods. More than that, computers, with the appropriate software and telecommunications hookups, create and process what they transport.

Replacing the New with the New

The average replacement cycle for cars has lengthened tremendously over the past decade and will probably grow longer still as car-makers try to outdo each other and hold on to their share of a shrinking market with better warranties and other quality-related promises that would never have existed in the booming big-car era.

By comparison, we all know how fast computers turn into electronic junk. My fancy machine was practically obsolete the day I bought it, while my car has a few miles left on it yet. And though most of us are quite satisfied with a single automobile, chances are there's more than one computer in our lives.

As a true emblem of the old economy, the auto industry is slowly fading into the sunset. Yet month after month, the business press trots out the latest car and truck production statistics (every ten days in the U.S., where apparently people just can't wait a whole month for now-meaningless information), as if the economy's health still depends on how many fenders roll off the assembly line. Nothing could be further from the truth. When it comes to what drives our economic present and future, computers are in and cars out.

From about the middle of the last century to the end of the First World War, cheap steel was the key ingredient in the economic growth formula. Then along came cheap energy as the driving force of the mass-manufacturing era. Today, we live in a world that spins around on cheap microchips. To get a sense of how important these tiny bits of silicon have become in our daily lives, I set out one day to count how many of them were running things in my own home.

I started in the most logical place: the kitchen. The first thing that caught my untrained eye was the Panasonic microwave oven. "That's got to be good for at least one microchip," I said to myself. "And the wall oven couldn't turn itself on and off with what seems like a mind of its own without a chip in there someplace, though I swear every time it ruins the brownies it's just plain possessed." By this time, the dog was looking at me quizzically, so I stopped talking out loud.

The intercom unit on the wall above a little desk looked as if it might contain another couple of microchips. But the darn thing hasn't worked since the day we bought it, so I could be wrong about that.

Moving on into the living room, I zeroed in on the CD player, stereo, tuner, amplifier and tape deck. All definitely new age, crammed with chips. Anyone who's been in an electronics store in the past couple of years knows about the microchip-driven techno-gadgets that are available to us just so we can listen to our old Beatles records, with every skip and scratch preserved for posterity!

SHIFTING
GEARS
═══════
THRIVING
IN THE
NEW
ECONOMY

Next stop on the tour was the family room, the technological capital of any household. Two electronic thermostats control the temperature. Both went on my steadily growing chip list, along with the gizmo that controls the lighting.

Our family space was laid out with great forethought to be a couch potato's haven. But this cocoon of comfort is really a microchip-driven nerve center. There's a large television, a cable converter (why does every household need three of those remote-control gadgets, when there's only one TV?), a VCR and the old stereo and tape deck that date from the Pleistocene Age of electronics — the mid 1970s.

By this point, we're talking about a major investment in new technology, and we haven't even got off the main floor! Throw in the security system and a couple of garage-door openers ... I began losing count after coming up with twenty-three microchips in what I consider a very normal home. With my point about our daily dependence on the humble microchip proved beyond any doubt, I never even bothered going upstairs to count our motley assortment of clock radios (some of which are so ancient they actually have dials!). A fax machine and computer in my husband's study, along with the rest of our household's paraphernalia, never made it to my list either.

And what about our telephones? We've got this computer hookup that enables us to plug into all sorts of outside databases. We can shop at Sears, do our banking and leaf through the Yellow Pages electronically, all for a mere nine dollars extra a month — all driven by cheap chips.

ENGINE No. 2: HEALTH AND MEDICAL

Monthly medical starts in the United States have been soaring — up almost 10 percent in real terms from their level of a year ago.

People are always asking me what a "medical start" is. I coined the term to describe the construction of general and special-care hospitals, clinics, outpatient treatment facilities and chronic-care, nursing and convalescent homes. It also includes commercial buildings devoted solely to housing doctors and their labs, but it doesn't embrace retirement residences.

Medical starts produce infinitely greater economic spinoffs than housing starts, which measure the construction of homes and are wrongly considered to provide a vital reading of an economy's health today. Manufacturers and retailers in the old economy rubbed their hands in glee at the thought of the $500 dishwasher and $1,000 fridge that would be fitted into a new home. But compare that to a one to two million dollar CAT-scanner for each new hospital or diagnostic clinic. A couple buying a home might splurge on a brand-new bedroom set, broadloom or a pair of bunk beds for their kids, but such furious consumer action pales beside the tens of millions of dollars in orders that flow from a new two or three hundred bed hospital.

And if you're talking about one of those fancy California clinics that specialize in face-lifts or tummy-tucks, you're looking at hundreds of thousands of dollars just for the tasteful, soothing art on the walls (not to mention the vast sums expended on mineral water and special mudbaths). Compare that to the ten or twenty dollars a young home-buyer might spend for a Van Gogh poster or a portrait of Elvis to decorate the living-room wall!

The health and medical sector numbers scores of industries that are large and dynamic in their own right. Pharmaceuticals alone have become a $49-billion-a-year industry in the United States. (By comparison, the entire American household appliance industry is worth $17.4 billion.) Add diagnostic substances like the chemicals used to analyze urine and blood samples, pregnancy tests (thankfully, no one waits for the bunny to die any more) and the stuff they pump into you for X-rays and other medical unpleasantries, and you've got an almost $60-billion-a-year industry. That's huge by any standards. The whole U.S. dairy industry is worth less than $50 billion. Soft drinks are even lower, at $28 billion. And what drives much of this explosive growth is medical starts.

SHIFTING
GEARS

THRIVING
IN THE
NEW
ECONOMY

Yet none of the experts who regularly monitor the economy track this vital sign. Housing starts and retail sales remain leading economic indicators, tabulated and studied to death, the way ancient soothsayers once examined chicken bones, and with about the same results. Leaving out a major engine of the economy is like trying to do a thorough medical examination without checking the patient's pulse and blood pressure.

Even in Canada's public health system, where hospital beds are being closed and services curtailed because of high costs, the medical industry is thriving. (This is perhaps even more true in the unbelievably expensive American private enterprise structure.) Of course, as in any other business, public or private, inefficiencies build up that have to be squeezed out, and the incompetent and the greedy have to go. But just because a scalpel is being applied to the care side doesn't mean public pressure for the services is easing.

As in the powerful postwar housing boom, the demand is fueled by obvious demographic trends. The graying population may no longer need as much new housing, but it does insist on plenty of high-quality health and medical services. And as we all get older, the demand can only rise. People are taking better care of themselves and living longer, which means more, not less, use of the medical system.

The way the housing industry developed in the postwar years provides another useful benchmark for the health business. When demand for houses soared, major roadblocks to mass construction had to be overcome. For houses to be thrown up quickly and affordably, the building trades had to be brought together under the roofs of general contractors.

Similarly, the medical industry is being streamlined to make the delivery of services a great deal more efficient. While it would be wrong to expect a surge of new spending on the care side in Canada and other countries where costs are spiralling out of control, you can be sure that millions will be pumped into the diagnostic end of the medical biz. To survive, hospitals in major centers will have to have the very latest in equipment and techniques or risk losing the race to smarter, better-equipped competitors.

We'll also see new medical techniques and breakthroughs, like artificially reproduced genes that will speed healing and solve some of the current disease puzzles. This is already happening, and Canadian companies are getting their share of a business with untold potential for growth. To take just one example, a Mississauga, Ontario, company, has reproduced a protein that plays a key role in skin regeneration after burns or other serious damage. And every major company in the industry is working on similar "miracle cures."

ENGINE No. 3: COMMUNICATIONS AND TELECOMMUNICATIONS

When people talk of the rising importance of the service sector in our economy, the big mistake they make is in identifying it as *the* new economy. I don't know about you, but I have trouble keeping a straight face when I try to picture hair salons, donut franchises, banks or shoe-repair shops as part of the new economy. Service businesses have been around since the beginning of commerce itself; they can hardly be labelled collectively as our economic future. Yet I hear it all the time: "We're soon going to be nothing more than a service economy, filled with jobs that pay low wages!"

Well this "McJob" syndrome is simply not going to shape our economic existence. For one thing, the lowest salaries are almost always in the non-union, unskilled factory jobs of the old economy. A portfolio manager in charge of billions of dollars in mutual funds is part of the service economy. So is actress Julia Roberts. And for that matter, what is the President of the United States if not an employee in the service sector? None of them will ever be confused with the hamburger-flippers or store clerks who come to mind when the discussion turns to service jobs.

When we're talking about services strictly designed for the new economy, we're walking in the land of giants — tracking the footsteps of the huge telecommunications, cable and entertainment

SHIFTING
GEARS
THRIVING
IN THE
NEW
ECONOMY

companies. For example, 890,000 Americans work in the telecommunications service industry, which, incidentally, chalked up revenues of $175 billion last year. That's a lot of healthy zeroes in anyone's book!

On the manufacturing side, 390,000 people turn out radio, television, broadcasting and communications equipment that ranges from the most complex of satellites to the simplest of walkie-talkies. Another 85,000 people make equipment for the telephone industry, and that is certain to grow.

The market for portable cordless phones alone will easily be worth tens of billions of dollars. I'm not talking about the already outdated phones that could be carried around the house without tripping over a long cord, or the costly cellular models that have become virtually standard equipment in cars and briefcases. The newest in phone technology is remarkably light and cheap. No bigger than one of my three TV channel-changers but less complicated to work, the flip-top phones can be tucked into an ordinary pocket.

Canada's Northern Telecom and other major telecommunications manufacturers must be drooling at the potential of a market that didn't exist until this decade. But then, the entire way we transport everything has changed dramatically in recent years. Who could have imagined the ubiquitous fax machine, voice-mail or electronic messages via computer even a few short years ago?

To get an idea of the stunning changes, think of what it must have been like to try to conduct everyday business a hundred, or, if you're a real history buff, two hundred years ago. Imagine sending a package to another city before the age of railways. Overland travel of a couple of hundred miles was a major trek. As recently as the 1950s, getting a parcel across the Atlantic could take weeks. I still remember as a kid how long it took to ship a Christmas gift to Ireland. Believe me, that was no Priority Post! Sending money presented its own daunting obstacles, but today, funds can be transferred halfway around the world in split seconds as the telecommunications industry revolutionizes the business of transportation.

In the old economy, people and products had to be carted around physically, which turned transportation into a mighty engine of growth. That's still important, but the big growth these days is happening in industries that carry the ideas, information and know-how directly. The age of communications and telecommunications is upon us, hurtling along with such force that it makes the engines of the old economy look slow and cumbersome by comparison.

There's a TV commercial that perfectly illustrates this world of change. In the ad, a harried sales manager cancels a holiday because of all the meetings he has to attend. At the airport, he bumps into a friend who has completed his weekly managers' meeting by a multicity phone conference before stepping on the plane for a vacation with his wife and kids.

Corporations have added 1-800 phone numbers to support their products across thousands of miles. Presidents routinely use videoconferencing to address entire workforces scattered throughout different parts of the world. Cellular phones have popped up everywhere, promising to keep us all in touch with people we never want to hear from again. Outside of fiction writers and a few bold scientists, who could have imagined a few short years ago that all this would be commonplace, along with all the sundry other technological innovations we take for granted today in the new economy?

Entertainment, too, is vastly different thanks to the technology of the new economy. Once upon a time, the big event of the season for many a small town was the arrival of the circus, with its exciting and exotic range of entertainment. Now, even in the most remote of hamlets residents have access to a mind-boggling array of television programs coming in by satellite on dozens of channels, or, if they prefer, stacks of movies at the local video-rental outlet. The companies that deliver these services are the ones worth betting a future on.

As just one example of how much the entertainment world has changed, we need only look at the sprawling Walt Disney empire. With its electronics-filled theme parks drawing millions of visitors on

SHIFTING
GEARS
────────
THRIVING
IN THE
NEW
ECONOMY

three continents, as well as huge international television, film, cable, record and video operations, Disney is covering all the bases in the global village. It's no coincidence that Japanese electronic giants Matsushita and Sony have moved to acquire huge Hollywood bases — the software to go with their long-established edge in hardware.

Canadian entertainment companies like Alliance Entertainment and Nelvana are dipping their toes in the global market as well. Where once they might have been perfectly content with modest Canadian television contracts or perhaps a Hollywood bit part, now they scour the world for production partners and sell their programs in dozens of markets opened up by the explosion in cable and satellite TV.

ENGINE No. 4: INSTRUMENTATION

Machine tools were a powerhouse of the old economy. Equipment like lathes, milling machines, grinders and stamping machines represented economies of scale, the production of vast quantities of identical parts and materials for an economy based on mass-manufacturing.

The new engine of instrumentation provides "economies of scope," which enables us to place a custom-designed car order, and a few weeks later pick up a finished vehicle that meets our exact specifications. Try doing that without computer-assisted design and manufacturing — a key feature of production in the new economy.

The new manufacturing technology has changed the products we use and how we use them. Remember when cars used to rattle and shimmy, when their doors never ever closed properly, when television sets and toasters and irons and ovens and washing machines fell apart the day after the warranty expired? That still happens with some makes, but they are sure to be crushed by competitors using the most modern of instrumentation to reduce costs and eliminate flaws.

Electron-beam welding, a process that allows the fusing of different metals like copper and steel with almost the same strength the metals had on their own, was once so expensive it could only be used for the turbine blades of jet engines. Now, the method is so highly automated that it can be used in everyday car parts, turning them out with a rapidity and precision never seen before. How does that affect us? Apart from lasting longer and running better, the cars made with these parts can run as smoothly at high speeds as they do when we're crawling along in rush-hour traffic.

A lot of the innovations were driven by the space race of the '60s and '70s. It's pretty tough to call Joe's Garage for a precision part when you're orbiting the moon.

Anyone who still thinks instrumentation is a sidelight to the big show needs to take another look at the numbers. Machine tools are a $4.2-billion business today. That barely stacks up against modern instrumentation, whose shipments last year exceeded $40 billion. The most basic parts of the new engine, such as industrial control devices, are worth more than $23 billion. Last year, companies sold over $10-billion worth of surgical instruments alone.

Yet faithfully each month, business journalists cling to machine-tool orders as if they really meant life or death to the economy. Crackers and cookies are a $7.1-billion business — nearly twice as large as machine tools — but when was the last time your morning paper played up a drop in biscuit orders? They correctly surmise that the fate of the nation is not at stake because the cookie business might be crumbling. Why can't they understand that machine tools now rank in the same "so what?" class? Here's what the U.S. Department of Commerce had to say: "In 1991, shipments of the entire machine-tool industry were less than what most of the top Fortune 100 companies shipped individually."

Machine tools are still valuable; manufacturers will always need them. But they will never again be an economic force, as a tour of any modern plant quickly shows. The first thing you see when you walk in the doors is the incredible degree of automation — the key difference between the old and the new, the successes and the failures in manufacturing today. Companies in the old economy have had little choice but to adopt the new technologies. (Old dogs *can* be taught a few new tricks when their lives depend on it!)

SHIFTING
GEARS
─────
THRIVING
IN THE
NEW
ECONOMY

There's a steel mill in Belgium like many others in the world now that reveals how old industries can be adapted through technology to survive in the new economy. The entire mill is run by a single person standing in front of a panel full of controls in an air-conditioned pulpit. Well, actually computers run everything. He mostly just stands and watches, contentedly sipping his *café crème*.

One process, called roll-changing, involves mill rolls weighing 12,000 to 14,000 pounds apiece. This used to require a staff of ten and the help of an overhead crane. The rolls have to be changed once or twice during an eight-hour shift, and the process used to take anywhere from one to two hours, which could eat up almost half of the working time. The Belgians installed an automatic, computer-controlled roll-changer, reducing the whole job to a few people, a couple of buttons and fifteen minutes. To stay competitive, other steel-makers around the world have adopted similar technology.

As cheap labor becomes less and less of a factor in manufacturing, Western plants can use instrumentation to regain or widen their competitive advantage, particularly in the new industries that require the most sophisticated instruments — robotics, computer controls, laser technology and the like. Similarly, the surging demand for environmental monitoring equipment for gas emissions, water purity and the ozone layer presents an exciting opportunity for growth. The people who can measure the garbage and its risks are becoming major economic players.

When I was a kid, concern for the environment meant not throwing the McDonald's container on the grass or tossing a cigarette out the car window when driving through a national park. The environment scarcely seemed a likely breeding ground for a high-tech industry with an insatiable demand for the most sophisticated of measuring instruments.

That's what change is all about. Smart companies make the adjustments, but too many others ignore a simple maxim: Nothing lasts forever.

NO TREE GROWS TO THE SKY

For every industry that successfully makes the leap from one circle to the next, there's another that falls straight off the edge or barely makes it across the chasm, hanging on by its financial fingernails for a while before slipping into the black hole of oblivion. But there are plenty of clues that disaster lurks — if you know where to look for them.

Ross Perot, who built a fortune out of processing data for governments and corporations, certainly knew where to look after the sale of his creation, Electronic Data Systems, brought him into the embrace of General Motors. The car giant bought Perot's multibillion-dollar enterprise in 1984 as part of a concerted effort to make its transition from the old economy into the new and avoid permanent relegation to a rapidly fading economic circle. The idea was to team up with a vibrant, technology-driven company that could breathe some life into GM's old-economy culture and help it step gingerly into the new economy.

It couldn't have taken Perot more than five seconds in his new environment to realize that he had made a terrible mistake. It's hard to imagine an outspoken maverick like Perot fitting into

SHIFTING
GEARS

THRIVING
IN THE
NEW
ECONOMY

anyone else's organization, no matter how flexible, but he had a right to assume that people staring disaster in the face might listen to an outsider with a spectacular track record in a part of the economy they didn't understand. Instead, his ideas and criticisms were brushed aside like so much dirt on the windshield. Perot's attempts to shake the car-maker out of its old ways branded him a nutcase. Whether he qualifies as a walking Christmas cake or not, it's always easier to attack the messenger than to listen to unpalatable truths. Blame the unfair Japanese, or government policies, or the fickleness of the buying public. It's only human nature to blame anything and anyone but the face in the mirror.

Like some faded movie hunk, a lot of once-Schwarzenegger-like companies have gone flabby, while smarter, tougher competitors turn out all the box-office hits. Instead of exciting new products and bold innovations, IBM made headlines for inner turmoil and morale problems. GM became the butt of jokes over desperate management shuffles, while Citicorp, once the epitome of global banking might, couldn't seem to do anything right. All lost buckets of money; yet, for the life of them, they couldn't seem to figure out why. That's because the executives who run these companies are only now coming to realize an absolute truth: No tree grows to the sky.

Hard as it might be to accept, nothing goes on forever, not even for the best and the brightest. IBM, GM, Citicorp, American Express, Philips and so many others have fallen into the trap. As much as they would love to, they've discovered that they can't *will* customers to buy their products merely because of their famous names. The burial grounds are full of once-great corporations that died lingering, painful deaths because they couldn't make the same leap as their customers.

Companies, industries, entire economies that don't shift gears with the changing times are doomed. It's as simple as that. They can install a revolving door in the executive offices, slash costs to the bone and make pronouncements about their commitment to the future all they like — but unless they can figure out how to make and sell products people actually want to buy, the boldest actions will have no more impact on the sad, downward spiral than if the owners of the *Titanic* had fired the captain after the ship hit the iceberg.

You Know You're in the Old Economy When...

Anybody who's ever sat through a job interview knows the vague but powerful feeling of unease that hits when something is somehow not quite right with the company doing the hiring. It might be the products, or the managers, or the questions being asked, or the general appearance of the offices. A little voice whispers: "Get out of here ... now. Before it's too late!"

Not being in Ross Perot's financial position, most of us ignore our built-in radar. But that can be the mistake of a working lifetime. Select the wrong employer in the wrong part of the economy and you might as well rent a big billboard telling the world that you've given up on your financial and career prospects. Worse yet, you stand an excellent chance of being back on the street again before you've had time to update your resumé.

My research shows that if you're employed in the old economy, the odds are better than 50 percent that your job will disappear — no matter how many years of loyal work you've put in. There's nothing theoretical about what government and business economists like to call "downsizing." This nice, tidy word translates at the personal level into incredible fear, anguish and pain. The cost in terms of self-esteem can be staggering, as millions of helpless victims lurch from one job in the old economy to the next with nothing to show for their exhausting efforts but a collection of pink slips and unemployment checks at the end of the day.

I once participated in a public meeting on the state of the economy. One of the people speaking was a clean-cut guy in his early thirties, an earnest sort who had been in and out of three jobs in the past six years. His clear, intelligent eyes shone with pain and defeat and helplessness, and his voice was etched in despair.

SHIFTING
GEARS

THRIVING
IN THE
NEW
ECONOMY

The unfortunate man had started out at a steel company in his hometown, the same one where his father and grandfather before him had spent their entire working lives. Naturally, if naively, he assumed that he would enjoy the same security. He married his high school sweetheart and they began planning for a family and a home of their own.

It was about then that the layoff notice arrived. "I could see that the writing was on the wall. I had low seniority. There was no chance I'd get called back."

Filled with the optimism of youth, the newly unemployed steel-worker dutifully signed up for a government retraining program and emerged as a qualified machine-tool operator. Despite the cries that there are never enough skilled workers, he couldn't land a job. "I was trained for a $22-an-hour job that didn't exist," he says ruefully. Eventually, he did find work, as a low-paid, general factory laborer, lost it and went back into retraining yet again. He found another job, but it too was on a lower rung of the old economy, and he lasted only eighteen months.

Like hundreds of thousands of others pounding the mean streets of North America and Western Europe, the disillusioned man doesn't work regularly any more, if at all. His head no longer dances with images of picket fences, large suburban spaces and laughing children. And his heart doesn't sing. After diligently following the next-to-useless advice of well-meaning politicians and job counsellors, he faces a bleak future of more and more training for jobs that don't exist — or won't much longer — because they are wedded to a stagnant or dying economy.

The old economy is a dark pit in which millions of people are wasting the best years of their lives. The staggering cost of so much lost potential should make us all weep, because it's all so unnecessary.

There are plenty of ways to tell which companies — and entire industries — are treading water and which are going under; which ones are decrepit old warriors on their last legs and which are would-be survivors. The key is never to trust the bottom line or the company's public statements. Rely on your instincts, and on what your senses, common and otherwise, tell you. Believe me, you will know when you've entered the land of the old economy.

Based on my own observations, you're definitely in the Death Valley of the job market when

- The parking lot is nearly empty. Either no one works there any more or the ones who do can no longer afford cars.
- The factory's empty and has a dirt or plank floor. Don't laugh. Dirt floors used to be standard in heavy industries, to absorb the weight of all the massive old equipment.
- There isn't a worker under forty-five, and early retirement schemes are so oversubscribed there's a waiting list.
- The decor is some variation of avocado green and orange, because the last time they could afford to paint the place was twenty years ago when those colors were all the rage. The same goes for tin desks, linoleum on the office floor and those old five-drawer heavy metal filing cabinets. If the cabinets are made of wood, or the company's using cardboard boxes for its records, you're really in trouble.
- Layers upon layers of management have built up, with more vice-presidents than lead hands on the shop floor.
- The talk's all about what used to be, instead of what's ahead. If the interviewer starts reminiscing about the glory days when the place was humming on round-the-clock shifts, and violins start playing over the intercom, it's time to politely get the hell out of there. If there's a historical plaque on the building, don't even bother going in unless you're looking for very temporary work. The place has already been designated as a monument to the past.
- You ask what programs are in place to protect against viruses and they send you to the company nurse instead of the systems manager.
- Management says: "We tried that and it didn't work."

SHIFTING
GEARS

THRIVING
IN THE
NEW
ECONOMY

- The union leader is a whole lot smarter and more experienced than the company president.

- The bulletin board is covered with notices for retraining, retirement, rationalization, restructuring, relocation. (Why is it that so many "R" words carry the smell of corporate death?) What you're looking for is a place where the notice boards are filled with news of staff additions and promotions and celebrations of growth.

- "Just-in-time" means making it through the gate before the foreman notices.

- The art work consists of big pictures of the ancient company founder and his successors glowering down from the walls in their three-piece attire, holding pocket watches as if they're still timing workers' lunch breaks. Better to see a portrait of the founder in jeans, or, preferably, no picture at all, because the president has far too much work to do to sit still for one.

- The company is more than two decades old and is still being run with an iron hand by the founder.

- The equipment is older than most of the people who use it. Be particularly wary if the old Underwood typewriters are still clacking away beside computers that have never been unwrapped from the original plastic. The same goes for new factory machinery. If it's still in the packing cases, the company has given up pretending to keep up with the competition.

- At least three-quarters of the workers are men. That may sound like an odd indicator, but the simple fact is that in the new economy — the one with all the growth prospects, the big salaries and the security — women account for 48.4 percent of the knowledge-intensive jobs (professional, managerial, scientific, technical). That's better than their 45.9 percent share of the total workforce.

Experts continue depicting women as stuck in job ghettos with fragile security — which is the case in the old economy — but the unemployment rate for knowledge workers in North America is below 3 percent. In the old economy, where jobless levels stand at

20 percent or more, women factory workers are outnumbered four to one by men. That might be a good ratio in a singles bar, but it's a sure sign that you should be considering another place to work.

• The pay is really low. This may seem obvious, but consider that the median weekly wage for American factory workers in 1991 was $351, while technicians in the new economy pulled in $500. The average full-time worker in the textile industry, which is about as old as the old economy gets, takes home $233. At the top of the textile pay scale sits the winding-and-twisting machine operator, at $298 a week.

That's less than the typical going rate for lifeguards or aerobics instructors who work for municipal recreation departments. Even religious workers (priests, ministers, rabbis and the like, who presumably have foresaken vast material gains) make more than the average textile-machine operator or construction worker.

The Cold Light of Reality

But it could always be worse; you could be working for a company studied firsthand by a friend I'll call George, an international steel analyst who has tracked the declining industry for years. He's toured plants all over the world, and can spot the sure losers faster than I can say "cold-rolled steel." None, in his experience, has been a better bet for the scrap pile than a certain North American operation.

This company has been in decline for years, but is being kept alive on a government support system, presumably in the hope that the 1880s will return at any moment. George says the government and the workers would both be better off if the assistance went directly into the workers' pockets, and everybody forgot about trying to make steel.

"I went out to this one mill. You could tell it had no future as soon as you drove into the parking lot. There were no cars in the visitors' space — and this was a regular working day."

SHIFTING
GEARS
━━━━
THRIVING
IN THE
NEW
ECONOMY

He checked in at the gate to pick up his pass and the requisite hard hat and safety glasses. "There were only three hats, because they don't ever expect guests, you know, people selling equipment or engineers from other companies." Other plants keep boxes of the protective gear on hand.

"I drove out into the heart of the complex. There was no traffic whatsoever. It was like one of those ghost towns in the old movies." Inside, George spotted other tell-tale signs of trouble. "All the paint was peeling. You couldn't tell what was paint and what was rust. They never bothered doing any repairs. There were big holes in the building, but there was nothing to steal. All the equipment weighs tons, and it was useless anyway."

Modern machinery lay in the original packing cases five years after it had been delivered to the grime-encrusted mill. That's great news for the packing-crate industry or the used machinery business, but it doesn't say much for the company's faith in the future of its mill. A manager had to put down a piece of burlap on the grease-covered visitor's chair so that George could sit down.

He's sure he saw only a couple of employees under the age of forty. There might have been others, but they looked and acted much older because of the strain of working day after day for a company without a real future.

"All the young, up-and-coming talent was gone. What are you left with? They had engineers using thirty-year-old equipment. I couldn't believe it. There's new technology that would cut their costs by maybe 40 or 50 percent. They said changing would be risky. What if the new equipment didn't work? What would they do then? Can you believe that? They're going down the tubes and they don't want to change the way they do things. It's like keeping an old airplane going with elastic bands. I was ready to throw my briefcase through the window."

Industry Life Cycles

George knows from years of experience that this steel company isn't even trying to make it to the next circle of growth. Like someone who contracts a terminal illness in old age, it's just waiting for the sad but inevitable end. The problem is that a lot of hard-working people will go down with it. Some companies in just as bad shape have a much stronger will to live. With some hard work, enough money and a little luck, they will pick themselves off the dirt floor and climb back on to a renewed growth track.

Every industry — and every company in it — goes through its own life cycle, always with what I've identified as five distinct phases to their expansion and inevitable decline and fall: growth, inflation, disinflation, deflation, and the rock-bottom, or, in economists' jargon, "the trough."

Growth: This is the golden time when the marketplace can't get enough of a company's products and sales skyrocket. Pharmaceutical, software and environmental companies are in this happy stage of the cycle right now. You can afford to lower prices when orders skyrocket.

Inflation: Production still climbs, though at a much slower pace. In the meantime, companies have come to the wonderful discovery that seemingly endless demand and a lack of effective competition enable them to set their own pricing. Companies can keep the dollar value of sales rising at the old clip simply by raising their prices whenever they need more revenues.

This is the stage at which every corporate planner orders a ruler from the supply room and draws one of those lines on the chart heading straight up, as if the demand will never hit a ceiling, prices can be raised forever and the road ahead is permanently paved with success. No wonder executives start believing in their own infallibility. They expand with wild abandon and become convinced they've discovered the key to perpetual profits.

93

" . . . NO TREE GROWS TO THE SKY"

INDUSTRIAL LIFE CYCLES

Growth	Inflation	Disinflation	Deflation	Trough
Demand is strong	Prices rise faster than volume	Price rise slows; volume falls	Prices and volumes fall	Stable prices; slow growth

Personal services

Computers

Federal government

Financial services

Medical

Auto

Mining

Oil & Gas

○ Points show where each sector is today

Disinflation: Everything still looks rosy from the outside, but behind the brave words of the corporate chieftains lurks genuine fear. They've discovered to their shock and horror that in real life nothing grows forever. Under the sheer weight of all the overcapacity piled on in the expansion phases, competition really starts to bite. Prices still go up, but not the way they used to, and nowhere near enough to cover the huge additional costs caused by all those extra plants added in the glory years. As a result, profit margins slide noticeably.

The clue that a company or industry has hit this painful stage is the emergence of catch-phrases like "lean and mean," as in: "We're going to become lean and mean, so that we can tackle all the unfair competition grabbing an increasing piece of our market." Translation: "Maybe, if we lay off lots of workers and cut out some extravagances, like sales meetings in exotic locations, our shareholders will be happier with our performance."

This is a tough time for the best of managers. But it's only the scene-setter for the horrors to come.

Deflation: By this stage, companies have given up on lean and mean. They're just plain *mean*. Sales plunge and prices fall as smarter, tougher, lower-cost competitors catch up, and everybody cuts each other's throat. Just ask Chrysler's Lee Iacocca about the strain of managing through the toughest period of the life cycle. Of course, the task would be easier if years of ever-rising revenues had not convinced them that, even as they heard the muffled sounds of chainsaws in the distance, their trees would indeed grow forever.

After contemplating different methods of ritual suicide, a typical company invariably decides to mothball its old factories, downsize its workforce by something close to 50 percent, sell off the crown jewels — some of its best divisions — while screaming for trade protection or a corporate savior.

It's a hallmark of this stage that mortal enemies come to exchange vows of eternal love. Witness the huge bank mergers in the United States — Chemical Bank with Manufacturers Hanover (commonly known as "Manny Hanny"), and BankAmerica with Security Pacific. Their desperate boards figure that twice the sales at half the cost will enable them to grow. But they are only postponing the final reckoning.

Trough: This should not be confused with that other "trough," where some businesses have been known to gather for government handouts during this depressing — and depressed — period of the life cycle. "Keep us going at any cost," they whine, "or you will have a lot of unemployed voters on your hands."

Industries like oil and gas are at the bottom of the well right now, but they will have plenty of company as other fading stars (Hello, big banks!) slide down the ladder. At this point, life carries on much as it would for an accident victim in shock — too numb to do much about anything. Those that survive the ordeal will emerge bloodied and bruised, not to mention refinanced, rationalized and reorganized (here come those painful "R" words again) to catch the next wave of growth.

THE SEVEN-YEAR JOURNEY

You can set your watch by the predictable reactions of business executives to the various steps in their downward march to the dreaded trough. Examining the growth and subsequent shrinkage of several hundred industries, I found that the decline and fall are typically completed after seven years. This is a span with strong biblical overtones, and many troubled titans start questioning God's existence as the shrines they built come tumbling down around their ears at the sound of the new economy's trumpets.

The first year after a company peaks, the president announces without fail that it's just a temporary squeeze, adding with a brave smile: "This shakeout is a very healthy thing that's happening to our industry.

We couldn't possibly have kept pace with the surging demand. We welcome the respite to give us a chance to catch our breath."

That's easy to swallow, if you still believe in, say, the Tooth Fairy. After all, isn't every company just itching to get rid of those nasty sales and profits when they become too big to keep track of?

By Year 2 of the slide, the story changes. A nearly apoplectic CEO is angry about the godawful recession, the terrible taxes and the brutal competition. But, like every government leader facing a lousy economy and a frightened electorate, our valiant chief assures the directors and shareholders that there will be light at the end of the tunnel — some time in the second half of the year.

Then Year 3 arrives, and the light turns out to have been on a freight train, heading the wrong way. By now the executive in charge of the wreck is talking incoherently about dark international plots to destroy his company. His eyes have a strange, glassy look to them and his knuckles are white as he grips the boardroom table and rails against enemies real and imagined.

The central bank, he's sure, is out to ruin him by keeping interest rates up on all that money he borrowed to finance expansion as the company tried to grow its tree to the sky. The politicians are in a massive conspiracy to keep the dollar high and import barriers low. Oh yes, and then there are those Japanese. Always blame the Japanese. It sounds plausible to the workforce, looks good in the media and keeps shareholders at bay for a while longer.

I attended an annual meeting of a large resource company a while back. The CEO was giving one of those impassioned speeches that are a trademark at this point in the decline. Everything — and I mean everything — was a threat to this bold visionary and his company. There were no opportunities out there any more, just costs, costs, costs, and they all had to go. He spent so much time bashing the government that he couldn't possibly have had the time to listen to positive proposals that might have worked.

It's an insidious process, this business of blaming everyone but yourself for your troubles. Instead of planning how to recoup market

SHIFTING
GEARS
───────
THRIVING
IN THE
NEW
ECONOMY

share by introducing creative marketing ventures or, better yet, innovative products, too many corporations would rather lash out at the external forces that are supposedly ruining them. What they are really facing is change, but they refuse to recognize, even at this point, that they have to respond to it. To some companies, innovation is a life-threatening experience and "new" is a four-letter word!

At another annual meeting, this time of a large insurance company, I remember the CEO devoting more than half his speech to the government's terrible management of the deficit, after which he promptly announced that corporate dividends would be increased despite recent losses. His attitude was typical: "Maybe if we ignore all the things happening around us, they will go away."

Most CEOs know deep down that the company has to be saved from itself. Yet they demand to know when someone — anyone — is going to *do* something. In the good times, the same executives would have gone on for hours about the glories of the free market, but all of that stops the day the free market threatens to drive their companies right into the ground. A doctor stands by at the annual meeting to check the CEO's blood pressure and keep him away from sharp objects. Friends and relatives recommend a long vacation in some place calmer, like Belfast or Beirut.

It's only in Year 4 that it begins to dawn on the executive committee that there might have been a major structural shift in their markets. But it takes time to figure out exactly what's changed and how it affects what they do. Like patients when they first get the grim news that they have a serious illness, the corporate decision-makers look toward the heavens and ask plaintively, "Why me, God? I was on the golf course minding my own business. What did I do to deserve this?"

By Year 5, the company, by now likely under new leadership, has found what it's sure is the answer to its prayers. "What we really need in here are some bright Harvard Business School graduates with sophisticated financial skills. Those are the guys who will save us from ourselves," the newly appointed CEO tells shareholders.

In Year 6, the new management adopts the nifty financial tricks proposed by the Harvardian (or Whartonian) number crunchers who now run the company and couldn't care less what it does for a living. These numerical jugglers never venture onto the plant floor. They wouldn't know a machine tool if it hit them on the head. A screwdriver is an alcoholic drink and a monkey-wrench is something that screws up a brilliant proposal to raise millions of dollars in new financing.

Like corporate raiders, what these whiz kids do know plenty about is the art of financial engineering. They use their financial acumen to capitalize on a company's existing value. But that's not the same as building on that value and getting back to the business of growth. It really gets under my skin when I see people devoting so much corporate energy, time and scarce resources to figuring out how to cash in on what's already there, instead of creating new value.

These MBAs, all of whom seem to wear eyeglasses (I'm absolutely convinced they wear the glasses as part of their uniform, even if they have 20-20 vision), take in hopeful shareholders with their assurances that everybody will be better off if the company is broken into pieces. So they start selling vital appendages, often leaving what's left too crippled to climb on to a new growth track. No one ever focuses on how to start growing again — which should be the pre-eminent corporate goal during life on the trough.

All the financial mumbo-jumbo in the world never created a single job. That's why it's more than annoying when corporate raiders try to pass off a cheap imitation of healthy growth as the real thing.

The Financial Workout

A number-crunching type I'll call Peter the Pumpkin Eater bought a company that produced photocopiers and did, you guessed it, a financial workout. This guy had never made himself a cup of coffee, let alone a photocopy of anything, since his days as a starving university student. Yet off he flew from his aerie in Manhattan's Upper East

SHIFTING
GEARS

THRIVING
IN THE
NEW
ECONOMY

Side to reorganize a company that made machines he couldn't even turn on or off.

What the Pumpkin Eater did know was how to issue junk bonds — the junkier the better. The fact that eight hundred workers depended for their livelihoods on his lack of manufacturing and marketing expertise was irrelevant to him. All of them were to be sacrificed in his so-called rescue strategy. Peter, of course, walked away with millions.

Peter and his ilk did not disappear with the end of the '80s, despite the S&L scandal, the spectacular fall of corporate dice-throwers like Robert Campeau and Robert Maxwell and the disgrace and jailing of junk-bond king Michael Milken and some of the other vultures who prey on companies living on the trough. The day of the rapacious raider may be over, but rest assured, there are plenty of opportunists out there with a new snake oil to peddle to desperate corporations trying to get up from the bottom the easy way.

By the way, everybody calls the '80s "the Decade of Greed," but surely it was really "the Decade of Serendipity." Without the nuttiness unleashed by people like Milken, T. Boone Pickens, Ivan Boesky, Campeau and hundreds of lesser lights, a lot of companies could have picked themselves off the trough a lot faster, instead of draining their treasuries in search of a nonexistent magic elixir.

Having rejected the instant-fix solutions to their deep-seated problems, companies typically begin facing up to the hard realities of their grim situation in about Year 7 of the famine. But what on earth do you do when the moon blots out the sun and lightning flashes from the darkened sky?

THE BLESSING AND THE CURSE

The good news is that losers can become winners again. Life on the trough is both a blessing and a curse. It's a blessing because the company has survived, which alone merits a medal. But it's also a curse, because survival is not nearly the same thing as growth.

Getting back to the healthy expansion that will ensure the corporation has a future depends on how well it plays "Let's Make A Deal." There are only three ways off the trough, all of which seem simple enough. The only problem is that it's not a game. This is deadly serious stuff, and selecting the wrong door can be fatal.

Choosing **Door Number One** means turning out new products or services that people actually want to buy.

It's not enough for companies to scratch their heads in wonder at the consumer's silly refusal to purchase whatever they ordain. "But we must be right, we're the industry leader" doesn't go over well with customers who have a wide range of other options, usually at lower prices. And if the company slashes its prices on things no one wants, what good does that do? Would there be a big lineup for butter churns merely because the world's last maker is offering great bargains?

There's a story, related to me secondhand but made famous in a competitor's television ads, of the time a group of GM executives first came to the frightening realization that their institution was up to its armpits in a Honda-infested swamp. After a long day poring over their sliding sales figures, the executives headed for the staff parking lot in the fading twilight. There, among the rows of Buicks, Oldsmobiles and Chevrolets, they had trouble finding their own cars, because everything seemed the same.

That worked for Henry Ford's Model-T and Volkswagen's Beetle for a couple of decades, because there was little else to choose from in the price range. GM was convinced that it could shape the market in its own boring image. But then, when real competition hit these shores, the auto giant simply didn't acknowledge that it had a problem until it was too late.

Choosing **Door Number Two** means finding new markets. And you were wondering why companies are drooling at the prospect of Eastern Europe going capitalist? For a while, in the '80s, the savior was supposed to be China, with a market of a billion people clamoring for Western goods. No one bothered to ask how they'd

**SHIFTING
GEARS**

THRIVING
IN THE
NEW
ECONOMY

get the products to the bulk of the population, given the country's poor transportation and distribution networks. The point was that for companies like the dying American Motors, China represented potentially its last door to salvation.

In some cases, China did prove a godsend. James Ting's International Semi-Tech Microelectronics found a ready market there for personal computers he couldn't sell in North America or Europe. Ting subsequently used the base to build a global electronics empire firmly embedded in the new economy.

But Doors One and Two don't offer something for everybody. Which is where **Door Number Three** comes in. This is the door to new processes, which only works if companies make a genuine commitment to becoming the lowest-cost supplier on the planet. It's the toughest of the three strategies, because making the decision to grind your costs into the ground for, say, the next forty years is not something most corporations have the stomach for.

But if a desperate company has little to look forward to other than a future of shrinking markets for declining products, it's still reasonable to bring in new processes that will boost quality while shredding costs to the bone. Steel-makers can turn red ink to black by introducing new thin-strip casting technologies while slashing old capacity until there's nothing left to cut out.

If there's nothing behind any of the three doors — if there is no way to climb back to the growth track because of a lack of vision or knowledge — the smartest thing to do is to sell out to a company that does have a strength in one of those areas and hope that the corporate dowry you bring to the marriage will be enough to keep you in the good books of the buyer. After all, there's no point pursuing new products if the last time your company came up with one was forty years ago. Don't suddenly turn to your sixty-four-year-old head of research and order the R&D department cranked up. The knowledge base won't be there, and the poor man, who has spent the past twenty years reading retirement brochures, might have a heart attack from the strain!

And forget about foreign markets if you have to buy the marketing vice-president a subscription to *National Geographic* to help him find out where Japan is. Likewise, Eastern Europe isn't going to work for people who can't live without both hot and cold running water (at the same time), or if foreign is anything east of Missouri. You're better off sticking to your knitting and hoping for a friendly acquisition.

A COMPANY IS THE SUM OF ITS PARTS

Sometimes you'll find that it's just a particular brand or product line that's stuck in the trough. We all know products that were terrific money-makers in their day, only to run out of sales steam when times and tastes changed. The key to survival is innovation and creative marketing.

Take the case of Brylcream, a hair product from my early youth that was devastated when male teens started wearing their hair longer in the '60s and rejected all the stuff that reminded them of their parents. The brand owner, Beecham, spent a fortune reformulating and repackaging (into plastic tubes from glass jars). Its 1968 launch of the "New Brylcream," one of the most expensive ever mounted to that point, succeeded in attracting a younger customer and breaking sales records in new markets. The company aggressively pursued foreign markets, expanding sales into the Middle East, Asia and Africa, selling the former "greasy kid stuff" in twenty-three countries.

But that was then, and this is now. Once again, the product seems to be languishing as executives content themselves with holding the leading share of a declining market.

You can't imagine how aggravated I get when name brands stumble and sink into decline. Where were the owners of these great names when things changed? I'll tell you where. They were either asleep or mesmerized by those growth lines drawn straight upward on their sales charts, convinced their product — and theirs alone — would sell forever.

SHIFTING
GEARS
‾‾‾‾‾
THRIVING
IN THE
NEW
ECONOMY

Marketers could all take a lesson from the poultry business. Poultry slaughtering was one of the stalwarts of the old economy. But look at the large processors today like Perdue Farms, Cuddy Farms and others. They have succeeded in converting their businesses into thoroughly modern players, reaping the benefits of new processes while aggressively exploiting new markets for innovative products. Why sell ordinary stewing hens that need careful cooking for hours when you can market ready-to-pop-in-the-microwave gourmet chicken at much higher prices, taking advantage of major shifts in consumer preference to reap huge profits? We're all still eating — more than ever, in fact — but not in the ways we used to. Today we graze instead of dine, which is why sausages have become one of the fastest-growing products in the new economy. Just look around the next time you go to a ball game.

Coca-Cola, which markets the world's best-known brand name, isn't garnering record profits because it sat around saying silly things like, "The world may change, but it will never affect us." Where would the company be today if it had looked at aspartame as just a passing fad? Instead, the soft-drink giant moved aggressively into market openings created by the demand for diet and caffeine-free beverages and opened up new sales opportunities overseas.

In short, Coca-Cola did three things right that enabled it to glide easily from the old to the new economy:

1. Designing new products that people actually want to buy.
2. Opening new markets. Who else could get its T-shirts on the backs of kids in Lebanon?
3. Developing new processes allowing faster, better and cheaper production.

As Coca-Cola discovered in its brief but disastrous effort to change its classic recipe, you don't even have to alter the basic product if you're good at positioning yourself to take advantage of changing consumer demand. Kellogg now markets its famous Corn Flakes to grab baby-boomers who are health-conscious but have been muesli-ed to death and who will scream if they see another nut in their cereal bowl!

The kiss of death is to say "the world can change but it won't affect my product, my company, my industry." Just ask the property developers and the financial institutions that put billions of dollars at risk because of the old-economy thinking so prevalent in the financial services world of bankers, brokers and insurers, and the industries that are so closely tied to them.

THE ROADBLOCKS

The reclusive, billionaire Reichmanns made headlines around the world last spring when their Olympia & York property empire ran into a severe financial crisis. The news rattled global markets, sent investors scurrying for cover and prompted crisis meetings at the highest level of government. If a mighty company like O&Y could be pushed over the edge, was nothing safe from the ravages of this terrible economy?

Much of the press attention was devoted to the potentially huge losses faced by the banks that had lent O&Y billions in the good times. But plenty of sympathy was reserved for the highly respected Reichmanns themselves. Perhaps, it was suggested, they had just bitten off a little more than they could chew by taking on the enormous Canary Wharf office development in a derelict section of East London. And who could have predicted that the cold winds of recession would whistle for so long through their prized real estate and resource holdings?

If the journalists, pundits and all the other experts had had even a basic knowledge of the economic changes under way since the early '80s, they wouldn't have been surprised in the least by the woes that have hit real estate developers worldwide. On the contrary, they would have wondered how the industry could have fended off real trouble for so long. More than anything else, the development industry tripped into a financial quagmire because they hitched their railcar to the fading old economy, on a spur line running to nowhere.

Just as we are what we eat, real estate operators are who they lease to, blossoming or suffering with their major tenants. And all the financial maneuvers in the world won't change the fact that a single developer became the premier provider of property to an industry that's past its peak and on the way down to the dreaded trough. They pinned their future on banks, brokers and other players in the financial services arena, so much a part of the old economy.

Back in 1982, when O&Y landed thirteen of the foreign banks then entering Canada as long-term tenants of its flagship First Canadian Place in Toronto, the strategy seemed impeccable. The financial sector was booming and space was at a premium. The euphoria of the period masked the true picture, however.

Financial services went into the classic *inflation* stage in the 1980s. The next step, as we have seen, is always *disinflation*. Remember the hallmark of that period — "lean and mean" — companies cutting bodies and other operating costs left, right and center merely to survive. As a supplier, the real estate industry is one of those costs. It's never good for business when a major customer turns to you and says, "Help us cut our expenses." Just the kind of tenant you want occupying millions of square feet of your best office space, right?

There's not one neat financial trick left in the book that can save the premier provider of space from pain. It will be the parade of the terrible Rs all over again: restructuring, refinancing, reorganizing, retrenching, repositioning, reducing risk. All retrograde stuff. The first commonsense rule of business is to tie yourself to an industry that's growing, not shrinking. It's a lesson neither the property developer nor the lender learned fast enough.

SHIFTING
GEARS

THRIVING
IN THE
NEW
ECONOMY

Who Says Banks Are Forever?

When bankers wake in a cold sweat from nightmares peopled with credit disasters like Alan Bond, Robert Campeau, Robert Maxwell, Peru, Donald Trump, they are comforted by their belief that the worst will soon be over. If only the Reichmann crisis can be sorted out and the real estate markets revive, they will again be feeding happily at the top of the financial food chain.

They couldn't be more wrong. Their troubles have only just begun, and their worst nightmares are about to come true. Unless they make some radical shifts in their thinking and strategies — and quickly — the banks will be reduced to a brief footnote at the end of financial history.

Here's a tidbit of information that would probably surprise the developers and others who have bet so much on the future of the existing financial services industry. Banks, the premier providers of credit to the old economy, now account for only 6.4 percent of all the money raised annually, by all the corporations and individuals combined, in the United States. I can think of half a dozen U.S. pension funds that could make up that market share at the drop of a hat. Anyone with a market share of under 7 percent of anything either has a new product about to make a big breakthrough or an old one that is languishing on the shelves.

It's not that banks no longer matter, it's just that they don't matter as much as they once did. Yet we still live with this utterly silly notion that the banking system is the lifeblood of the economy. That's why there was such panic when it appeared that the banks might be hurt badly by a collapse of the Reichmanns' O&Y. And apart from our understandable personal interest in preserving all the money that we've handed to them for safekeeping, it really doesn't matter, in a broad economic sense, whether the *current* financial structure is preserved.

Private banks were the driving force in financing the commodities-processing circle in the last century, just as commercial banks bankrolled the mass-manufacturing era earlier in this one. The nature of banking has evolved before and will again in the new economy. The plain truth, though, is that the banks appear unable or unwilling to make the leap to the current circle of growth, acting more often as roadblocks to expansion.

It's no coincidence that the banks are up to their eyeballs in loans to the real estate sector. It's their kind of industry — lots of fixed assets, like buildings, that look good on paper. Not like the newfangled companies in the high-growth bracket. Those are built on brains. How the heck do you assess gray matter when you're used to measuring value in bricks, mortar and inventory? Their seeming inability to figure out what makes the new economy tick helps explain why the banks and other traditional providers of financial services have remained locked within the ever-narrowing confines of the old economy.

Banks are the first to admit that they are only as successful as the individuals, companies, industries and economies they serve as financial intermediaries. In the days when the commodities-processing circle dominated the business universe, private banks deploying large pools of family wealth provided much of the financing needed by the great railway, mining, textile and steel barons, always on a project-by-project basis. Often it was a case of an incredibly wealthy family (like the Rothschilds or Andrew Mellon) or groups of families financing themselves, for the bankers also wore the hats of mighty industrialists. Every major family had its private bank or easy access to one.

The guardians of these private fortunes would have been shocked at the notion of lending money to anyone who wasn't an intimate in their circle or who could not be vouched for by someone who was. And to the old-style bankers, living a comfortable life in the C Circle, the thought of actually taking deposits from the masses must have seemed utterly bizarre.

"Baron, did you hear what these commercial banks in the new world are doing? They have branches taking money from any

SHIFTING
GEARS
THRIVING
IN THE
NEW
ECONOMY

customer who wanders in their doors. Then, they pool the money together and lend it to complete strangers. They must be daft!"

The banking aristocrats who failed to adapt to the enormous financing needs of the mass-manufacturing era became nothing more than wealthy bit players, destined to live a life of contented obscurity on the trough. The field was left to more aggressive lenders, who went on to become household names: Bank of America and First National City Bank (Citibank) in the United States, the Royal Bank of Canada and Britain's Barclays Bank.

These, and dozens of other big banks that soared along with the mighty engines of the M Circle, have coasted for years, weathering ill-conceived forays into foreign lending and other adventures. Many are still chalking up record profits, and yet they are as much in danger of fading into obscurity as those long-ago private bankers who were unable to recognize change when it passed by their mahogany doors in search of more welcoming arms.

The players in the new economy keep their payroll and other accounts at the banks, but they go elsewhere for the serious money. Banks don't like lending to people with no fixed assets. Your average banker displays a real preference for having his money secured by vintage 1950s plants and equipment than for taking a risk on an idea, an invention, an innovation or a list of patents. Vintage is good if you're talking about wine or furniture; it's not so hot when it describes how a bank does its lending. Whether you're a company or an individual looking for a line of credit, the measures are similar — and so are the forms — they were designed to measure, in the main, net worth in the form of hard assets.

When bankers do take unusual risks on a particular industry, as First Boston did on the film industry in the 1930s, they often reap big rewards. Where they so often get creamed is in following the herd. Too often, bankers get roped into a harebrained financial scheme by someone with the right style and connections. A brilliant inventor with an ill-fitting suit and no vast portfolio of questionable old assets hasn't got a snowball's chance.

The main source of financing in the new economy is the massive pool of assets accumulated by pension funds in recent years. As any high-tech entrepreneur knows, it's easier to sell an idea to a multi-billion-dollar fund with a raft of sophisticated international investments than to the local banker. Venture capital groups and pension funds are less likely to have hangups. Typically, the funds are approached by smaller companies eager to grow. They frequently stand to get a terrific return on their investment and stay in as shareholders, often for the long haul.

That was the experience of James Ting, the founder of International Semi-Tech Microelectronics. The Hong Kong immigrant struck out in the North American banking and investment communities when he went looking for funds in the mid-1980s to build his dream of a multinational electronics empire based in Canada. Where did he go for the millions he needed? Hong Kong investors — who liked his ideas, liked him personally and didn't worry much about his lack of old, hard assets — and the huge British Merchant Navy Officers Pension Fund, which became one of Semi-Tech's largest shareholders, after Ting himself.

Ting's experience was by no means unusual for those in the new economy. Can you picture a techno-whiz like Bill Gates strolling into the office of his local banker in jeans and running shoes and coming out with millions in loan guarantees? Even if the overmatched banker understood Gates's strategies and innovative software products, there would be no traditional collateral. How could the poor banker possibly justify betting his career on someone else's brains? Today, Gates's fabulously successful Microsoft can write its own ticket at the bank window. But why bother, when there are much cheaper and more reliable ways of obtaining money?

Banks say it's not their role to provide venture capital, to take flyers on the unknown and the unproven. After all, they have shareholders and depositors and regulators to worry about. But that didn't stop them from plunging madly into dubious loans to debt-ridden Third World countries in the '70s. Then, in the '80s, they

SHIFTING
GEARS
—————
THRIVING
IN THE
NEW
ECONOMY

put their vast resources at the disposal of incredible gamblers like Maxwell, Campeau and everyone else who had an urge to buy companies they couldn't afford with money that wasn't theirs.

The real reason the banks haven't financed the new economy is that they have never understood it or known how to properly gauge its risks. But banks are changing, and it's a good bet that an industry that has already mastered a quantum leap in technology — to electronic funds transfer — and that has been at the forefront in developing a raft of new financial services will deal with the new challenges that it faces.

The Last Days of Wall and Bay

The capital markets played a hugely important role in financing the transition from the commodities to the mass-manufacturing circle. Without Wall Street, the foundations of the great American manufacturing fortunes might never have been laid, and they continue to provide a marvelously inexpensive source of money. Bill Gates would not be the billionaire he is if his company had not met a spectacular reception when it sold shares to the public. Ting and others can also thank the international markets for turning them into multimillionaires and providing a steady source of new funds.

But apart from a handful of exceptions, it's abundantly clear that many of the people who arrange corporate financings don't have much more understanding of how the economy has changed than many of their cousins in banking.

I still remember the day I walked into the corporate finance department of a major New York brokerage firm. My experience there has not been repeated elsewhere, but it certainly showed how out of touch some organizations can be.

As soon as I stepped off the elevator, I knew I had entered an alien world, unwelcoming to anyone without a vested interest in the old economy. The air was redolent of old money, which would have been all right if the firm had been more than five years old. The effect was deliberate. Like many newcomers, these guys wanted to convey solidity, longevity, discernment, good blood-lines, connections.

The floors were inlaid with rich, highly polished hardwood designed for men in wing tips or silent Gucci loafers. My heels marked me as an unwelcome intruder, their *click-click-click* echo-ing throughout the expensively appointed offices. I instantly felt like someone who had mistakenly worn a pink dress to a funeral.

After I passed inspection from the receptionist, I was ushered into what I later discovered to be one of three large boardrooms. The one the partners appeared to favor looked — and it's hard to describe it any other way — as if it had been removed lock, stock and plush chairs from a private club in New Orleans. The place was filled with expensive antiques, including the old-thinking young men in dark blue pinstripes and print silk ties sitting around the oval mahogany table.

I had to suppress the urge to ask two important questions: Why would a firm of young gunslingers want to pretend it's been around for a century or more? and How the heck do they ever get any business done in such surroundings? For that matter, I'd like to meet the customers who think this sort of display means some-thing, because it's a sure bet they don't understand much of what has been happening outside their windows in the past decade.

The reality is that this firm makes most of its dwindling profits by channeling your money and mine, including our hard-earned pension contributions, straight into the old economy. Imagine a stock portfolio filled with modern-day equivalents of buggy-whip makers. I couldn't imagine some whiz kid in jeans and Nikes get-ting past the reception desk. Nothing scuffs up those glorious old floors like a pair of running shoes or disturbs a carefully cultivated old-fashioned atmosphere like a bold, new idea.

SHIFTING
GEARS
—————
THRIVING
IN THE
NEW
ECONOMY

INSURING THE FUTURE

Once upon a time, merchants gathered in a London coffee house to put up the money to insure cargoes being shipped from the far corners of the world. Eventually, they formed syndicates to back all sorts of shipping risks.

The availability of such insurance was crucial to the growth of the commodities-processing circle, in which shipping was a driving force. The system worked well for decades, until the time of transition to the mass-manufacturing circle. Like everything else in the economy, the nature of insurance and the demands on it then changed substantially. Eventually, insurers were asked to come up with life, health and pension benefits for the millions of production workers at the heart of this circle, while continuing to guarantee the shipment and security of raw materials.

Eventually, the industry tapped into an increasingly affluent public, creating life, car and accident insurance on a mass scale. Each time they ventured into a new area, they were stepping into the unknown. Imagine trying to price the first auto insurance policy. Everyone knew those newfangled horseless carriages weren't safe at any speed!

The economy is again in transition and undergoing profound shifts. The technology circle offers vast opportunities which, to date, have been left largely untouched by the giants of the insurance industry, who inadvertently act as yet another roadblock to growth. Turning themselves into a conduit for the new economy could bring insurers immeasurable gains. True, they have been expanding into banking-like activities and other financial ventures, but these are linked mainly to the shrinking old economy or the viciously competitive consumer market.

When it comes to the new economy, many companies haven't left the starting gate yet. The longer it takes them to come around, the more time they will spend poking around on the trough, competing with all the other "past-their-peak" financial institutions for the same mined-out clients who no longer need their services and couldn't afford them if they did.

I was once approached by the executives of a small Canadian insurance firm who had come up with a great idea — a truly innovative form of environmental insurance. My job was to provide advice on the mining industry, for which the product was being specifically designed.

If anybody needs environmental insurance these days, it's mining companies, and they know it. In the past, the industry had put no cash aside for the costly cleanup after a mine was stripped of its valuable minerals. By that point, it isn't unusual for such expenses to exceed the value of the company that operated the mine.

The idea, as explained to me, was elegant in its simplicity. It was modeled after ordinary life insurance, which accumulates value over the duration of the policy. A mining company would take out insurance that would pay off years later on the inevitable death of the mine. There would then be enough cash available to clean up the site and return it to a semblance of its original state.

The little insurance company lacked the market clout or size to issue such policies on its own, but no matter how hard its executives tried, they couldn't persuade larger institutions to join them in syndications. You might think an industry willing to gamble on ships at sea could find a way to measure new risks on land. Not every piece of property is going to end up as a toxic headline with nightmare costs. Governments are keen on seeing companies make provisions for environmental cleanup costs that taxpayers might otherwise be stuck with, and yet such opportunities are still "lost" to the market.

The insurance world might not want to know about something new, different and, well, risky. But if insurers won't take on legitimate business risks, who will? If the London risk-takers who thought fire insurance might be a good idea after the Great Fire of 1666 had taken the same view, there would have been a great deal less confidence about the rebuilding. And shipping would have remained the

SHIFTING
GEARS
━━━━━
THRIVING
IN THE
NEW
ECONOMY

preserve of the brave and the foolhardy, instead of becoming a major force of the mercantile and later the commodity era.

Like the environment, the technology circle is one vast pot at the end of the rainbow for any company willing to go for the gold. In the burgeoning health and medical services field, for instance, an innovative insurer could do extremely well with what I call geriatric insurance and other products for the aged, a natural in light of the growing size and market influence of the graying population. What about illness-specific insurance for Alzheimer's, Parkinson's disease and other calamitous infirmities? A policy that would pay once a medical diagnosis had been confirmed? It could be a great comfort to the unfortunate victim of the disease to know that costly medical care — with the dignity the patient could now afford — would be forthcoming as a result of their private policy.

Certainly, governments aren't anxious to be saddled with the cost of lengthy institutional care. And if insurers are capable of calculating the actuarial risk of losing, say, one big toe and an earlobe, what's stopping them from figuring out the probability of a customer being felled by Alzheimer's or a stroke? Big dollars await the private companies willing to go beyond conventional medical and travel insurance.

Then there are the crucial knowledge assets of the new economy. So far, insurers have not been able to "get their hands" around them, or cover them with an "umbrella" or protect them behind "the rock."

If you run a widget company in the fading, old economy and happen to whisper at the golf or tennis club that you've got a factory or a piece of equipment that needs insuring, a pack of agents will descend on you before you can put your gear away. Like bankers, insurance people love all the old stuff — machines, bricks, mortar. The fact that the profit margins in such businesses are infinitesimal these days is just a small aside.

Then try to picture the same scene with one small difference. Instead of a widget manufacturer, it's the president of a computer company who is looking to insure the brains of the organization. This executive could probably drive a golf ball through the locker room without hitting anyone admitting to even being in the insurance business.

Insurers thought they were being particularly innovative when they came up with "key man" insurance, basically a life insurance policy on an important employee. But this is only of value if the poor guy drops dead. What if something much more terrible happens and the vital staff member jumps to a competitor?

A U.S. company once bought out a British high-tech firm with an enviable record of innovation. Six months later, the new owners belatedly decided to check out the patent record of their prize acquisition. There were plenty, but most of the company's key patents were attributable to a single scientist, who happened to quit after the American company took over. This immensely valuable human resource — really the *raison d'être* of the whole company, though he didn't appear on the books as a corporate asset — had set up his own business and was busily filing a new batch of valuable patents that would no doubt lead to directly competitive products.

Thousands of other companies are potentially in the same boat, companies whose principal assets are simply not protected. How much creativity does it take to provide a measure of security for a company's knowledge? No more, I would maintain, than to insure the more traditional inventory, equipment and buildings. Losing that British scientist was just as catastrophic to the company's owners as having a plant burn down in the old days, and will one day be just as insurable. If I can buy business interruption insurance, why not R&D interruption insurance?

A related surefire product has got to be knowledge-worker unemployment insurance. When governments first introduced unemployment protection, it was a stroke of brilliance — a cushion to prevent the unfortunate from ending up on poverty row. But for the scientist or engineer used to a high income and the lifestyle that goes with it, jobless benefits don't stretch very far. Just as private

SHIFTING
GEARS
THRIVING
IN THE
NEW
ECONOMY

insurers supplement basic medical coverage, there is a huge market for private job insurance. And the risks are relatively low because employment prospects are so much better than in the old economy.

As for that little insurance company with the bright idea of environmental insurance for the mining industry, it went out of business. It died trying to scale the impossibly high walls erected by those unwilling to accept the risk that always accompanies change. It will soon be joined in the graveyard by considerably larger and wealthier companies — the fate of all who refuse to adapt to a vastly different climate. Wake up, Hartford, before you spend the best years of the decade on a downward slope to nowhere.

Another roadblock for the new economy is the mass of elected officials at every level of government. Despite the best of intentions, they manage to dig us deeper into the old economy with every move they make, because they don't have a clue that the new economy even exists.

The mayor of one troubled municipality telephoned one day and asked me to draw up an economic development proposal. But I was warned in advance that there would be strong resistance to change among some officials. This struck me as particularly bizarre once I had had a chance to look over the town. You could have shot a cannon down Main Street and not hit anything of economic importance.

The town's three major employers were all firmly wedded to the old economy, which meant a steady stream of losses and layoffs. Shifts were eliminated, plants closed, suppliers dumped and millions of dollars squeezed out of payrolls — dollars that used to flow into the community for all manner of goods and services. Real estate prices plunged as worried families put their houses on the block and hunted for jobs in more promising territory. By the time I got there, the once thriving community was well on its way to becoming the 1990s' version of the old nineteenth-century ghost town, the one that was deserted when the silver mine was played out, the cattle herds stopped coming or the new rail spur line was ripped up.

It reminded me of a town in New Hampshire that in its heyday was the butter-churn manufacturing center of the universe. This was the Cuisinart of its day, *the* hot kitchen gadget that no self-respecting home could afford to be without. The rise of commercial dairies put the industry out to pasture. But it didn't happen overnight. Where were the town's leaders when all this was going on? Sitting around saying, "Things may change, but we won't be affected," that's where.

Few politicians ever imagine that the same thing could happen to a modern industrial community in the late twentieth century, but for all the millions poured in by governments to shore up fatally stricken manufacturers, the sword of doom hangs over literally hundreds of communities that dot the moonscape of industrial North America. Factory after factory that provided a stable tax base and steady employment to three or perhaps four generations are shutting their doors for good. Without a strategy to shift gears to the new circle, the towns that depended on them are heading for oblivion, as surely as those long-ago mining and cow towns.

The good news is that these communities are far from helpless. They don't have to sit idly by and watch the toil and sweat of decades go for nought. With careful planning and an aggressive selling job, all of them have the ability to turn misfortune into a joyous, albeit painful, rebirth.

The main engines of the new economy are expanding by leaps and bounds, and it's there that municipal development officers should be placing all their time and effort. What good does it do to attract yet another player from the old economy to an outdated industrial park with terrific tax breaks and bags of other government goodies? At best, it postpones the inevitable reckoning for a couple of years while depriving the community of potential tax and other revenue that would come from a growing company in a healthy industry.

That doesn't mean every community has to clone itself into a mini-version of Silicon Valley. If semiconductor smarts or biotech brains aren't a big local feature, that's no reason for the elders to

**SHIFTING
GEARS**

THRIVING
IN THE
NEW
ECONOMY

wring their hands in despair and hire moving vans for cities like Saskatoon or Seattle, where high-tech industries have been carefully nurtured. There are still enormous opportunities to attract valuable cabooses hooked up to the mighty engines of the technology circle.

You don't need a truckload of computer PhDs to run a sausage factory or to make pallets and skids, to name two of my favorite high-growth industries in the new economy. The humble sausage has acquired a new lease on life thanks to changing eating habits (grazing instead of dining), better quality manufacturing techniques and an increased supply of inexpensive raw material, as packing plants trim more and more fat from steaks and roasts to satisfy health-conscious carnivores. Similarly, how much high-tech training do you need to turn out pallets and skids, even the new ones made out of composite materials? This is a booming business, now that virtually everything in the new economy is shipped just-in-time to manufacturers on portable platforms. (Just-in-time, used to perfection by the Japanese for years and now in wide use here, means parts and materials arrive at the factory door only when needed. This eliminates the costs of carrying huge inventories, made even more onerous by the cost of financing them.)

Plenty of other growth opportunities are waiting out there. You can almost hear them beckoning above the steady whine of the doomsters and naysayers who see a dark cloud behind every dark cloud.

Logic implies that it's in a politician's interest to embrace what's good and healthy for the people who do the voting. But sometimes that means making the hard choice to let go of an obsolete industry that's been a community fixture for decades. That's easier said than done. The old-economy companies on the trough have far more ability to marshall pressure for government aid and other breaks than fledgling companies with no track record or long history of political support. That's precisely why governments at every level commit billions in futile efforts to resuscitate the dying and already dead rather than spend a fraction of those amounts fostering industries with top-notch prospects.

To visualize what's going to be happening here (in fact, already is), a trip to Sheffield, England, would be instructive. This was once an enormously prosperous metal town, synonymous with the finest steel. But you'd never guess that from a drive through the area today. It's enough to turn anyone into a political agnostic. Cows graze on pastureland where the mightiest steel mills in the world once stood. Now, I'm all for the reclamation of farmland, but what are the people in this community supposed to live on? While the local politicians were probably sipping their port and congratulating themselves on a job well done, the local tax base crumbled to dust, and the potential for thousands of well-paying permanent jobs went down the drain.

It doesn't have to be that way. Economic diversification is not a new idea. That's why Pittsburgh didn't fall apart when the great steel-makers started shredding production. Nelson, B.C., did it right by diversifying away from the mine site. And so did the province of Quebec, despite all the bad publicity it gets.

Quebec is known in some circles as a hotbed of separatism and seething nationalism, but it should be known instead as a hotbed of the new economy. That's right. Quebec, the place that gives poorly informed international investors migraines, has created the optimal conditions for tremendous growth. The province has fostered booming biomedical and aerospace businesses and has the second-largest electronics industry in Canada.

The roots of Quebec's success can be traced to an innovative stock-savings plan introduced by Jacques Parizeau in 1979, when he was finance minister in the Parti Québécois government of René Lévesque. The idea was to encourage the development of loyal home-grown industries that might otherwise have had to go elsewhere for financing. It was a simple tool that helped a lot of aggressive, young players get around formidable financial roadblocks.

Other jurisdictions have tried similar incentives, but with less spectacular results, perhaps because they lacked the nationalist zeal that fueled Parizeau's strategy and sparked those who leaped

SHIFTING
GEARS

THRIVING
IN THE
NEW
ECONOMY

at the opportunity. But I suspect the real reason is that Quebec kept things very simple. British Columbia has introduced a venture capital program for financing-starved companies, but the complexity of the programs is a roadblock. As soon as the high-priced lawyers, tax accountants and corporate finance experts became involved, the money never seemed to end up where it should — in the hands of the innovators and wealth creators, who have not only *seen* the future but *are* the future.

WHAT'S A KNOWLEDGE WORKER?

E very new era has a unique knowledge base that distinguishes it
from the old economy that came before. New technologies and
new skills open up the opportunity to develop new products, new
processes, new markets and, eventually, entirely new industries.

In the commodity-processing circle, explosive growth and
undreamed-of prosperity were made possible by the new technologies of a "batch system" of production that overcame the limited
output of a single craftsman or small group making a one-of-a-kind
item (a clock or an article of clothing or a single machine). Batch
production made it possible to produce literally hundreds or thousands of the same piece using a machined reproduction of its original, and it became the basis for an industrial revolution in which
production soared and costs fell to a fraction of those for one-of-a-
kind originals.

The new knowledge base changed the very nature of work (from
craft to batch), the workplace (from cottage to factory) and the way
in which management directed its workforce through the first structure of labor-management relations and the birth of unionization.

SHIFTING
GEARS
───────
THRIVING
IN THE
NEW
ECONOMY

In the mass-manufacturing circle, new technologies once again created vast new opportunities. Thanks to the latest marvels of technology, manufacturers could integrate components into a single end product. Demand for the workers of the M Circle developed rapidly, and their wages far outstripped the average wage of the time. Before long, pension and health benefits, life insurance, paid annual vacations, cafeterias and employee parking lots became standard perks.

These workers were so appreciated that the U.S. Department of Labor set up a specific category for the new "production workers," and each month (to this very day) it has measured the number of jobs created in the mass-manufacturing economy. Tracking this category allowed economists to tell quickly how many new production jobs were being created in the high-growth manufacturing economy.

In the technology circle of growth, production workers from the old economy have been displaced as the vital cogs in the industrial wheel by professional, scientific and senior managerial employees. Although the U.S. Bureau of Labor Statistics does not yet track these knowledge workers in their monthly statistics, it would be a good idea if it did. The bureau would discover that more than 35 million people qualify as knowledge workers in the United States — 30 percent of the total labor force. By contrast, production workers account for just over 10 percent of total employment, down from 23 percent in 1960.

Who is a Knowledge Worker, Anyway?

Everyone agrees that knowledge is the prized asset of the '90s. The national preoccupation with raising the standard of education, the focus on training and retraining for workers already in the workplace and the boom in courses of every conceivable description attest to the awareness that new technologies and skills have replaced the old.

In many companies within the new economy, the only corporate asset of consequence is the knowledge base, yet, unlike factories or land or equipment, knowledge is not measured on a company's balance sheet. What good is an asset if you can't measure it, or worse, if you don't know it's there? Which leads to two questions. First: What exactly is a knowledge worker, and are you one of them?

To qualify as a knowledge worker, you have to fit into one of the following three employment groups:

1. Professionals, such as doctors, engineers, lawyers, accountants and actuaries. These are knowledge workers in the new information age. The demand for their specialized skills and information has created dramatic growth in professional services.
2. Engineering, scientific and technical workers. This category is not strictly related to the level of education attained, but is based on the extremely specialized skills acquired. Many production workers from the old economy have gone on to become knowledge workers in the new economy through specialized training.
3. The very senior ranks of management. These are the power-wielders, the true decision-makers in any corporation, and for all our sakes, they had better be up to speed in the new technologies, or we're all in trouble.

The second question is: If you don't qualify as a knowledge worker, does it mean you have no knowledge?

Eighty years ago, much the same fears were expressed about the rise of the production worker on the factory floor who pushed the fledgling mass-manufacturing economy forward on all cylinders. If you didn't work in one of the giant plants, did it mean you weren't productive? Hardly. And the same goes for knowledge in today's society.

Knowledge is the Asset of the Nineties

Employment opportunities for knowledge workers have been among the truly bright spots in the latest recession. From June 1989 to June 1992, 1.3 million new knowledge jobs were created — which is a darn sight more encouraging than the 919,000

SHIFTING
GEARS
THRIVING
IN THE
NEW
ECONOMY

manufacturing production jobs that were lost over the same period of time.

KNOWLEDGE VS. MANUFACTURING PRODUCTION JOBS

(Thousands)

Year	Knowledge Workers	Manufacturing Production Workers
1984	28,029	13,285
1985	29,106	13,092
1986	29,917	12,877
1987	31,088	12,970
1988	32,711	13,221
1989	34,043	13,269
1990	34,499	12,979
1991	34,806	12,467
Net Job Creation/(Loss) between 1984-91	6,777	(818)

Of course, there are smart and not-so-smart industries in this world, and plenty of companies in each category. The challenge is to tell which ones are which from the outside looking in. Smart companies have a way of standing out. The way they operate, the kinds of workers they employ, their corporate strategies are all like flashing neon highway signs: CLEVER COMPANY AHEAD. WATCH FOR FALLING COMPETITORS. If would-be employees or investors did their homework, they could identify a host of corporations as stand-out winners in the knowledge-based world of the '90s and spare themselves the aggravation and anguish of linking their fortunes to the wrong company.

Not everybody who sets up shop in a rapidly growing, high-IQ industry like computers or pharmaceuticals is automatically assured of making it, however. Potential alone isn't enough to guarantee success, or even survival, in a hotly competitive universe. And it's equally true that some companies in the fading old economy will continue running rings around their worn-out competitors as they equip themselves with the technical and scientific expertise necessary to develop the next generation of products for the new economy. They will keep making big money while others are driven out of their steadily shrinking markets.

What sets the smart apart in both the old and the new economies is not the number of their factories or the quality of their equipment or the way they market their products. It's knowledge and the way it's employed. I quickly discovered, however, that no one, anywhere, was evaluating this most crucial of corporate assets. Analysts could tell me everything I wanted to know about efficiency, productivity or finances, but nothing about knowledge, about whether a company would know a great idea if one fell from heaven and landed in the president's lap.

That's why I developed what I call the **Knowledge Ratio**™, which calculates the number of knowledge workers as a percentage of total employment in an industry, individual company or organization. While a Knowledge Ratio is simple to calculate, its impact is profound because it lets an employee or investor know whether a company can sustain its growth.

Although corporate IQs have never been measured scientifically, I couldn't pass up the challenge. It seemed the one sure way to tell whether a particular company or an entire industry had any real future. So I set out to determine the knowledge levels of 339 industries, the number for which the U.S. government had collected sufficient raw data.

Months later, as the first numbers started spewing out of the computer, my pulse began to race and I could feel my heart pounding. Page after page of calculations showed with blinding clarity that the knowledge base of an industry, or any company within that industry, could indeed be tabulated with the precision of a laser beam.

The numbers for some of the industries confirmed what you and I already knew intuitively. Makers of high-tech products and

SHIFTING
GEARS

THRIVING
IN THE
NEW
ECONOMY

equipment — like guided missiles and space vehicles, computers and pharmaceuticals — topped the manufacturers' IQ list, while such older industries as furniture, textiles, steel, food-processing and logging clogged the bottom. (Logging ranked well below fishing, probably because you can find trees without having to bait the chainsaw.) Also, companies with a higher than average Knowledge Ratio for their industry stand out from the pack with higher margins and earnings than their competitors.

It was a relatively simple task to classify the entire industry base of an economy in three categories:

- **High-knowledge-intensive industries** have Knowledge Ratios of 40 percent or higher, meaning that at least four out of ten workers are actually bone fide knowledge workers. That still leaves plenty of room for other people, such as receptionists, accounting clerks and warehouse workers.
- **Moderate-knowledge-intensive industries** cluster between 20 percent and 40 percent on the Knowledge Ratio scale. For the most part, this category constitutes the home turf of the old mass-manufacturing economy.
- **Low-knowledge-intensive industries** stand below 20 percent on the scale, meaning that less than a fifth of the people employed in these industries are full-fledged knowledge workers. This category includes what many people think the service sector is all about — low-wage industries that will drag the country down to a lower standard of living.

The Surprises

Some big discoveries were in store for me as I sifted through my research results. Who would have imagined that funeral parlors would score higher than the Federal Reserve Board, the U.S. central bank? The possible consequences for global financial markets of such comparisons are enough to set any economist's teeth on edge.

For that matter, providers of funeral services rank ahead of religious organizations. And both have a higher Knowledge Ratio than credit and collection agencies, which, believe it or not, rank as the smartest in the entire financial services field. Maybe the moral is to have the money buried with you when you go!

Here's a list of the best and brightest in financial services, ranked from the lowest Knowledge Ratio to the highest.

1. Insurance. Bowling alleys and old folks' homes score higher than the insurance industry — which leaves a lot of room for insurance companies with an understanding of how the world is changing and what it's changing into to run rings around their competition.

2. Real estate. A few points higher than insurance, but nowhere near as smart as chiropractors.

3. Brokerage industry. Higher up the ladder than real estate, but it distresses me that Wall Street is not even close to Hollywood when it comes to knowledge. Maybe that's because so many of the financial middlemen, like Michael Milken, are in jail or banned from the business. In the end, the movie and book industries probably made more money from Wall Street scandals than many of the unwary people who invested in some of the bad deals.

4. Savings and loan institutions. The fact that the survivors of the great S&L debacle in the United States have a higher Knowledge Ratio than the average brokerage house somehow doesn't give me a feeling of great comfort.

5. Banks. A higher industry IQ than S&Ls, but not as high as day-care centers. Should we worry or be thankful when the people who mind our kids are smarter than the people who look after our money?

6. Credit agencies. This ranking would probably change if the world's largest new credit agency, the KGB, were included. The former Soviet spy agency has adapted to the new economy in its own way by providing credit checks on would-be Russian bank borrowers.

Apart from these and other tidbits, two vital facts jumped out at me from the numbers. First, the smartest in manufacturing are nowhere near the levels of the best and the brightest in the service sector. The old notion that services cluster in the low-tech, low-knowledge end of the economy fell apart under the weight of hard evidence. Any list of North America's smartest industries must include engineering, research, education and computer programming — all members in good standing of the burgeoning service sector.

The second big surprise was the broad range occupied by service industries on the IQ scale — running the gamut from ultra-smart at one end to the lowest industry IQs at the other. And yet some people still talk about the service economy as if it were a single entity. A vast number of widely different industries are thus tarred with a broad brush of ill-concealed contempt, because none of them supposedly has the smarts or the savvy to do a "real job" in manufacturing.

Farm devotees used to say much the same thing in the last century about the huge factories that were changing the face of the work landscape. The only jobs that were of any real value, so this myopic view went, were those tied to the land. As hardworking and under-appreciated as farmers are, no sensible person would argue today that the clock be turned back to the preindustrial age.

So why do so many intelligent people insist that service jobs are somehow inferior, a refuge for those who can't cut it in the big, tough world of manufacturing? In the new economy, knowledge and information are the key sources of power; and these, to a remarkable degree, reside in the service sector. Only 5 million of the 35 million Americans who qualify as knowledge workers — the people who make change happen — work in manufacturing.

WHERE U.S. KNOWLEDGE WORKERS HANG OUT

(1991)

Total Number of Knowledge Workers	35 million
In Personal and Business Services	19 million
In Manufacturing	5 million
In Wholesale and Retail	2.7 million
In Financial Services	2.4 million
In Government	2.3 million
In Transport, Communications, Utilities	1.7 million
In Construction	1.2 million
In Mining	217 thousand
In Agriculture	201 thousand
In Forestry and Fisheries	37 thousand

AMERICA'S HIGH-KNOWLEDGE INDUSTRIES

That leaves the bulk of knowledge workers in the labor force working in services of one shape or another. Here are a few of the elite:

1. Engineering and architecture. Only one industry classification ranks higher and that's "miscellaneous professionals," which includes one-person companies and their answering machines.
2. Research institutes. The think-tanks really do live up to their name most of the time.
3. Commercial research and development labs. For the right price, these people will test your bright ideas, and, for an even righter price, they'll develop the whole thing for you.
4. Consulting. Take it from me, consultants are not a bunch of unemployed people waiting for real jobs in manufacturing.
5. Broadcasting. It's not just Tom Brokaw and Peter Mansbridge who are responsible for raising this service into the elite of the

131

SHIFTING
GEARS
‾‾‾‾‾‾‾‾
THRIVING
IN THE
NEW
ECONOMY

workforce. The faces and voices that float into our living rooms are backed up by an astonishing number of technical experts.

THE MODERATE-KNOWLEDGE SECTORS

Just below the cut-off line for the industries, institutions and entire economies that meet my high-knowledge criteria sits the U.S. government. Most taxpayers could have guessed that without my help. But determining which department sits where requires a little more careful research. Using the Knowledge Ratio, it's now possible to calculate government IQs as precisely as those for the private sector. Which is probably only useful if you're planning on a career in the civil service or writing a David Letterman monologue.

Here is a list of U.S. government departments, ranked from the lowest up. With no similar data available from Canadian or other governments, it wouldn't be fair for me to draw parallels, but feel free to make your own.

- Justice, public order and safety. The only departments that couldn't make it into the moderate-knowledge sector. Anyone who witnessed the behavior of municipal, state and federal law officials during the Los Angeles riots in the spring of 1992 will know that the major intellects hang out somewhere else in government.
- National security and international affairs. The fact that CNN often seems to know what's going on before the people who run the CIA and the State Department (numerous foreign heads of state, including King Hussein of Jordan and Russia's Boris Yeltsin, have turned into virtual CNN couch potatoes) tells all you need to know about why this group is not among the best and the brightest — despite what the Henry Kissingers of the world might lead you to believe.
- Environment and housing. The performance of these departments over the years speaks for itself.

- Employment. Maybe the people who work in this department have more knowledge than the numbers show. After all, they have jobs while so many others don't.
- Executive and legislative branches. According to so many media reports, this ranking might drop in a hurry if Dan Quayle ever makes it to the Oval Office.

And the smartest departments are:

- The Internal Revenue Service and, although not as knowledge-intensive as the funeral industry, the folks who run the Federal Reserve Board.

Judging from the mess most countries are in these days, it's safe to assume that their own governments are operating with similar or even lower Knowledge Ratios.

The best example of a smart leader in a stupid environment was Mikhail Gorbachev. He and dozens of like-minded technocrats knew from the time they were in university that the Soviet system simply didn't work, and had probably guessed that their government's IQ was somewhere just above the average winter temperature in Siberia. But the group kept the knowledge to themselves until they were in a position to do something about it.

I once met a nuclear physicist of Gorbachev's era who told me point-blank that everyone in her class knew the system had to go, but until one of their own could rise past the sclerotic old guard holding the keys to power, there was nothing they could do about it. "The change was inevitable. I knew it. We all knew it. We had people in our class, they became generals. They knew. My own father was an admiral, and he knew it."

I haven't measured the IQ of the old Soviet Union or, for that matter, the new Russia. But the method used for individual industries or government departments applies equally to entire countries.

Canada actually has a very high intelligence score, but for all the wrong reasons. Canada's IQ shot up because so many of the nation's low-knowledge industries from the old economy don't live here any more. They have been devastated, and the fact is that only the smart survive the economic cataclysms. But even more telling is that 304,000 of the 339,000 — or 90 percent — of all the jobs created in Canada in the past seven years come from high-knowledge-intensive industries. And over 27 percent of Canadians are already employed in High-Knowledge Industries, as the pie chart on page 138 demonstrates.

America's Lowest-Knowledge Industries

As much as we may rail on about governments or certain of their policies or the laws they pass, they still rank far above many industries when it comes to Knowledge Ratio.

The industries with precious few knowledge assets to their credit are easy enough to peg. The following are at the bottom of the list:

1. Beauty salons and barber shops. Cutting hair doesn't require a PhD from MIT. Unfortunately, there's no way to scientifically measure the commonsense wisdom dispensed in these havens from a harsh world, where you can read *People* magazine without your fellow rocket scientists looking at you askance.

2. Car dealerships. These aren't as knowledge-intensive as shoe-repair shops. But then how often do your shoes break down on the highway?

3. Shoe repair shops. I didn't say cobblers were among the brightest. They're just smarter than car dealers.

4. Detective agencies. Tracking errant spouses or serving subpoenas requires special skills, but it's not exactly a complex mental exercise.

5. Retailers. It should come as no shock that pharmacies top this broad group. But drugstores are the only retail outlets that have even moderately high IQs. Everyone else is at the low end.

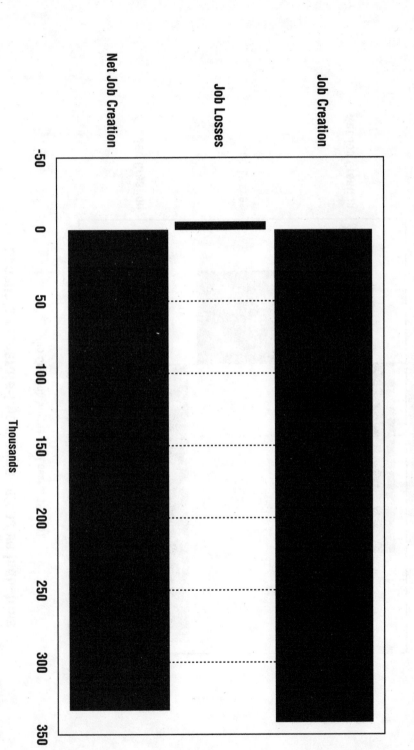

Canada's High-Knowledge-Intensive Industries

Job Creation Versus Job Losses: 1984-91

Job Creation

Job Losses

Net Job Creation

-50   0   50   100   150   200   250   300   350

Thousands

Canada's Moderate-Knowledge-Intensive Industries

Job Creation Versus Job Losses: 1984-91

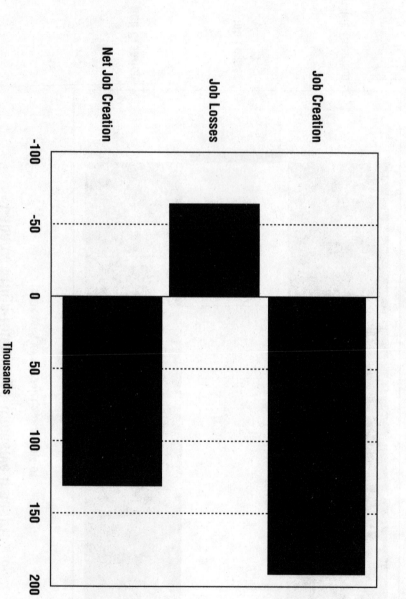

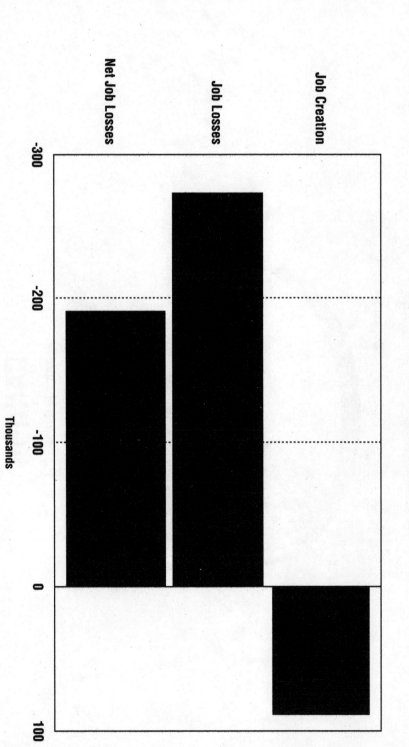

Canada's Low-Knowledge-Intensive Industries

Job Creation Versus Job Losses: 1984-91

Job Creation

Job Losses

Net Job Losses

-300   -200   -100   0   100

Thousands

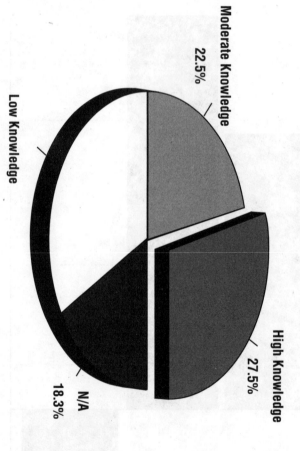

CANADA
Knowledge Ratios 1991

Moderate Knowledge
22.5%

Low Knowledge
31.7%

High Knowledge
27.5%

N/A
18.3%

THE HEAD COUNT

I haven't yet met the senior executive who didn't want to know exactly where his or her company ranked in the league of knowledge and which competitor had a higher ratio. You would be amazed at the lengths to which some companies will go to give themselves a boost up the knowledge chart!

Take the case of a savings and loan company that sought my advice. After I had explained that the key to their corporate IQ level was the number of knowledge workers they employed (rather than the mere fact that they had survived the S&L debacle with their good name intact) the executives rushed to their staff rosters. They began checking off anyone who had ever so much as taken a high-school bookkeeping course.

One senior vice-president who had been engrossed in detailed calculations in the corner for a good twenty minutes announced proudly that he had just figured out his company's exact IQ — on the back of an envelope. His own number was, predictably, sky-high. In fact, it was 50 percent above the industry average!

As gently as possible, I explained that he was vastly oversimplifying the calculations, which led him to mess up his own head count. The real numbers revealed that not only was their IQ lower than the industry's as a whole but it had been slipping for years. Whoever said "a little knowledge is a dangerous thing" would have felt justified in that meeting.

Once people know where their employer stands on the list, the next question is exactly how to go about measuring corporate or institutional brainpower, without a messy dissection of the top officials. (That might be satisfying to some disgruntled employees, but hardly scientific, or a good selling point for my consulting practice!)

In deciding whether you meet the criteria for a knowledge worker, forget about education for a moment. It's valuable all right, but if you're a PhD driving a taxi, you don't qualify. The key is what you and your employer do with the brains — whether, in fact, you've been *empowered* to use the knowledge that you've acquired.

Back in the early days of air travel, airlines hired registered nurses as flight attendants. Imagine employing that kind of specialized talent to run up and down aisles making passengers comfortable and pouring coffee for fourteen hours at a stretch. If an emergency arises, it's nice to have someone with the skills to deal with it, but as the airlines have since discovered, these can be taught to people who haven't invested years and years in costly medical training.

It only goes to show that some things are a lot slower to change than others. If hospital nurses and other skilled workers were empowered to use their knowledge productively, they would increase their institutions' total brainpower — and with it their ability to provide the modern care we've all come to expect, at a cost we might be able to afford.

Thinking Assets

Because nothing is more vital to a company than its knowledge assets, it stands to reason that the more knowledge a company can draw upon the better its chances of surviving and thriving in the new economy. But it's equally important to measure the return a company derives from its knowledge base. There's nothing worse than listening to a chief executive bragging about how brilliant his staff of 500 engineers and scientists is when you know full well that 450 of them spend their working days reading the sports pages and doing crossword puzzles. It would be like General Motors boasting about its vast array of manufacturing plants, when many of them are in mothballs.

Just as not every so-called asset in the old economy was of value to an industry that didn't know how to make use of it, it's equally true that not every knowledge worker is capable of earning his or her keep. And merely employing a large number of bright people won't boost a company's prospects one iota. A slaughter-house can hire as many out-of-work lawyers as it wants, but unless it develops a radical new way to kill chickens, it will be a monumental waste of talent and won't do much for the productivity of the knowledge base — the key factor in determining whether all the smarts in the company actually mean anything.

Educated people who aren't using their noodles productively, like the taxi-driving PhD, show up in every nook and cranny of both the old and new economies. As you would expect, however, the industries of the old economy are the worst offenders.

In the old economy, it was normal for a company to measure its Return on Assets. They did so by seeing how much profit they were able to squeeze out of their factories, buildings and anything else in which they had hefty investments. In the new economy, what I call the **Return on Knowledge Assets** (or ROKA for short) — how effectively knowledge is put to use — can be measured with as much exactitude as the Knowledge Ratio.

Knowledge Is Power and Money

If you're tired of working in a low-knowledge industry, curious about where your neighbors fit in or plain eager to know where you're spending so many of your waking hours, check out the knowledge rankings at the back of the book. The next time a headhunter calls with the career opportunity of a lifetime, it might be worth your while to find out exactly what you're getting yourself into. Knowledge Ratios mean more than who fits where on the scale. They are also a guide pointing to success or failure in the new economy.

Don't assume, however, that you should automatically turn down a job in a relatively low-knowledge industry. Opportunities abound for smart people in such situations, particularly in companies committed to improving their corporate IQs.

Take something as basic as the hardware, plumbing and heating supplies business. As might be expected, it carries a low Knowledge

SHIFTING
GEARS
THRIVING
IN THE
NEW
ECONOMY

Ratio of eleven. That means only eleven people out of every one hundred employed are actually knowledge workers. But a closer look at this old industry reveals that a technological revolution is going on practically under our noses. The latest thing is a "smart toilet." The Japanese have invented a toilet that will take your blood pressure, pulse, temperature and weight while you wait. North American manufacturers are already turning out technological wonders with electrically heated seats, computerized temperature controls, spray nozzles and dryers.

And if you think the toilet's smart, wait until you slip into the bathtub of the future. Already past the drawing board stage is a tub that will fill itself to your personalized temperature. And you don't even have to be at home. You can call in from your car phone while you're stuck in freeway traffic and have a glorious hot tub ready when you pull into the driveway.

Just as the color television became a product every consumer had to own, resulting in the replacement of millions of black-and-white models, so smart bathroom fixtures may open vast replacement markets. But remember one of life's important rules: Never acquire anything that has a higher IQ than the company that made it.

Which brings me back to an earlier point. What if you're by yourself in a relatively low-knowledge environment? Can you still make a difference? Or should you just give up and start counting the days to the delivery of the first pension check?

The answer is that knowledge can be applied to improve any company's chances. Just make sure you're in a high enough position to actually shake things up without shaking yourself out. If the desire for change isn't there, you'll be in big trouble. There's no faster way to an ulcer than to be the only live wire in a company that is firmly committed to the past.

The good news is that knowledge workers tend to have a much firmer hold on their jobs than others in the labor force. While overall unemployment has hit double digits in many regions, the jobless rate for knowledge workers is a mere 2 to 3 percent. Another point to keep in mind is that the higher an industry's Knowledge Ratio, the better the pay tends to be. Successful companies, used to paying top dollar for the best and the brightest, are less likely to flinch when other employees come seeking a share of the rewards. In any case, it has to be better than working for a boss in a low-knowledge industry who spends most of his or her days hacking and cutting just to keep the business alive. You know you're really in trouble if you hear the boss blaming everything on the minimum-wage law. "If only we could go back to paying people thirty cents a day, we might be competitive" is a sure clue that your time in that company will be very short indeed.

How to Manage Knowledge Workers

As many executives can attest, knowledge workers can't be managed in the same way that worked well in the framework of the old economy. For starters, how do you tell people what to do when they have more specialized knowledge than you do?

The standard management model in the old economy called for a vertically structured organization with one leader and many followers. Any worker reluctant to fall into line with the company's procedures would be off the production line faster than the blink of an eye, unless there was union protection against arbitrary management actions. In the old economy, management regularly locked horns with labor, and confrontation was deeply rooted within the corporate structure.

It was clear from a company's financial statements that labor was considered part of the cost of doing business — often the biggest cost and one to be trimmed at every turn. In the old economy, if you weren't an asset (and labor never was, because the company's auditors said so) then it stood to reason that you were a burden — a liability to be managed, often through the collective-bargaining process. Land, factories, machinery and equipment

SHIFTING
GEARS

THRIVING
IN THE
NEW
ECONOMY

were considered the real assets of the company, and analysts would carefully calculate the rate of return on these. Knowledge did not come into the equation.

Unlike the old assets, which depreciated in value through time, the value of knowledge workers might actually rise as they apply the latest technological advances in their fields. Pay for performance, and the development of work teams where the role of boss and employee have become blurred beyond all recognition, will eventually lead to a management and accounting revolution.

⚙ LISTENING TO MOTHER

Picture a visitor to a strange land who witnesses a complicated-looking game. It looks something like baseball, but it obviously isn't. Somebody stands on a small hill and throws a huge white ball as hard as he can toward some fellow crouching down, wearing a mask and other protective equipment. Another masked person dressed in an oversized blue suit leans over him. A player on the opposing team stands to the side, swiping at the ball with a large stick as it goes by.

Most of the time nothing happens, but every once in a while, the person hits the ball with the stick through a basket in the middle of the field and runs full-speed down a white line toward a sack, leaps four hurdles, does a somersault and leaves the game.

Try as he might, the outsider can't make heads or tails of what's going on. The rules are a complete mystery, and he can't understand why the crowd cheers at certain times and not at others.

It's much the same feeling people get these days when they look at the economic changes occurring all around them. Strange things have been happening out on the field of play, where the traditional game has been undergoing changes that haven't been properly explained to the participants or the fans.

SHIFTING
GEARS

THRIVING
IN THE
NEW
ECONOMY

After watching a few baseball games, even the novice can figure out the difference between the pitcher and the catcher. And eventually, the statistics dutifully compiled to measure success or failure in the game — batting averages, runs batted in, fielding percentages, wins and losses — start to make some sense (though why someone who misses the ball nearly three out of four times should be worth $3 million a year is still beyond me). But what if, as in the strange variation on a familiar game described above, the rules had changed and the old statistics no longer provided an accurate picture of who was winning and who was losing? It's simply not possible to be an active player — or even a knowledgeable spectator — in a world that you don't know how to track any more.

Over the years, various averages and ratios have been carefully crafted to keep tabs on the old economy. Applied intelligently, they gave us a useful reading on the health of an individual company, an industry, an entire economy. But as we have seen, the rules of the game have changed, and it's time for a new set of measurements. Without them, we can't know with any certainty where we should be working or investing; who is likely to survive and who isn't; who will prosper in the future and why. Which players are worth their $3 million salaries, which ones should get only $300,000 and which would be overpaid at $3,000 a year.

In the old economy, the most impressive companies were the ones with the best physical and financial assets — machinery, equipment, land, buildings, cash on their balance sheets. A whole convention of financial ratios and accounting methods evolved to measure these attributes. They could tell us whether a corporation was growing rapidly or not; whether it had genuine value; whether, in fact, it had a future.

But today, key players in the new economy have different kinds of assets. Software companies don't have giant football-field-size assembly plants or vast fleets of trucks. Their best assets are two-legged, human, very mobile — and impossible to evaluate using the old measurements. Start running phenomenally successful software-developer Microsoft through the old financial drills and you'll soon be exclaiming, "Holy cow! This company doesn't make any sense! Why would anyone want to invest in it? It can't possibly survive!"

So how do we track the new economy? How do we know which companies, industries and economies are making it and which aren't? Is there, in fact, life beyond the old statistics that we once regarded as so crucial to understanding how our economic world worked?

Accurate assessment is more than merely an academic issue, of interest only to the economists, accountants and statisticians who ply their trade in the deep, numbing waters of numbers and projections. It's absolutely critical to the everyday functioning of the new economy. Without the right tools, how can a bank or pension fund decide whom to lend money to? How can an insurer properly assess risk or develop valuable new products? Certainly not by the old measurements, which give a badly distorted picture of who's hot and who's not.

Measuring the New With the Old

Banks, insurers, stockbrokers and governments don't intentionally set out to become roadblocks. As far as I've been able to determine, there's no massive conspiracy to block progress, no deliberate attempt to hold economic growth in check or keep new industries from gaining access to the financial and investment support they need. It's just that, like the visitor attending a strange ballgame in a foreign land, many financial intermediaries and government officials don't understand the new rules. They no longer know the purpose of the game and can't for the life of them figure out how the umpire keeps score.

Suppose, for example, that bankers and insurance executives had spent years devising meticulous formulas to evaluate the worth of baseball players; but then they found that they couldn't transfer the same methods to any other sport. How could they possibly tell

SHIFTING
GEARS
THRIVING
IN THE
NEW
ECONOMY

if football star Joe Montana was earning his keep? Experts looking at a game of football for the first time with baseball criteria filling their heads would be truly perplexed.

"This game makes no sense," the baseball maven would conclude. "The only standards I understand are for baseball, and every time I try to apply them to football, it's simply ludicrous. Who gets the error on a dropped pass? Is a field goal the same as a run batted in? If quarterback Montana is effectively the team's pitcher, how do I figure out his earned run average? Then again, maybe Montana's really the catcher, because they always call the person in the mask the quarterback of baseball. Football is the dumbest game I've ever evaluated. Has anyone seen the kid selling the hotdogs?"

Similarly, every time the experts take out the financial tools used to track the stars of the old economic circles and apply them to the new economy, they wind up disoriented, bewildered, frustrated and just plain wrong. The old methods aren't up to the job of figuring out whether one corporate athlete in the new economy is outperforming another, whether an industry is of championship caliber or an also-ran. And they are completely inadequate for any real assessment of an entire economy's prospects.

That's why I've developed twenty-five measuring devices that will do the job. These new devices will evaluate the ups and downs of the new economy as accurately as the old tools measured the old. Best of all, most of what I use to measure corporate performance can be easily adapted to assess the condition of any municipality, province, state or country.

We've already seen the value of Knowledge Ratios, which I designed to grade corporate IQs, and the Return on Knowledge Assets, which shows whether a company is using its brainpower productively. Previously, these could only be evaluated haphazardly through anecdotal evidence. It was easy to tell that Merrell Dow Pharmaceuticals Inc., with its rapid growth into the transdermal medication market, had plenty of brains hard at work. But what about all the fledgling drug companies out there looking to attract bright investors and employees? The knowledge measurements provide a valuable clue as to whether they've got something on the ball or not.

There are plenty of other ways of telling which companies are likely to become the Wayne Gretzkys and Michael Jordans and which will be lucky to survive the cut in training camp. The key is to remember the lessons of childhood, the simple truths you were taught to guide you along life's highway of hairpin curves, rock slides and inevitable potholes.

What Mother Always Told Me, Part 1:
"Looks can be deceiving."

The most important new tool to determine whether a company has a *real* future is what I call the **Peak-to-Growth Ratio** (PGR). This shows what portion of a company's sales are going to the vibrant new economy, compared with what it markets to the tired old one. The PGR for any company (revenues from its businesses in industries that have not structurally peaked, expressed as a percentage of revenues from its businesses that are on the downward slope) is also the acid test for how well the managers are doing their jobs.

If anyone ever tells you it's impossible to measure the quality of management, then they obviously have never seen or heard of the PGR. Without this tool, investors and employees can be taken for a ride, as gullible as any visitor to the local carnival.

Think of how easy it is for management to make itself look particularly good, at least at first glance. All it takes is a hard-driving team intent on selling off major divisions, shredding costs and sending short-term profits straight up. This is obviously a highly focused management with a mission, instantly attractive to the uninformed and the uninitiated.

But guess what? Though shareholders might not realize it until it's too late, it's the wrong mission. Endorsing a management that's

SHIFTING
GEARS

THRIVING
IN THE
NEW
ECONOMY

dedicated to slashing and burning its way to success would be like giving one's blessing to a squadron of kamikaze pilots before their suicide missions. Would a self-respecting banker lend $50 million to a daredevil pilot with no sense of direction, a death wish and a broken compass? It seems ridiculous, but that's exactly what's been happening. Then, when the press carries the funereal news of yet another corporate demise, the bankers and shareholders bemoan their bad luck — or the bad economy or bad government — while watching their dollars swirl down the drain.

Take two companies in the food industry. Both have annual sales of approximately one billion dollars and both have been going through painful changes in the past five years. Their debt-to-equity ratios (the debt they've taken on compared with the equity that they own — better known as the "owe-to-own" ratio) aren't out of line with the industry average. Both companies are comfortably profitable, with earnings that would give any investor or employee that warm and fuzzy feeling. But looks, as mother always said, can truly be deceiving.

One company — I'll call it Sausages Are Us — is on the way up. The other, called Bread is Better, is past its peak and headed downward toward oblivion. But how can we tell the winner from the loser?

Sausages Are Us used to be in the meat-packing business, when it was known as Consolidated Butchers Inc. The company had a big investment in milk and butter and had diversified into ice cream, cookies and crackers. Then its managers bought out the company and began turning heads when they changed the old name and sold off, one by one, the divisions that had made CBI strong.

Watching these aggressive new managers go at it, local townfolk could only shake their heads and wonder how long the company could survive. "Who gets into poultry slaughtering and sells off a lucrative dairy business? These guys must have feathers for brains!"

But that was nothing compared to the big acquisition binge. Management used the cash from the sale of the old divisions to buy a dozen small sauce and salad-dressing companies in rapid succession. The money-making cookie and cracker business was peddled to Bread is Better Corp., or BBC. To everyone's astonishment, the money from the sale was immediately plowed back into the cheese business, the only part of the dairy holdings retained by the managers.

The common thread — and the only one that really matters — in Sausages' new strategy was that the company was pulling out of businesses tied to the old economy and brilliantly shifting gears into the new. What the company sold off were operations that, regardless of their profitability, had seen their best days. The replacements were businesses with plenty of room to grow in the new economy, providing Sausages with strong underpinnings for the future.

A Peak-to-Growth Ratio would have revealed that more and more of the company's earnings were coming from businesses still on the way up. Every time another old-economy division was shed, the ratio would climb by leaps and bounds.

BBC, on the other hand, was sticking with its bread and butter through thick and thin, even adding more companies in products such as crackers, where it had acknowledged expertise. It didn't matter to BBC's out-of-touch management that crackers — and every one of the company's other lines — were well past their peak, or that the company had failed to recognize major shifts in its main markets. All that mattered to BBC was the bottom line, which still looked great.

But for how long? The company's PGR would have shown bankers, investors and employees that BBC was in deep trouble, long before the actual — and inevitable — decline in profits set in. Armed with this sort of information, they would certainly have made better choices about where to put their money. And if the company's executives had realized what they were doing to themselves, they would have made vastly different decisions. After all, few captains of industry really have a vested interest in sinking their own ships and torpedoing their futures.

SHIFTING
GEARS

THRIVING
IN THE
NEW
ECONOMY

WHAT MOTHER ALWAYS TOLD ME, PART 2:
"NEVER PUT ALL YOUR EGGS IN ONE BASKET."

Few companies in the real world would disagree that producing products people actually want to buy is a darn good way to build a thriving business. Those that do take issue with this fundamental truth tend not to last long without the support of long-suffering relatives or taxpayers.

But as General Motors, Ford, IBM and countless other corporations have discovered, the products that people want today are not the same ones that were hot sellers in years gone by. When is the last time you saw a long lineup outside a corset shop? When, for that matter, is the last time you saw a corset shop, or even a corset?

I remember suffering through an entire year of business management courses in university. We learned such useful tidbits as how to manage inventories, the importance of good labor relations and at least a zillion ways to finance the growth of a company. But I can't recall even a half hour devoted to the basic fact of business life that survival depends on making stuff that people are willing to pay money for.

To determine a company's odds of turning out new products that might attract a market, there's no better place to start than by tracking its patents. The **Patent-to-Stock-Price Ratio**, which takes the number of patents and divides it by the price of a company's stock, is one of the most telling gauges of any company's chances of success.

Take two companies in the plastics industry. Both report earnings of about $300 million a year, and their stock was recently trading at roughly fifty dollars a share. But what does the investor really get for the fifty dollars? The answer is something quite different for each company.

Say Company A has filed only three patents in the past year, while its competitor, Company B, has submitted thirty. Which one is a smarter bet for the future? And why would anyone even consider .

investing in a company without first finding out whether it's investing in itself? These are questions I'm constantly asking, because the
average investor really doesn't know. If analysts tracked patent
ratios, as I have, along with the usual measures of financial success,
there might be fewer unpleasant surprises.

If an oil company came along and said it had high hopes of hitting a gusher, even a novice might be moved to ask, "Well, how
many wells are you drilling?" If it turns out that your dentist has a
more active drilling program than the oil firm, it would probably
be wiser to buy shares in the dentist's practice. I'm forever com-
plaining that I never win a lottery, and people are forever telling
me, "Wouldn't it help if you bought a ticket?" It's the same in the
corporate world. If companies aren't filing patents and trademarks
— their own version of the lottery — then they'll never hit the
jackpot with new products.

The Patent-to-Stock-Price Ratio reveals that investors in Company A's $50 shares are paying over $16 for every patent filed.
With Company B, the investor is paying just over $1.60 per patent.
It doesn't take an Einstein to see which investment offers more
bang for the buck, or which company has a better chance of finding
that elusive road to success.

The next important step is to measure the productivity of a company's innovations. For patents to be worth more than the paper
they're written on, they had better lead to new products. That's
where other measurements, such as the **Research-to-Development
Ratio** and the **R&D-to-Patent Ratio**, become awfully handy to
have close by.

Everybody knows that first you do research and then you
develop it. But some companies get it all backwards. They
couldn't tell the difference between research and development if
their existence depended it. And, ironically, it does.

Many companies have the notion that a new product simply
means a slightly different version of their profitable old product.
How many times have we seen "New and Improved" stamped on

SHIFTING
GEARS
─────
THRIVING
IN THE
NEW
ECONOMY

the same old box of laundry detergent, tube of toothpaste or candy bar? If all the R&D money is going into development, then the company is looking at a bleak future. It's fine for a candy company to have all of its scientists working on a cantaloupe-flavored version of the same old fluff. But the potential gains from entirely new products that leave the competition in the dust are surely going to outweigh the market advantage of adding a few wrinkles to the same old thing.

Imagine the fate that would befall a record company if it kept slapping "New and Improved" labels on its vinyl forty-fives while the rest of the world was rushing to compact discs and digital tapes. It's enough to send chills of terror down a marketing expert's spine. But as preposterous as the record example might sound, far too many companies stick with the reliable old standbys long after the market has signalled its desire for something truly new.

If General Motors had shifted to front-wheel drive and other innovations when they were first proposed to top executives, the giant car-maker almost certainly would have preserved more of its shrinking share of the North American market, earning additional millions and saving thousands of jobs in the process. Yet GM decided that the public would continue buying whatever it chose to sell — in this case, boats on wheels with poor gas mileage. This mistake has been underlined by the success of the Japanese and repeated over and over by once-innovative companies that have grown fat and complacent and let the R slide right out of R&D.

What Mother Always Told Me, Part 3:
"In life, nothing is static: you either move forward or you move backward."

Although Mother wasn't thinking about capital spending, it's certainly one of the key items that economists look at when deciding whether a company, industry or whole country is moving ahead with the times or falling behind. But capital spending, as we've seen, can mean paving the employee parking lot or renovating the cafeteria. While most certainly welcomed by the workforce, this type of spending is hardly going to ensure a brighter corporate future. (One Canadian firm I know paved the lot twice in one year so that it wouldn't have to return any of its earnings to its foreign parent. It never dawned on the executives running this place that the dollars could have been invested more wisely in new technology.)

My **Technology Spending Ratio** measures what proportion of total spending actually goes into technology, particularly information-processing (easy to spot because it's loaded with microchips and computer displays) and machinery for the service industry, like the laser scanners at the grocery checkout counter.

When you consider that just over 40 percent of total capital spending in the United States today is technology-related, it's not unreasonable for employees or shareholders to have a keen interest in measuring how their company stacks up against its competition. As an investor, you would be mightily impressed if the company announced that its capital spending was going to be double that of its competitors in the year ahead. But elation would quickly slip into despair if it turned out that your investment dollars were slated for a new assembly line that was an exact replica of the existing one installed in the '60s, while the main competition was devoting its smaller budget to sophisticated new processes.

Buying a computerized voice-mail system of the type that's taking the place of the receptionist's antiquated switchboard, or investing in numerically controlled machines on the factory floor that display production information in nanoseconds, is no guarantee of success. But more often than not, the companies with the technological edge have the advantage in the marketplace as well.

SHIFTING
GEARS

THRIVING
IN THE
NEW
ECONOMY

What Mother Always Told Me, Part 4:
"Don't be penny-wise and pound-foolish."

The world of business, fuelled in large measure by the expansion of financial markets beyond their narrow domestic confines, has adopted a global perspective. Whether a company has made the leap and tested foreign markets or not, all have to be aware of the inescapable fact that money no longer recognizes national boundaries.

The **Credit Access Ratios** (CAR) tells a useful story about which companies are putting all their eggs in one financial basket. They may be penny-wise — but they're pound- (and franc and yen) foolish.

Imagine the following scene: Alan Greenspan, chairman of the Federal Reserve Board, which controls U.S. interest rates, wakes up one morning in a terribly cranky mood. He's gone through one congressional hearing too many, and if he hears just one more word about his money supply policies being too tight — or too lax — he'll jump off the nearest Washington monument.

Greenspan telephones his Ottawa counterpart, John Crow, and learns that he too has had it up to here with the politicians and lobbyists. Suppose they make a joint pact to resign and open a little bed-and-breakfast place in the Cayman Islands?

The Canadian and American dollars would immediately drop off the cliff, and interest rates would soar. Companies tied to the fortunes of their national currencies and monetary policies would break out in a cold sweat, and their treasurers would be checking into rest homes in the countryside. But the financial officers of smart companies with high Credit Access Ratios wouldn't even need to increase their Valium supply. They would be sitting pretty, knowing that most of the money their company relied on had no link to domestic interest rates or dollar value.

Companies rarely tie themselves to a single supplier, so why on earth would they leave themselves vulnerable to only one source of capital? Only the very small and the very weak lack the ability to take their search for money beyond their national financial markets.

The higher the Credit Access Ratio, the more financially diversified and more secure the company will be from sudden domestic upheavals. Even for the inexperienced investor, there's nothing easier to track than a public company's CAR — just look at its published financial statements and calculate the percentage of credit and bank loans from international sources. Two companies might have an identical amount of debt, but the one with the lower CAR rating will always be much more vulnerable to the whims or suicidal tendencies of any one central bank or government.

A second financial measuring tool that's exceedingly useful is the **Credit Electricity Index** (CEI). I don't know what was going through my head when I named this one, but take it from me, it's nowhere near as complicated as it sounds.

The CEI shows how vulnerable a company is to changes in interest rates by taking the proportion of floating-rate loans as a percentage of its total debt. Corporations can find themselves whipsawed by rising and falling interest rates. One company might be fretting right now about lower rates, because it bet that they would stay high and locked in to what later turned out to be overly expensive financing. A competitor that made a better guess would be sitting back and wondering what all the fuss is about.

Another pet item in my financial tool kit is the **Insider Funding Ratio**, or, as I sometimes think of it, the "commitment index." I find it extremely useful to know what percentage of a company's financing has been provided by people on the inside — people like senior management and the board of directors — compared with what outsiders have invested. The more money coming from the pockets of insiders, the more committed the company is likely going to be to success. Often, really big, hard decisions have to be made, the outcome of which could determine whether a company lives or dies. It's a great comfort to know that the people who run the company have a lot more riding on the decisions they make than I do.

SHIFTING
GEARS

THRIVING
IN THE
NEW
ECONOMY

What Mother Always Told Me, Part 5:
"Seek and ye shall find."

There's no one ratio that can measure the vast changes that are taking place around us each and every day. I would have loved nothing better than to have uncovered the Holy Grail in the form of one blindingly brilliant ratio that would unveil every secret of a company's future. But that would be about as futile as trying to identify the common denominator of the universe.

Still, there are myriad ways of coming up with a reasonably accurate picture of a company and its prospects in the new economy. Take the **Global Penetration Ratio**, which measures total market share worldwide.

Suppose a highly successful beer company boasts of having 95 percent of the market in northern New Brunswick. That might sound impressive; this is a company with a seemingly iron grip on local consumption. But what if its share of the whole North American market is only 0.0000000003 percent? It's nothing but a big fish in an extremely small pond. Then, one day, a giant brewery starts pouring its heavily marketed suds into New Brunswick. Chances are that the big fish in the little puddle will be eaten alive by the huge shark before the head on the draft has settled.

As an employee, an investor, a banker, an insurer, it's important for you to know exactly what a company is bragging about when it says it's "really big." Is it the biggest vacuum-cleaner manufacturer in southern Texas, or in the whole state or the continent or the entire world? What, in other words, is its Global Penetration Ratio (a company's sales as a percentage of the total global Gross Domestic Product for its industry). If an executive has no idea what the heck I'm talking about when I mention global penetration, I know the company has serious problems.

Plenty of companies pay lip service to "globalization," but precious few actually measure their global market share to determine whether or not it's rising. It's one thing to say "We've got a terrific international business. We sell into a hundred countries." But what if the company is only talking about supplying one-quarter of 1 percent of the entire global market for its type of product? If sales are rising and the global penetration is falling, it might be time to sit down with the vice-president of international sales and ask what's going on out there. Chances are that a host of tough new competitors have entered the fray, and just because you haven't found them doesn't mean they won't find you.

The **Export Ratio**, which I often call the National Trade Bloc Export Ratio, measures the percentage of a company's sales outside of its usual trading bloc. In a world that has so visibly fragmented into different blocs — the North American Free Trade Area, the European Economic Community, Asia-Pacific — it's more important than ever to get a fix on how well a company is doing outside of its traditional market.

Take two Canadian companies in the same industry. Both eagerly tell you in glowing terms that they are truly global players because 57 percent of their sales are now international. The only difference between them — and the Export Ratio would show this clearly — is that in the first company, all 57 percent is earmarked for the North American market. Big deal — so the geniuses running the company have discovered Buffalo! That's hardly as impressive as the competitor who has managed to sell a hefty portion of what it makes to the Japanese, the Germans or the Malaysians.

Let's face it, selling into the comfortable home market or to nearby trading partners doesn't embody nearly as much value and know-how as playing in someone else's bloc.

What Mother Always Told Me, Part 6:
"You can never be just a little bit pregnant."

Last but not least among my favorite ratios is the **Revenue Per Voting Share Ratio** (RVSR). Once upon a time, public companies

SHIFTING
GEARS
━━━
THRIVING
IN THE
NEW
ECONOMY

figured out that they could split their shareholders into voting and non-voting groups. The end result is that not all shareholders are created equal: some have plenty of say, while others have no influence whatsoever. If, as a non-voting shareholder, you decide that the corporate management is seriously off-track, you can't do much about it, apart from selling your stock. And if other investors share your opinion of corporate ineptitude, there won't be many takers.

The serious question answered by the RVSR is how much control the shareholders have over the revenue streams flowing into their company. If the company generates sales of $100 million a year, the RVSR would show just what proportion should be allotted to shareholders with a vote in its affairs. In a world where corporate revenues are often equated with corporate power, it's important to know just how much of that revenue stream is in the hands of an entrenched management — and out of yours, as an ordinary investor. You can never be just a little bit pregnant — you either have control as a shareholder or you don't.

Armed with the right devices to measure the new economy, the game starts to make sense again. The industry stars perform the way they're supposed to, and the over-the-hill players stick out like an old pitcher who has lost his fastball. The new ratios can't guarantee that your investments will turn into gold or that your employment future will be secured, but you might just be able to avoid betting your hard-earned money, your career or your family's well-being on the wrong team playing in the wrong league.

The measures of success that make sense today will almost certainly become obsolete in the next circle of growth. The ultimate challenge is to get a sense of the way the universe will unfold. In the next great circle of growth, the Fourth Circle, the economy will be driven by a whole new set of engines — and the people who know how to take its measure will have a head start on everyone else.

THE FOURTH CIRCLE

It's in our nature to seek stability. Change is unsettling; it's disturbing; it puts us on edge. And it's never going to stop. Sooner or later, as surely as night follows day, we're going to wake up and find that the new economy has turned into the old economy.

As inconceivable as it might sound, the shiny new information and technology era of today will one day seem as tired and sadly dated as steel and textile mills do now. Makers of computer and telecommunications equipment will come to be described by not-too-distant historians as "the old warhorses" that once upon a time helped drive the economy of the late twentieth and twenty-first centuries to dizzying new heights of prosperity. People will look back with curiosity and wonder at archaeological relics like computer keyboards, software manuals and cellular phones. They will sift through the remnants of what we currently regard as the ultimate in medical technology and marvel that any serious doctors could have relied on such antiquated tools as CAT-scanners or ultrasounds to diagnose health problems like brain tumors and kidney stones.

The seeds of change into what I call the "fourth circle" of economic growth have already been planted and are beginning to poke

**SHIFTING
GEARS**

THRIVING
IN THE
NEW
ECONOMY

through the soil. Still small and fragile, some of these seedlings will perish in the harsh and unforgiving climate of dramatic change; others will survive, but their growth will be stunted and their fruit bitter. But more than a few will evolve into the towering redwoods of the future, every bit as mighty as computers in the current technology circle or automobiles in the preceding era of mass-manufacturing.

The Way We'll Be

I talk to a lot of young people about the future. It's all they usually ask about. The present holds little interest, and the past and its lessons scarcely count. The brightest and most adventurous among them are inevitably looking for a road map to the future — detailed directions to the fast track.

Twenty or thirty years ago, these whiz kids headed straight into computers and other technology-driven industries. It didn't matter that they were small and relatively insignificant in the economic scheme of things, lacking the stature and comforting security of the brand-name corporations that the vast majority of their peers would one day want engraved on their business cards.

Most of us would rather have the warm, fuzzy feeling of belonging to an established corporation, but that's rarely where the action and excitement are located at the dawn of a new economic era. For the explorers and the risk-takers among us, a steady income and a nice pension plan take a back seat to the thrill of achievement and the heady climb up the ladder of economic success.

I remember vividly one particular conversation with two teenagers. The pair, who were just embarking on their university studies, called me out of the blue to find out more about my research. When these clean-cut kids arrived at my office, the first thing that struck me was that they were both wearing business suits. I couldn't help wondering if, as in the popular mythology, they had long-haired, jeans-clad parents living on an organic farm somewhere. But that did not turn out to be the case.

They had been sent by their parents to Canada from Africa when they were still in high school. The idea was that they would complete their schooling in a Western country and acquire the skills needed to make it anywhere. Neither looked out of place sitting in a corporate conference room, and both were incredibly focused on doing exactly what their parents had planned for them — finding careers with real futures, where they might make a difference.

The students had come to me for a road map to that future, one noting the landmarks they could look for to ensure they were on the right course. I immediately launched into a description of the new economy, the four engines that were driving it, why the world was changing and what it was changing into. It was a talk I'd given many times before, though usually to people more their parents' age.

Most of the time, what I have to say about the new economy comes as a startling revelation to people of their parents' generation. They grew up in an age of certainties, most of which are simply not so certain any more. But for the college tyros sitting across from me, all this was interesting but hardly earth-shattering stuff — and, in fact, it didn't address the purpose of their visit. To them, it was perfectly obvious that the world had changed drastically, that computers and electronics and the like were huge employers still on the way up while other manufacturers were on the slow boat to oblivion. After all, most of their friends were going into these industries. They didn't know a single top-notch student rushing to get in on the ground floor of one of the big forestry or auto companies.

After listening politely for several minutes, one of the students stopped me cold with a gentle but unmistakably direct question, the kind that only the very young or the very old can get away with. What the brother and sister combo wanted to know was what awaited them down the road, what the seedlings of the future were going to be and where they could be found.

"We want to go someplace where we can learn the ropes, where we can get experience that will mean something," one of my young

SHIFTING
GEARS

THRIVING
IN THE
NEW
ECONOMY

visitors said. "We want to start with an industry that we can grow with, that will let us make our mark. The starting salary is not the issue."

It was the same feisty, independent-minded attitude that propelled young talents to start up the Apples and Microsofts and Hewlett-Packards of this world, when it would have been so much easier to sign on with one of the corporate behemoths that was living off past glories but offered a terrific package of benefits.

The students' probing questions prompted me to describe to them the "fourth circle," or at least what I knew of it. And at that point they sat enthralled, like children hearing a great bedtime story for the first time. It was then that they realized what prospects, what opportunities await the bright and the ambitious in the real world of the twenty-first century.

THE E CIRCLE

We are entering a world that will be dominated by engineering, in all its many modern guises. The future will revolve around science-fact that not so long ago was science-fiction. The new engineers are already revolutionizing such fields as farming and medicine. But these are nothing compared to what's on the horizon, when the driving force of the global economy will no longer be inexpensive microchips in plentiful supply but cheap genes by the bushelful. The engineers are at the same stage today as computer designers were back in the '40s: "Wow, you've come up with a machine that can do complicated math equations. And you say it only takes up one large room and will be cheaper to run than the national economy of Peru?"

Among the potential big engines of growth in the fourth circle:

• genetic engineering and biotechnology
• artificial intelligence
• the business of space
• new materials, including ceramic composites and combinations of metals or plastics with fibers.

THE IMPACT OF THE NEW ENGINES

It's readily apparent that the new technologies will revolutionize a staggering number of today's industries, promising to breathe new life into some that are rapidly fading in economic importance. Here's a small sampling of how the future is changing the present in a wide range of industries and applications.

• Health care. This sector has already taken its seat as a driving force of the third circle, but compared with the changes being wrought by the wonders of biotechnology and genetic engineering, we haven't seen anything yet. The range of diagnostic tests on the market today would have staggered the most fertile of imaginations twenty years ago. It's hard to find a news magazine that doesn't feature yet another lengthy account of this or that major breakthrough in genetic engineering. Such stories are so commonplace that jaded readers are starting to yawn: "Ho hum, another discovery."

But what's coming down the discovery pipeline is certain to open the eyes of even the most blasé among us. As in the early days of computers and space travel, biotech breakthroughs will boggle the mind. The age of medical treatment will disappear, to be replaced by an emphasis on prevention. And in the process, the very way in which our medical institutions, insurance programs, government policies and the structures designed to manage them will change forever.

• Food and agriculture. Tomatoes ripen on the vine without getting soft and mushy or rotting, and there are grain crops that can resist the nastiest of wheat germs. The first crop of genetically engineered wheat is appearing on world markets this year. But that's only the beginning. Scientists have isolated antifreeze genes in fish, which promise to revolutionize the frozen food market, and they've come up with new enzymes to produce ultra-low-calorie beer — proof positive that great scientific minds are not going to waste!

165

SHIFTING
GEARS

THRIVING
IN THE
NEW
ECONOMY

Apart from the obvious benefits in the marketplace for the successful inventors and producers, the new engineering will provide food that will be both safer to eat and safer to grow. Artificially created growing conditions, possible in outer space, and genetically engineered foodstuffs hold out the promise of feeding the world, using far less to produce much more than ever before in history. People who can invent watermelons with no seeds and edible plates and cups to reduce waste can do anything once they set their minds to it!

- Space commerce. Experiments have been performed in outer space that simply wouldn't work anywhere on Earth. More than two hundred American companies have already linked up with NASA for the great commercial explosion in outer space. Scientists are testing the production of ultra-light materials, large protein crystals and pharmaceuticals under ideal conditions only found beyond the Earth's atmosphere.

- Energy. The debate has raged for years over whether science would have the wherewithal to save the planet from ourselves. Well, we'll find out for sure in the fourth circle, as industry turns its collective brainpower to workable solutions for seemingly intractable problems. Superconductivity — the ability to transport electrical energy without losing so much of it along the way — might result in an energy and transportation revolution. Under normal circumstances, about 20 percent of electricity is lost in transmission through high-tension wires. Getting the loss close to zero would reduce energy costs substantially. But even without the availability of the superconducting ceramics needed to carry the power, energy companies are taking advantage of new biotechnology developments to literally clean up their acts. Already on the market are enzymes that remove the sulfur from petroleum, resulting in cleaner-burning fuels.

- Bioremediation is a process that has been used for years in sewage treatment. Oxygen and enzymes are pumped through liquid waste to speed up the natural disintegration of the guck. Mining companies similarly use micro-organisms to leach metals from ore. This process, known as bioleaching, is already used in the production of a quarter of all U.S. copper and is becoming important in gold and uranium mining.

- New materials. Super-adhesives derived from mussels are replacing screws and metals in surgical repairs on the human body. These adhesives (we're not talking Crazy Glue here) promise faster healing and fewer problems getting through airport metal-detectors. Bioceramics enable hip replacements that last longer and more closely resemble God-given joints.

Space-age fibers capable of resisting intense heat and designed for the shields on the Space Shuttle are finding their way into commercial use. This goes far beyond the well-known transformation of Teflon from a rocket coating to the household frying pan.

A range of light and incredibly strong materials, some reinforced with metal, are being tested in machine tools and other equipment. If these composite-fiber materials can be successfully adapted for use in automotive and aircraft parts or, say, containers to store toxic chemicals, we could be looking at a market worth hundreds of billions of dollars and the emergence of a new textile industry that has precious little to do with the making of clothes or bedsheets.

Partly driven by concerns about waste and recycling, manufacturers in Europe are already working on car bumpers and other components made out of textile fibers. Think of it! Early in the next century, textile companies could be locating beside mines and auto plants to get closer to their customers!

- Education. It's likely that we'll look back at our education system and wonder how we ever managed to educate ourselves. The textbooks — not to mention the teacher reading the day's lesson — will eventually be consigned to the shelves containing other charming relics of the past, like quill pens and ink wells. Virtual reality — computer technology that actually allows us to experience sights and smells and sounds — could

**SHIFTING
GEARS**

THRIVING
IN THE
NEW
ECONOMY

turn a lesson in medieval history into something that goes far beyond anything that a modern textbook with the most vivid and elaborate of pictures and drawings could match.

Artificial intelligence and "fuzzy logic" systems, already in use experimentally in insurance and banking and defense, will find their way into education. "Fuzzy logic" does not, in this case, describe how your mind works first thing on a Monday morning. Fuzzy logic, an offshoot of artificial intelligence, allows the computer and its user to evaluate a range of outcomes beyond the simple yes or no, true or false confines of today's software.

Using the computer version of fuzzy logic (rather than their own) students could work their way through a range of problems in science, law or home economics on their school computer. With fuzzy logic, they could arrive at an expert opinion on, say, how Canada would be governed if the Criminal Code were abolished or how social values might have evolved in the United States if the Vietnam War had never occurred.

Students would no longer be the intellectual prisoners of teachers who might have limited knowledge of certain disciplines. Both student and teacher would, instead, have instant access to the finest minds in any given subject to help them arrive at their own conclusions and opinions. Education would no longer be a partly mechanical exercise in memorization and repetition. Fuzzy logic and virtual reality will open vistas never dreamed of by the most progressive of educators. They will come to dominate the lives of our grandchildren, replacing television and video games as a major focus in their lives — with infinitely more satisfying results. School will never again be treated as the dull period between the morning cartoons and the afternoon reruns.

My two young visitors, the ones who had prompted this description of what I think the future holds, were less interested in how the education system might change than in what lies far beyond the halls of academia — in the realm of law, government, management and the structure of commerce and finance. In this respect, the fourth circle will be much like those preceding it, owing a great debt to the people quietly laying the groundwork for what is to come.

All economic circles have certain defining characteristics, and the next great circle will be no different.

- Each era has its *virtuosos*, often so far ahead of their time that their work goes unrecognized until many years later.
- Each era can be defined by the *technology* that underpins its vast growth. Today it's computer science, but the technological key in the fourth circle sits in the biology cupboard. This makes the choice of subjects for students looking to get on the fast track relatively straightforward.

Where knowledge of computers is vital for anyone eager to get ahead in today's electronic world, understanding biological processes will be critical for advancement in industries as seemingly disparate as artificial intelligence, mining and food processing. That does not mean our schools have to turn out troops of biologists, any more than today's students all have to become computer programmers. But everyone will need to understand the rudimentary building blocks of the next circle.

- Each era has its *management practices*. The challenge of managing in today's economy is nothing compared with what lies ahead in the fourth circle, when the very structure of work itself will change. People talk of how more and more employees of the future will be working outside the main office — in the home or in remote locations. But what happens when you have the task of managing a three-person team, all working from their homes in Detroit, New Delhi and a research lab in outer space?
- Each era has its *winners* and *losers*. It's not too early to predict that the losers of tomorrow will include many of the winners of today. If a successful company starts believing it has all the answers — or that its tree will grow to the sky — it is already

heading down the wrong track. If a Microsoft, for example, doesn't go beyond software and make the leap into artificial intelligence and commercialize fuzzy logic on a massive scale, then its star will inevitably fall.

On the other side of the coin, companies that are struggling today can catch the next wave of growth if they make shrewd decisions about what products will be in huge demand in the fourth circle. A tired mining company could restore its long-term luster by cornering the market on a particular enzyme or a process yet to be discovered. An IBM could reclaim its spot at the top of the technological heap with bold innovations in artificial intelligence. What it takes is vision.

• Each era has its *roadblocks* that have to be overcome for the next circle to reach its full potential. To make the leap into the fourth circle, we will again have to reach beyond our present limitations: the lack of global government; the limited — and limiting — range of existing materials (in terms of strength, weight and resistance to heat); the inability of our medical system to protect people (a key asset of both the third and fourth circles) by preventing disease, instead of merely treating it.

What is being established today is nothing less than a global information economy, but without the global legal, political and social structures needed to make it work efficiently. National governments are, by their nature, fiercely protectionist and paternalistic. They can talk all they want about international free trade in goods and services, but they simply don't have their hearts in it. At least not yet.

One of the chief limitations of the technology circle has been the lack of international protection for intellectual property (copyrights, patents, trademarks). There are now signs that career violators like Taiwan and Korea are finally willing to accept global rules that will protect the creators of everything from computer games to sophisticated instrumentation. But much more must be done to prevent the disastrous collision of transnational technologies and research efforts with national or regional walls erected by governments more interested in meeting narrow political goals than furthering development of the fourth circle.

- Each era has its *economic and financial pacesetters*. We have seen how Britain passed the baton to the United States in the mass-manufacturing circle. In the technology circle, it has been Japan and the United States, each uneasily dependent on the other for years. Who will lead the engineering circle? It's still too early to tell, but I have a strong suspicion that future historians will look back at this period and see the Group of Seven industrial countries as the forerunner of a vast economic and financial confederation.

The G-7 makes news headlines today about once a year when the leaders of the United States, Japan, Germany, Britain, France, Canada and Italy gather for a photo opportunity covered by several thousand journalists who have to scramble to find a shred of news. But out of the public spotlight, the senior ministers of the world's mightiest economies have brilliantly orchestrated nothing less than the transformation from the M Circle into the T Circle without precipitating a global depression. Only the quick action of the G-7 prevented the stock market crash of 1987 from widening into a global economic and financial collapse.

By creating a framework of economic and financial management, the G-7 has laid the groundwork for the global structures needed to make the fourth circle function. But the industrial powerhouses are far from unanimous in their views on how the economic universe should be unfolding. And if this confederacy isn't the answer, something else will have to be.

- Each era seems to *expand prosperity* to a wider number of people. In the C Circle, wealth filtered out to the colonies, while the M Circle provided the basis for the boom in the newly industrializing countries of Asia. The T Circle has reached out to encompass such have-nots as India, Brazil and

SHIFTING
GEARS

THRIVING
IN THE
NEW
ECONOMY

Mexico. And the next circle may go a giant step toward embracing the yet-to-be-developed countries of Africa and Latin America.

- Each era has its *reason for being.* The M Circle was clearly driven by personal spending, and it's little wonder that the consumer became the be-all and end-all of the economy. The notion that the consumer was king permeated every facet of business analysis and was reflected in how economic growth was measured. The corporate reason for living was to churn out goods and services for you and me and our children.

We may well look back on that period as an oddity of history. Growth in the C Circle was driven by business — not the yet-to-be-identified consumer — and in the T Circle, most of the high-growth industries wouldn't recognize a consumer if they bumped into one. The fourth circle will continue this historic pattern, with the consumer merely a sideshow to the main attraction, accounting for a tiny fraction of sales for the major growth industries. Many of the features of the fourth circle will, of course, not be clear until it has been given an opportunity to flourish.

Such is the future economic topography as I sketched it for those teenagers — a world full of golden opportunities awaiting people of ambition, brains, energy and enthusiasm and armed with the right maps and other tools to put them to work. The gloom-and-doom crowd who continue to predict the end of the world as we have known it and revel in the hard times afflicting so many industries and the people they employ (or used to employ) simply haven't yet grasped the fact that we are in the middle of an economic revolution, the greatest since the development of modern industrial economies in the last century. They would sow fear and darkness where there should be hope and light.

U.S Knowledge Ratios 1991

	RANK H = HIGH M = MODERATE L = LOW	KNOWLEDGE RATIO
AGRICULTURE	L	6.2
Agricultural Production, Crops	L	1.6
Agricultural Production, Livestock	L	0.7
Agricultural Services (Excluding Horticultural)	M	28.5
Horticultural Services	L	13.0
MINING	M	29.6
Metal Mining	M	23.8
Coal Mining	L	12.8
Crude Petroleum & Natural Gas Extraction	M	38.9
Non-metallic Mining & Quarrying (Excluding Fuel)	L	16.7
FORESTRY & FISHERIES	M	23.6
Forestry	M	32.9
Fisheries	L	14.1
CONSTRUCTION	L	16.5
MANUFACTURING	M	24.7
Lumber & Wood Products (Excluding Furniture)	L	11.2
Logging	L	7.0
Sawmills, Planing Mills & Millwork	L	11.5
Wood Buildings & Mobile Homes	L	15.0
Miscellaneous Wood Products	L	12.2
Furniture & Fixtures	L	10.8
Stone, Clay, Glass & Concrete Products	L	17.7
Glass & Glass Products	L	16.5
Cement, Concrete, Gypsum & Plaster Products	L	18.9
Structural Clay, Pottery & Related Products	L	13.3
Miscellaneous Non-Metallic Mineral & Stone Products	M	20.8
Metal Industries	L	18.0
Primary Metal Industries	L	17.7
Blast Furnaces, Steelworks, Rolling, Finishing Mills	L	16.3
Iron & Steel Foundries	L	13.8
Primary Aluminum Industries	M	21.3
Other Primary Metal Industries	M	20.1

173

	RANK H = HIGH M = MODERATE L = LOW	KNOWLEDGE RATIO
Fabricated Metal Industries	L	18.2
Cutlery, Hand Tools, & Other Hardware	L	16.8
Fabricated Structural Metal Products	M	20.0
Screw Machine Products	L	12.5
Metal Forging & Stampings	L	13.5
Ordnance	M	24.4
Miscellaneous Fabricated Metal Products	L	17.4
Machinery (Excluding Electrical)	M	33.2
Engines & Turbines	M	26.1
Farm Machinery & Equipment	M	25.7
Construction & Material Handling Machines	M	24.7
Metalworking Machinery	M	20.1
Office & Accounting Machines	H	45.1
Electronic Computing Equipment	H	60.6
Electrical Machinery, Equipment & Supplies	M	34.4
Household Appliances	L	17.6
Radio, TV & Communication Equipment	H	45.2
Transportation Equipment	M	30.2
Motor Vehicles & Motor Vehicle Equipment	L	19.1
Aircraft & Parts	M	37.4
Ship & Boat Building & Repairing	L	16.9
Railroad Locomotives & Equipment	M	21.2
Guided Missiles, Space Vehicles & Parts	H	60.8
Cycles & Miscellaneous Transportation Equipment	M	22.6
Professional & Photographic Equipment & Watches	M	34.8
Scientific & Controlling Instruments	H	41.3
Optical & Health Services Supplies	M	30.1
Photographic Equipment & Supplies	M	35.7
Watches, Clocks & Clockwork Operated Devices	M	27.3
Toys, Amusements & Sporting Goods	M	21.9
Food & Kindred Products	L	14.0
Meat Products	L	7.8
Dairy Products	L	15.3
Canned & Preserved Fruits & Vegetables	L	13.2

	RANK H = HIGH M = MODERATE L = LOW	KNOWLEDGE RATIO
Grain Mill Products	M	21.9
Bakery Products	L	10.8
Sugar & Confectionary Products	L	13.3
Beverage Industries	M	22.4
Tobacco Manufacturers	M	25.9
Textile Mill Products	L	12.1
Knitting Mills	L	13.6
Dyeing & Finishing Textiles (Excluding Wool & Knit Goods)	L	14.7
Floor Coverings (Excluding Hard Surface)	L	11.9
Yarn, Thread & Fabric Mills	L	11.2
Apparel & Other Finished Textile Products	L	10.6
Apparel & Accessories (Excluding Knit)	L	10.2
Miscellaneous Fabricated Textile Products	L	13.0
Paper & Allied Products	L	16.3
Pulp, Paper & Paperboard Mills	L	18.3
Miscellaneous Paper & Pulp Products	L	19.4
Paperboard Containers & Boxes	L	10.4
Printing, Publishing & Allied Products	M	30.7
Newspaper Publishing & Printing	M	36.4
Printing, Publishing (Excluding Newspapers)	M	28.6
Chemicals & Allied Products	M	37.7
Plastics, Synthetics & Resins	M	24.4
Drugs	H	45.8
Soaps & Cosmetics	M	34.7
Paints, Varnishes & Related Products	M	29.6
Agricultural Chemicals	M	29.4
Industrial & Miscellaneous Chemicals	M	39.7
Petroleum & Coal Products	M	35.3
Petroleum Refining	M	37.2
Miscellaneous Petroleum & Coal Products	M	21.7
Rubber & Miscellaneous Plastics Products	L	17.4
Tires & Inner Tubes	L	19.8
Other Rubber Products & Plastics Footwear & Belting	L	16.0

Miscellaneous Plastics Products	L	17.2
Leather & Leather Products	L	14.6
Leather Tanning & Finishing	L	18.8
Footwear (Excluding Rubber & Plastic)	L	12.2
Leather Products (Excluding Footwear)	L	15.4
TRANSPORTATION, COMMUNICATIONS & PUBLIC UTILITIES	M	21.3
Transportation	L	14.0
Railroads	L	15.4
Bus Service & Urban Transit	L	17.4
Taxicab Service	L	3.7
Trucking Service	L	9.0
Warehousing & Storage	L	17.5
U.S. Postal Service	L	7.4
Water Transportation	M	24.7
Air Transportation	M	25.0
Pipelines (Excluding Natural Gas)	M	21.1
Services Incidental to Transportation	M	24.6
Communication	M	38.3
Radio & Television Broadcasting	H	72.4
Telephone	M	31.0
Telegraph & Miscellaneous Communication Services	M	33.2
Utilities & Sanitary Services	M	27.3
Electric Light & Power	M	30.0
Gas & Steam Supply Systems	M	22.2
Electric & Gas & Other Combinations	M	29.1
Water Supply & Irrigation	M	28.4
Sanitary Services	M	21.7
WHOLESALE & RETAIL TRADE	L	11.3
Wholesale Trade	L	14.0
Durable Goods	L	14.4
Motor Vehicles & Equipment	L	11.0
Furniture & Home Furnishings	L	14.1
Lumber & Construction Materials	L	16.3

	RANK H = HIGH M = MODERATE L = LOW	KNOWLEDGE RATIO
Sporting Goods, Toys & Hobby Goods	L	14.0
Metals & Minerals (Excluding Petroleum)	L	12.8
Electrical Goods	L	19.1
Hardware, Plumbing & Heating Supplies	L	11.0
Machinery, Equipment & Supplies	L	14.6
Scrap & Waste Materials	L	10.1
Non-Durable Goods	L	13.6
Paper & Paper Products	L	17.2
Drugs, Chemicals & Allied Products	L	14.7
Apparel, Fabrics & Notions	L	13.6
Groceries & Related Products	L	10.6
Farm-Product Raw Materials	L	19.0
Petroleum Products	M	24.0
Alcoholic Beverages	L	11.5
Farm Supplies	L	11.5
Retail Trade	L	10.6
Lumber & Building Materials	L	9.7
Hardware Stores	L	5.2
Retail Nurseries & Garden Stores	L	5.8
Mobile Home Dealers	L	7.7
Department Stores	L	11.3
Variety Stores	L	6.8
Miscellaneous General Merchandise Stores	L	7.8
Grocery Stores	L	2.9
Dairy Products Stores	L	1.8
Retail Bakeries	L	1.3
Motor Vehicle Dealers	L	7.0
Auto & Home Supply Stores	L	3.9
Gasoline Service Stations	L	2.5
Apparel & Accessory Stores (Excluding Shoes)	L	5.4
Shoe Stores	L	7.1
Furniture & Home Furnishings Stores	L	8.8
Household Appliances, TV & Radio Stores	L	11.6
Eating & Drinking Places	L	16.6

	RANK H = HIGH M = MODERATE L = LOW	KNOWLEDGE RATIO
Drugstores	M	28.0
Liquor Stores	L	2.9
Sporting Goods, Bicycles & Hobby Stores	L	6.2
Book & Stationery Stores	L	11.1
Jewelery Stores	L	8.5
Sewing, Needlework & Piece Good Stores	L	5.5
Mail Order Houses	L	14.2
Vending Machine Operators	L	5.0
Direct Selling Establishments	L	3.6
Fuel & Ice Dealers	L	8.7
Retail Florists	H	44.8
FINANCE, INSURANCE & REAL ESTATE	M	30.6
Banking	M	37.0
Savings & Loan Associations	M	34.2
Credit Agencies	H	43.8
Security, Commodity Brokerage & Investment Companies	M	31.2
Insurance	M	22.0
Real Estate (Including Real Estate-Insurance Law Offices)	M	30.5
SERVICES	H	48.1
Business & Repair Services	M	35.3
Advertising	H	58.0
Services to Dwellings & Other Buildings	L	11.6
Commercial Research, Development & Testing Labs	H	76.3
Personnel Supply Services	M	32.1
Business Management & Consulting Services	H	74.4
Computer & Data Processing Services	H	72.0
Detective & Protective Services	L	8.0
Miscellaneous Business Services	M	36.3
Automobile Services (Excluding Repair)	L	19.2
Automobile Repair Shops	L	13.9
Electrical Repair Shops	L	15.9
Miscellaneous Repair Services	L	14.3
Personal Services	L	16.5
Hotels & Motels	L	17.5

178

	RANK H = HIGH M = MODERATE L = LOW	KNOWLEDGE RATIO
Lodging Places (Excluding Hotels & Motels)	L	12.2
Laundry, Cleaning & Garment Services	L	17.0
Beauty Shops	L	0.4
Barber Shops	L	1.0
Funeral Services & Crematories	H	63.0
Shoe Repair Shops	L	7.7
Dressmaking Shops	L	0.0
Entertainment & Recreational Services	H	44.1
Theaters & Motion Pictures	H	66.5
Bowling Alleys, Billiard & Pool Parlors	M	29.2
Miscellaneous Entertainment & Recreation Services	M	34.3
Professional & Related Services	H	58.6
Hospitals	H	59.0
Health Services (Excluding Hospitals)	H	45.5
Offices of Physicians	H	55.2
Offices of Dentists	H	48.8
Offices of Chiropractors	H	48.6
Offices of Optometrists	H	53.3
Nursing & Personal Care Facilities	M	28.4
Miscellaneous Health Services	H	53.3
Educational Services	H	64.4
Elementary & Secondary Schools	H	65.8
Colleges & Universities	H	61.3
Business, Trade & Vocational Schools	H	71.4
Libraries	M	37.7
Miscellaneous Educational Services	H	82.9
Social Services	H	45.6
Job Training & Vocational Rehabilitation Services	M	31.6
Child Care Services	H	46.9
Residential Care Facilities (Without Nursing)	M	36.6
Miscellaneous Social Services	H	52.7
Other Professional Services	H	67.2
Legal Services	H	60.9
Museums, Art Galleries & Zoos	H	45.7

	RANK H = HIGH M = MODERATE L = LOW	KNOWLEDGE RATIO
Religious Organizations	H	61.7
Membership Organizations	H	50.4
Engineering, Architectural & Surveying Services	H	83.9
Accounting, Auditing & Bookkeeping Services	H	66.7
Non-Commercial Educational & Scientific Research	H	79.9
GOVERNMENT ADMINISTRATION	M	39.9
Executive & Legislative Offices	H	55.8
General Government	H	43.0
Justice, Public Order & Safety	L	17.8
Public Finance, Taxation & Monetary Policy	H	60.2
Administration of Human Resources Programs	H	57.8
Administration of Environmental Quality & Housing Programs	H	54.7
Administration of Economic Programs	H	59.7
National Security & International Affairs	H	46.3

The Growth and Influence of Islam

IN THE NATIONS OF ASIA AND CENTRAL ASIA

Turkmenistan

The Growth and Influence of Islam
IN THE NATIONS OF ASIA AND CENTRAL ASIA

The Growth and Influence of Islam
In the Nations of Asia and Central Asia

Turkmenistan

William Mark Habeeb

Mason Crest Publishers
Philadelphia

Produced by OTTN Publishing, Stockton, New Jersey

Mason Crest Publishers
370 Reed Road
Broomall, PA 19008
www.masoncrest.com

First printing

1 3 5 7 9 8 6 4 2

Library of Congress Cataloging-in-Publication Data

Habeeb, William Mark, 1955-
  Turkmenistan / William Mark Habeeb.
    p. cm. — (Growth and influence of Islam in the nations of Asia and Central Asia)
  Includes bibliographical references and index.
  ISBN 1-59084-886-1
  1. Turkmenistan—Juvenile literature. I. Title. II. Series.
  DK933.H33 2005
  958.5—dc22
                              2004022663

Table of Contents

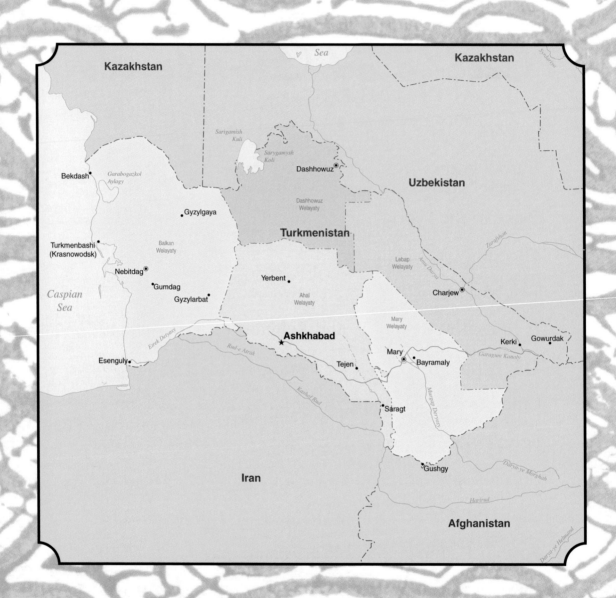

Kazakhstan

Kazakhstan

Sea

Uzbekistan

Sarigamish Kuli

Sarygamysh Köli

Dashhowuz

Dashhowuz Welayaty

Turkmenistan

Bekdash

Garabogazköl Aylagy

Gyzylgaya

Balkan Welayaty

Lebap Welayaty

Amu Darya

Zarafshon

Turkmenbashi (Krasnowodsk)

Yerbent

Ahal Welayaty

Charjew

Nebitdag

Gumdag

Gyzylarbat

Caspian Sea

Mary Welayaty

Kerki

Gowurdak

Ashkhabad

Garagum Kanaly

Mary

Etrek Derýasy

Rud-e Atrak

Tejen

Bayramaly

Esenguly

Murgap Derýasy

Saragt

Kesbat Rud

Iran

Gushgy

Darya-ye Morghab

Harirud

Darya-ye Helmand

Afghanistan

Dr. Harvey Sicherman, president and director of the Foreign Policy Research Institute, is the author of such books as *America the Vulnerable: Our Military Problems and How to Fix Them* **(2002) and** *Palestinian Autonomy, Self-Government and Peace* **(1993).**

Introduction

by Dr. Harvey Sicherman

America's triumph in the Cold War promised a new burst of peace and prosperity. Indeed, the decade between the demise of the Soviet Union and the destruction of September 11, 2001, proved deceptively hopeful. Today, of course, we are more fully aware—to our sorrow—of the dangers and troubles no longer just below the surface.

The Muslim identities of most of the terrorists at war with the United States have also provoked great interest in Islam as well as the role of religion in politics. It is crucial for Americans not to assume that Osama bin Laden's ideas are identical to those of most Muslims or, for that matter, that most Muslims are Arabs. A truly world religion, Islam claims hundreds of millions of adherents, from every ethnic group scattered across the globe. This book series covers the growth and influence of Muslims in Asia and Central Asia.

A glance at the map establishes the extraordinary coverage of our authors. Every climate and terrain may be found, along with every form of human society, from the nomadic groups of the Central Asian steppes to highly sophisticated cities such as Singapore, New Delhi, and Shanghai. The economies of the nations examined in this series are likewise highly diverse. In some, barter systems are still used; others incorporate modern stock markets. In some of the countries, large oil reserves hold out the prospect of prosperity. Other countries, such as India and China, have progressed by moving from a government-controlled to a more market-based economic system. Still other countries have built wealth on service and shipping.

Central Asia and Asia is a heavily armed and turbulent area. Three of its states (China, India, and Pakistan) are nuclear powers, and one (Kazakhstan) only recently rid itself of nuclear weapons. But it is also a place where the horse and mule remain indispensable instruments of war. All of the region's states have an extensive history of conflict, domestic and international, old and new. Afghanistan, for example, has known little but invasion and civil war over the past two decades.

Governments include dictatorships, democracies, and hybrids without a name; centralized and decentralized administrations; and older patterns of tribal and clan associations. The region is a veritable encyclopedia of political expression.

Although such variety defies easy generalities, it is still possible to make several observations. First, the geopolitics of Central Asia and Asia reflect the impact of empires and the struggles of post-imperial independence. Central Asia, a historic corridor for traders and soldiers, was the scene of Russian expansion well into Soviet times. While Kazakhstan's leaders participated in the historic meeting of December 25, 1991, that dissolved the Soviet Union, the rest of the region's newly independent republics hardly expected it. They have found it difficult to grapple with a sometimes tenuous independence, buffeted by a strong residual Russian influence, the absence of settled institutions, the temptation of newly valuable natural resources, and mixed populations lacking a solid national identity. The shards of the Soviet Union have often been sharp—witness the Russian war in Chechnya—and sometimes fatal for those ambitious to grasp them.

A vendor sells traditional furry caps at the Sunday market in Ashkhabad.

Moving further east, one encounters an older devolution, that of the half-century since the British Raj dissolved into India and Pakistan (the latter giving violent birth to Bangladesh in 1971). Only recently, partly under the impact of the war on terrorism, have these nuclear-armed neighbors and adversaries found it possible to renew attempts at reconciliation. Still further east, Malaysia shares a British experience, but Indonesia has been influenced by its Dutch heritage. Even China defines its own borders along the lines of the Qing empire (the last pre-republican dynasty) at its most expansionist (including Tibet and Taiwan). These imperial histories lie heavily upon the politics of the region.

A second aspect worth noting is the variety of economic experimentation afoot in the area. State-dominated economic strategies, still in the ascendant, are separating government from the actual running of commerce and industry. "Privatization," however, is frequently a byword for crony capitalism and corruption. Yet in dynamic economies such as that of China, as well as an increasingly productive India, hundreds of millions of people have dramatically improved both their standard of living and their hope for the future. All of them aspire to benefit from international trade. Competitive advantages, such as low-cost labor (in some cases trained in high technology) and valuable natural resources (oil, gas, and minerals), promise much. This is indeed a revolution of rising expectations, some of which are being satisfied.

Yet more than corruption threatens this progress. Population increase, even though moderating, still overwhelms educational and employment opportunities. Many countries are marked by extremes of wealth and poverty, especially between rural and urban areas. Dangerous jealousies threaten ethnic groups (such as anti-Chinese violence in Indonesia). Hopelessly overburdened public services portend turmoil. Public health, never adequate, is harmed further by environmental damage to critical resources (such as the Aral Sea). By and large, Central Asian and Asian countries are living well beyond their infrastructures.

Third and finally, Islam has deeply affected the states and peoples of the region. Indonesia is the largest Muslim state in the world, and India hosts the second-largest Muslim population. Islam is not only the official religion of many states, it is the very reason for Pakistan's existence. But Islamic practices and groups vary: the well-known Sunni and Shiite groups are joined by energetic Salafi (Wahabi) and Sufi movements. Over the last 20 years especially, South and Central Asia have become battlegrounds for competing Shiite (Iranian) and Wahabi (Saudi) doctrines, well financed from abroad and aggressively antagonistic toward non-Muslims and each other. Resistance to the Soviet invasion of Afghanistan brought these groups battle-tested warriors and organizers. The war on terrorism has exposed just how far-reaching and active the new advocates of holy war (jihad) can be. Indonesia, in particular, is the scene of rivalry between an older, tolerant Islam and the jihadists. But Pakistan also faces an Islamic identity crisis. And India, wracked by sectarian strife, must hold together its democratic framework despite Muslim and Hindu extremists. This newly significant struggle within Islam, superimposed on an older Muslim history, will shape political and economic destinies throughout the region and beyond. Hence, the focus of our series.

We hope that these books will enlighten both teacher and student about a critical subject in a critical area of the world. Central Asia and Asia would be important in their own right to Americans; arguably, after 9/11, they became vital to our national security. And the enduring impact of Islam is a crucial factor we must understand. We at the Foreign Policy Research Institute hope these books will illuminate both the facts and the prospects.

This ornate building stands as a reminder of the Islamic influences that have shaped the society and culture of Turkmenistan. Unlike other Central Asian states, most of the people of Turkmenistan share a common ethnic heritage.

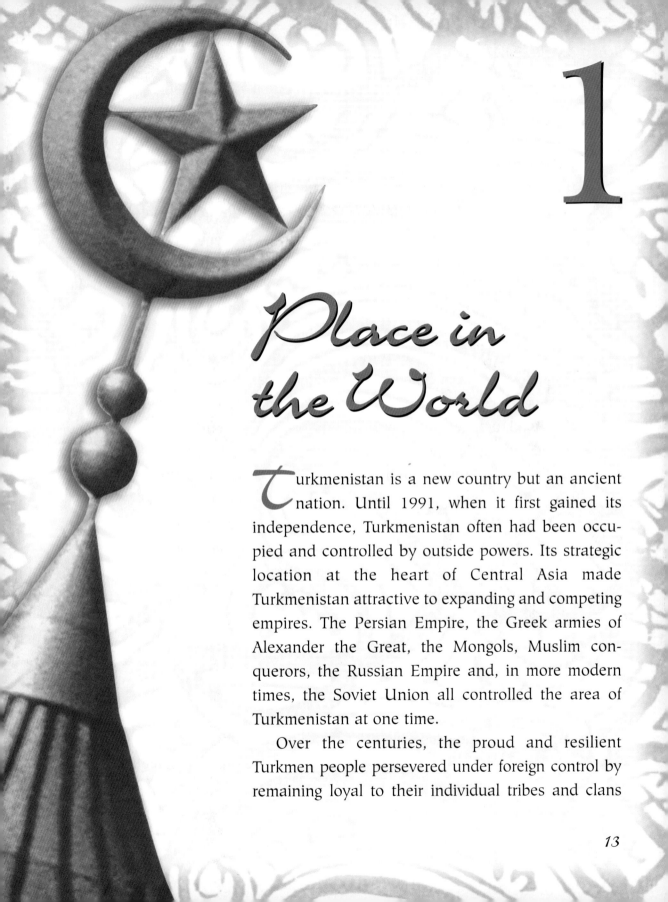

Place in the World

Turkmenistan is a new country but an ancient nation. Until 1991, when it first gained its independence, Turkmenistan often had been occupied and controlled by outside powers. Its strategic location at the heart of Central Asia made Turkmenistan attractive to expanding and competing empires. The Persian Empire, the Greek armies of Alexander the Great, the Mongols, Muslim conquerors, the Russian Empire and, in more modern times, the Soviet Union all controlled the area of Turkmenistan at one time.

Over the centuries, the proud and resilient Turkmen people persevered under foreign control by remaining loyal to their individual tribes and clans and maintaining many of their ancient traditions. While they have integrated into their culture many outside influences—most significantly, the Islamic religion—they have remained a distinct people, conscious of their unique identity. The Turkmen also share a broader identity with the Turkic peoples, closely related ethnic groups inhabiting much of the area from western China to modern-day Turkey who speak similar languages and share a common ancestry.

Turkmenistan is a rugged land, covered mostly by inhospitable desert. Its people have survived for centuries as nomads and herders. From the second century until the 14th century, the Silk Road traversed Turkmenistan. Merchants and traders used this route to transport silk, spices, and other valuable goods from China to the Mediterranean. Trading posts, which later developed into Turkmenistan's first towns and cities, flourished along the Silk Road, and generated new wealth for some Turkmen. But most of the people maintained their ancient nomadic lifestyle.

The Soviet Union first drew the borders of modern Turkmenistan in the early 20th century, establishing it as the Turkmen Soviet Socialist Republic. Under Soviet rule (1921–91), large-scale farming and some manufacturing were introduced to Turkmenistan, and the Soviets improved Turkmenistan's infrastructure. But for a majority of Turkmen, life remained essentially the same as it had been for centuries. The country continued to be poor, isolated, and largely unknown to the outside world. Upon the collapse of the Soviet Union, the independent country of Turkmenistan was established.

Oil, Gas, and Independence

Oil and natural gas were discovered in Turkmenistan in the 1950s and 1960s, and almost overnight this once-neglected land became an important economic center in the Soviet Union. By 1991, Turkmenistan was one of the world's leading producers of oil and gas.

Independence came to Turkmenistan almost unexpectedly, and without violent struggle or rebellion. As the Soviet Union began to collapse in the late 1980s and early 1990s, its constituent republics started to go their separate ways and declare independence. Turkmenistan followed suit, and in 1991 held a popular *referendum* in which the people overwhelmingly voted in favor of independent statehood.

As an independent country, Turkmenistan was open to the world's wealthiest oil and gas investors. Large international energy companies from the United States and Europe, which previously had not been allowed to operate in the Soviet Union, began negotiating deals with Turkmenistan to explore for oil and gas and develop resources.

Turkmenistan's strategic Central Asian location, its predominantly Muslim population, and its long borders with Iran and Afghanistan also contributed to the new country's importance on the world stage. Its significance was magnified after the September 2001 terrorist attacks against the United States by Islamic extremists and the resulting U.S.-led wars in Afghanistan and Iraq.

Turkmenistan's future is filled with great potential, but also wrought with great uncertainty. Given its huge oil and gas reserves and relatively small population, Turkmenistan has the potential to develop into a modern, wealthy nation. But as a country that is run as a virtual dictatorship and is situated in a volatile region, Turkmenistan also has the potential to succumb to the disorder and turbulence that surrounds it. Whatever the country's fate holds, the government desperately needs to introduce political modernization, personal freedoms, and greater democracy. Only then will the Turkmen people truly have the power to determine their future.

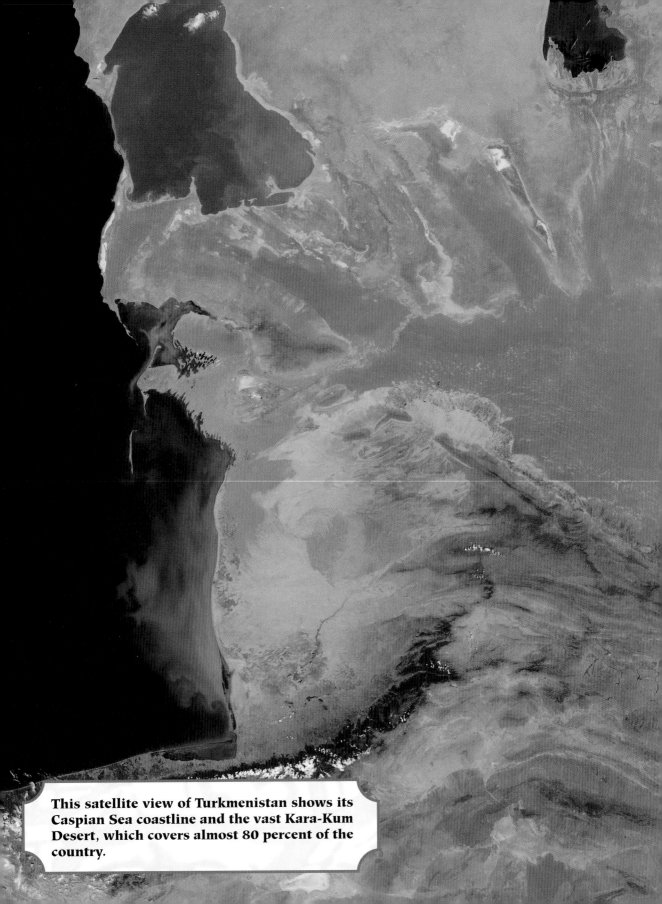

This satellite view of Turkmenistan shows its Caspian Sea coastline and the vast Kara-Kum Desert, which covers almost 80 percent of the country.

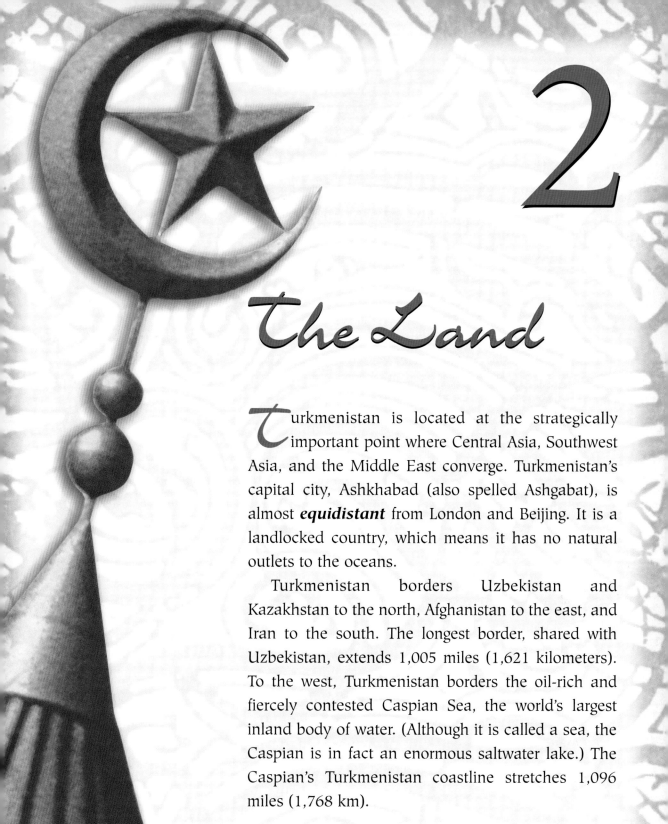

2

The Land

Turkmenistan is located at the strategically important point where Central Asia, Southwest Asia, and the Middle East converge. Turkmenistan's capital city, Ashkhabad (also spelled Ashgabat), is almost **equidistant** from London and Beijing. It is a landlocked country, which means it has no natural outlets to the oceans.

Turkmenistan borders Uzbekistan and Kazakhstan to the north, Afghanistan to the east, and Iran to the south. The longest border, shared with Uzbekistan, extends 1,005 miles (1,621 kilometers). To the west, Turkmenistan borders the oil-rich and fiercely contested Caspian Sea, the world's largest inland body of water. (Although it is called a sea, the Caspian is in fact an enormous saltwater lake.) The Caspian's Turkmenistan coastline stretches 1,096 miles (1,768 km).

With an area of 195,240 square miles (488,100 sq km), Turkmenistan is slightly larger than the state of California and slightly smaller than Spain. Most of Turkmenistan—over 80 percent—is covered by desert; the remaining land is made up of rugged mountains. Less than 4 percent of Turkmenistan's land is considered arable, or suitable for farming, and only about 8 percent is forested.

Mountains and Deserts

Turkmenistan's landscape is dominated by the Kara-Kum Desert, which stretches eastward across the country from the Caspian Sea and extends into Kazakhstan. The Kara-Kum (which means "Black Sand" in the Turkic language) covers nearly 140,000 square miles (350,000 sq km) of Turkmenistan. It is characterized by large sand dunes that are formed by strong blowing winds. Some of these dunes ascend to 70 feet (20 meters) or more. Other parts of the Kara-Kum are flat or descend into depressions—the Transcaspian Depression and the Vpadina Akchanaya both lie more than 260 feet (79 meters) below sea level. Some of the desert depressions contain expansive salt flats, which are all that remain of lakes that evaporated centuries ago.

Along the southern edges of the Kara-Kum Desert rise the Kopet-Dag Mountains. This narrow chain stretches from northwest to southeast for 375 miles (600 km) along Turkmenistan's long border with Iran, which contains the mountains' southern foothills. The Kopet-Dag features dry sandy slopes, plateaus, deep ravines, and foothills, along which are a series of *oases* fed by mountain streams. The highest peak in the range is Mount Shahshah, which rises 9,600 feet (2,912 meters); it lies just southwest of the capital city of Ashkhabad. The Kopet-Dag Mountains and nearby regions are geologically active and subject to powerful earthquakes—in 1948, one massive quake virtually destroyed Ashkhabad.

In northwest Turkmenistan, just inland from the Caspian Sea, lies the

Riding a camel, a ranger patrols the dunes near the Repetek San Desert Station in the Kara-Kum Desert.

Balkan Mountain range (not to be confused with the Balkan range of southeastern Europe). In the far southeastern part of Turkmenistan, near the borders with Afghanistan and Uzbekistan, are the rocky Kugitang Mountains. This range includes Turkmenistan's highest mountain, Ayribaba, which rises 10,356 feet (3,139 meters), as well as deep canyons and ravines. The Kugitang Mountains also contain the fascinating Plateau of Dinosaurs, which features over 400 well-preserved fossilized footprints

The Geography of Turkmenistan

Location: Central Asia, bordering the Caspian Sea, between Iran and Afghanistan.

Area: (slightly larger than California)
  total: 195,240 square miles (488,100 sq km)
  land: 195,240 square miles (488,100 sq km)
  water: negligible

Borders: Caspian Sea, 1,096 miles (1,768 km); Uzbekistan, 1,005 miles (1,621 km); Iran, 615 miles (992 km); Afghanistan, 461 miles (744 km); Kazakhstan, 235 miles (379 km)

Climate: subtropical desert

Terrain: flat-to-rolling sandy desert with dunes rising to mountains in the south; low mountains along border with Iran; borders Caspian Sea in west

Elevation extremes:
  lowest point: Vpadina Akchanaya depression, –270 feet (–81 meters)
  highest point: Gora Ayribaba, 10,356 feet (3,139 meters)

Natural hazards: earthquakes, drought, sandstorms

Source: Adapted from CIA World Factbook, 2004.

of dinosaurs. Scientists believe this plateau was a lagoon during the Jurassic geologic period, spanning from 206 to 144 million years ago. They theorize that the dinosaurs left footprints on the lagoon's sandy bottom while feeding on aquatic plant life. Another feature of the mountains is the famous Kugitang caves, an underground network more than 37 miles (60 km) long. For centuries, these caves were used as hiding places by smugglers and thieves.

Lakes and Rivers

In addition to Turkmenistan, the salty Caspian Sea borders Azerbaijan, Iran, Kazakhstan, and Russia. These five countries have held negotiations about how to share the Caspian's resources, which include fish (especially sturgeon, source of the world-famous Caspian Sea caviar) and vast undersea oil and gas reserves. The most important city along the Caspian, Turkmenbashi (known as Krasnovodsk until 1992), is the **terminus** for oil and gas pipelines as well as Turkmenistan's major shipping point for agricultural exports.

The most important river in Turkmenistan is the Amu Dar'ya, which flows northwest out of Afghanistan, eventually emptying into the Aral Sea in Uzbekistan. The Amu Dar'ya has been used for centuries by the Turkmen for **irrigation**. Because people draw water from the river and it flows through an area that receives little rain, it is usually very low and filled with sediment. As a result, it can only be navigated by the smallest boats. In ancient times, the Amu Dar'ya was known as the Oxus River, and played a prominent role in the military campaigns of the Persians and Greeks in Turkmenistan. According to early historical sources, the river originally flowed into the Caspian Sea; no one knows for sure when (or why) its course was later diverted to the Aral Sea.

One of the largest irrigation systems connected to the Amu Dar'ya is the Kara-Kum Canal. Constructed between 1954 and 1962 by the Soviet Union, this 852-mile (1,375-km) canal diverts large amounts of water from the Amu Dar'ya in an effort to irrigate agricultural land south of the river. Because the Kara-Kum diverts so much water from the Amu Dar'ya as it flows northward, it has become a source of contention between Uzbekistan and Turkmenistan. The Uzbeks are upset that they receive less water from the river than they once did. In addition, the diminished flow is causing the Aral Sea to dry up.

This view of the Kara-Kum Canal near Ashkhabad was taken at sunset. The canal brings water from the Amu Dar'ya to farmland in the south.

Climate

Turkmenistan has a subtropical desert climate, with long summers (May through September) that are hot and dry, and winters that are mild and dry. There is only modest variation in weather patterns from one part of the country to another. Precipitation falls principally between January and May, most heavily in the Kopet-Dag Mountains and their foothills. The country receives very little snowfall. Because the landscape features such vast desert areas, Turkmenistan is subject to almost-constant winds, blowing mostly from the north or northwest.

In Ashkhabad, which is located in the south, daily high temperatures in the summer months range from about 87° to 100° Fahrenheit (about 30° to 37° Celsius). It is not uncommon for Ashkhabad to have only three or four days of rain during the entire summer. In the winter, Ashkhabad's temperature rarely drops below freezing (32°F or 0°C), but it may rain for five or six days out of every month. By contrast, the city of Dashhowuz, located in the far north along the border with Uzbekistan, has cooler summers and chillier winters. Summer temperatures rarely hit 90°F (32°C), and winter temperatures can fall to 15°F or 20°F (–9°C to –7°C).

Turkmen workers post a giant portrait of the country's president, Saparmurat Niyazov, in Ashkhabad. Since Turkmenistan became independent in 1991, Niyazov has been the country's most powerful figure, and some opponents have accused him of creating a "cult of personality," by encouraging an atmosphere in which he is treated as an infallible leader and the embodiment of the national identity.

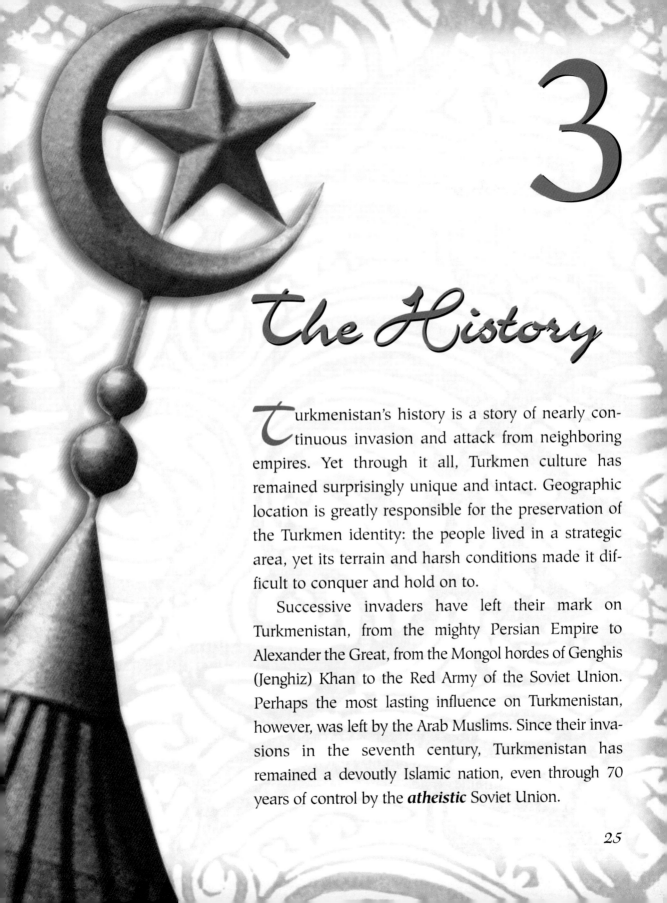

3

The History

$\mathcal{T}$urkmenistan's history is a story of nearly continuous invasion and attack from neighboring empires. Yet through it all, Turkmen culture has remained surprisingly unique and intact. Geographic location is greatly responsible for the preservation of the Turkmen identity: the people lived in a strategic area, yet its terrain and harsh conditions made it difficult to conquer and hold on to.

Successive invaders have left their mark on Turkmenistan, from the mighty Persian Empire to Alexander the Great, from the Mongol hordes of Genghis (Jenghiz) Khan to the Red Army of the Soviet Union. Perhaps the most lasting influence on Turkmenistan, however, was left by the Arab Muslims. Since their invasions in the seventh century, Turkmenistan has remained a devoutly Islamic nation, even through 70 years of control by the **atheistic** Soviet Union.

The Turkmen have always been a fiercely independent people, but Turkmenistan did not experience political independence until 1991. Self-rule came to the country unexpectedly, and Turkmenistan has been struggling for over a decade to develop its economy and ensure its stability in an unstable region. With a short history of democracy or representative government and a long history of tribal leadership, it is not surprising that Turkmenistan would come under the control of a charismatic and powerful individual. Saparmurat Niyazov, independent Turkmenistan's first and only leader as of this writing, rules with an iron fist. In 1999, he was appointed president for life. Turkmenistan's future prosperity depends in large part upon its ability to exploit its natural resources, use its income wisely to the benefit of its people, and gradually install a more representative form of government that will give all Turkmen a greater role in shaping their ancient nation's future.

Early History

Few details about present-day Turkmenistan's early history are known. The country's environment—which is prone to earthquakes, sandstorms, and wind erosion—has destroyed most archaeological remains and other evidence of human life. But archaeologists do know that Turkmenistan was inhabited as early as 10,000 B.C. by nomads and herders.

By 6000 B.C., small settled communities had begun to appear in the foothills of the Kopet-Dag Mountains, near the Caspian Sea, and along rivers and streams. Because of the lack of rainfall in the region, it was critical for these communities to be located near sources of water. The precise origin of these settlers is unknown, but they probably migrated to the region from the east, from what today are Mongolia and western Siberia. They lived by herding goats, hunting, gathering wild grains, and fishing. Many of these communities made their homes in caves, but archaeologists have found evidence that by around 5000 B.C., people had begun to construct mud brick houses clustered together in small villages. Today, houses in rural Turkmenistan have the same mud brick construction used by these early peoples.

These **prehistoric** communities eventually developed agricultural techniques, which allowed for a more settled lifestyle. They began to trade with one another and with nomadic peoples in the region. Pottery-making and textile-weaving joined agriculture and herding as important economic activities. The villages grew into towns, one of which was located at an oasis at the site of Merv, an ancient city in eastern Turkmenistan. By around 3000 b.c., the towns had made contact through trade with the rising civilizations in Mesopotamia, a region in the Tigris-Euphrates Valley within the modern-day country of Iraq. This contact brought about an influx of new ideas about culture, religion, and politics.

Little is known about the social structure of these early communities. They most likely began as **nuclear families** that were self-sufficient in most of their needs. But as isolated settlements grew into villages and then towns, extended families became the basis of social life. As extended families grew, they evolved into what are commonly referred to as tribes— large groups that share a common kinship as well as social customs.

By 1000 B.C., numerous towns and villages dotted the oases and foothills of Turkmenistan. Each was self-sufficient, and often dominated by a single tribe or clan. There was no formed concept of a nation or country, and, except for trade, no official relationship among the various communities.

Persians and Greeks

Tribes eventually began to move southward from the Caucasus Mountains region of what today is southern Russia into present-day eastern Iran. Two of these tribal groups—the Medes and the Persians—dominated Iran. After 500 years of competition and fighting, a Persian leader, Cyrus the

Great, defeated the Medes, unified Iran, and proceeded to create the most extensive empire the world had ever known to that time. Cyrus's empire, known as the Achaemenid Empire, included virtually all of Turkmenistan and stretched as far north as the Aral Sea. The Turkmen city of Merv (known today as Mary) was founded by Cyrus around 540 B.C.

One of Cyrus's successors, Darius I, solidified and expanded the Achaemenid Empire, establishing a remarkably advanced system of imperial administration. He constructed roads throughout the empire, minted gold and silver coins to facilitate trade, and established a professional army. Trade and commerce flourished throughout the Achaemenid Empire, bringing not only new goods but also new ideas to the people of Turkmenistan.

Darius's son Xerxes continued to expand Cyrus's territory. But in 479 B.C., his navy was defeated in a battle against the Athenians, and the Persians were driven from Greece. This defeat marked the beginning of the decline of the Achaemenid Empire. Turkmenistan remained part of the empire, but under a series of weak rulers who followed Xerxes, the Persians' influence and control began to wane.

In 336 B.C., Alexander the Great became the ruler of Greece upon the death of his father, Philip of Macedon, who had earlier unified the Greek city-states into one nation. Alexander was determined to crush the Persian Empire, and by 331 B.C. he had largely succeeded in doing so. He sacked the Persians' magnificent imperial capital city, Persepolis, and took control of Iran. But Alexander's thirst for conquest was not quenched, and he continued his march, first north, and then eastward toward India. In the process, he fought battles against Persians and local tribes as his armies crossed the Kara-Kum Desert of Turkmenistan. Alexander's forces conquered the oasis city of Merv, which had become a thriving center under the Persians, and renamed it Alexandria. Many of the Greek soldiers who had completed their tour of duty settled there permanently.

After Alexander's death in 323 B.C., his empire was divided among four of his generals. One of the Greek generals, Seleucus, became ruler of what had been the Persian Empire, including Turkmenistan. His descendants, known as the Seleucids, continued to rule this territory, but they were vulnerable to foreign invasions. By around 140 B.C. Greek control over Iran and Turkmenistan ended when the last Seleucid ruler was defeated by the Parthians.

The Parthians were a tribe from northern Iran and the Caspian Sea region; some archaeologists believe that they migrated there from their original settlements along the Amu Dar'ya in Turkmenistan. After defeating the Seleucids, the Parthians, under their great leader Mithradates I, proceeded to conquer most of the terri-

This page from a Persian manuscript shows the dying Alexander the Great surrounded by his entourage. Alexander's soldiers conquered cities in Turkmenistan and brought the region into his vast empire.

tory of the former Achaemenid Empire, including Turkmenistan. They soon gained a great reputation for their gold and silver coinage, much of which was minted in the city of Merv (which the Parthians then called Margiane).

Tourists walk along a desert road to the ruins of Nisa, an ancient Parthian city that was once an important center of trade in the region.

The Parthian Empire found itself under constant attack in the west by the Romans, and by around A.D. 240 had become so weakened that it lost control over Iran and most of Turkmenistan to a Persian tribe known as the Sassanians. Under the Sassanian Empire, the city of Merv maintained its role as an important center, both for coinage minting as well as cotton textile weaving. In the third and fourth centuries, Merv became a major intellectual center of Central Asia, and was the largest Sassanian city outside of the region that became Iran. It was also a major stop on the Silk Road, the important east-west trade route that crossed Central Asia.

The Sassanians ruled most of what is today Turkmenistan for around 400 years. They introduced a centralized form of administration and the Zoroastrian religion, one of the first *monotheistic* faiths. The new religion of Christianity—which in the fourth century was proclaimed the official religion of the Roman Empire—was also making inroads into Central Asia.

By A.D. 335, there were so many Christians in Merv that the pope made the city a **bishopric**. Buddhist artifacts also have been found in and around Merv.

By the late sixth century the Sassanian Empire was in decline, battered by a long series of wars against the Roman Empire to the west. In its weakened condition, the empire was ripe for invasion by two powerful new forces—Arab Muslim invaders from the south and Turkmen tribes from the east.

When the Sassanids ruled the region of modern Turkmenistan, they introduced the Persian religion Zoroastrianism. Fire was an important symbolic element in the religion, and featured prominently in temples like this one.

Muslims and Turkmen

The prophet Muhammad, an Arab merchant from what is today Saudi Arabia, founded the Islamic religion based on teachings that he attested were revealed to him by God (known as *Allah*). His recitations of these teachings became the Qur'an, Islam's sacred text. Although initially Muhammad and his followers were persecuted, eventually they gained control of Mecca and other important cities on the Arabian Peninsula. After his death in A.D. 632, Muhammad's followers set out from Arabia to spread Islam throughout the world. The religion's message was straightforward: "There is no god but Allah, and Muhammad is His prophet." (Habitually repeating this statement is a central practice of the faith.) The message was also ***inclusive***: anyone who professed this central faith and agreed to practice the other major principles of Islam was accepted as a Muslim, regardless of social status, tribal origins, or previous religious beliefs.

In 635, Muslim armies defeated the army of the Byzantine Empire (the eastern half of the Roman Empire, which had survived after Rome fell to barbarians in 476) in Syria, and turned their attention to the weakened Sassanian Empire. In a series of decisive battles, the Muslim forces routed the Sassanians. The last king of the empire, Yazdegerd III, met his death in 651 at the hands of Muslim armies at Merv in Turkmenistan, the last holdout of the empire. By the year 700, the former Sassanian territory, including Turkmenistan, was under the control of the Muslim ***caliph*** of Damascus, and most of the people had converted to Islam.

Starting around the ninth century loosely confederated nomadic tribes from Mongolia and southern Siberia began to migrate into Turkmenistan and as far west as modern Turkey. These tribes—known as the Oghuz— were Turkic-speaking people who embraced Islam. They absorbed the Iranians and other ethnic groups that inhabited Turkmenistan at the time.

Most scholars regard them as the direct ancestors of the people of modern-day Turkmenistan.

Turkmenistan remained officially under the control of the Muslim caliphs, but in fact real power lay in the hands of the many Oghuz tribal leaders. At the turn of the 11th century, an Oghuz leader named Seljuk established a dynasty based in Merv and began a series of military campaigns to the south and west. By the middle of the 11th century, the Seljuk Empire included the regions of present-day Iran and southern Turkmenistan. In 1055, Seljuk armies captured Baghdad, one of the Islamic world's most important cities, and other Oghuz tribes spread into Azerbaijan. In 1071 Alp Arslan, Seljuk's great-grandson, conquered most of Anatolia (modern-day Turkey). His descendants would establish the Ottoman Empire, one of the greatest and most extensive empires in history,

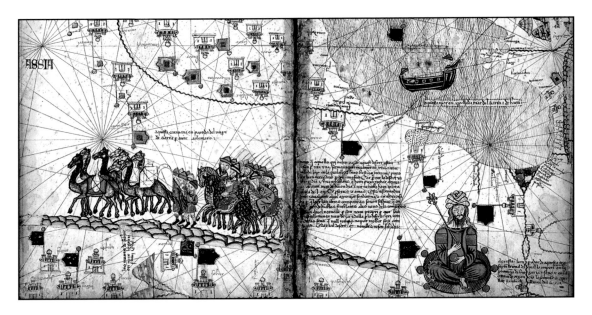

This detail from a map made in 1375 shows a caravan traveling the Silk Road. This was the name for a network of routes through Central Asia that connected China and Europe. Control over Turkmenistan, therefore, meant control of the lucrative trade, so many empires fought to assert their power over Central Asia.

in the late 13th century. The Ottoman Empire lasted for over 600 years; when it was dissolved in 1924, Anatolia was renamed the Republic of Turkey—an acknowledgment of the Turkic origins of its people.

By the 12th century, the various Oghuz tribes were commonly referred to as Turkmen. The city of Merv was the seat of the Seljuk Empire, and developed into one of the major centers of Turkmen culture. The growing economic importance of the Silk Road created great wealth for Turkmen traders, and Merv was adorned with beautiful palaces and mosques (Islamic places of worship).

In the late 12th century, the Seljuk Empire started to fragment as other Turkmen tribesmen—some of whom had at one time served in the Seljuk army—attacked it from the north and west. The Ottoman Empire was in the early stages of ascendancy and was emerging as a serious threat to the Seljuks. As the Seljuk Empire crumbled, Turkmenistan and much of Central Asia became susceptible to yet another foreign invasion—this time from the north.

Genghis Khan and the Mongols

Early in the 13th century, a Mongol tribal leader named Genghis Khan (also known as Jenghiz Khan) succeeded in unifying various tribes of eastern Asia living in and around present-day Mongolia. Genghis Khan was a military genius, and after unifying the Mongols he formed an army that swept across Asia and conquered a vast stretch of territory. At its height, the Mongol Empire stretched from modern-day Korea to European Russia, and as far south as the tip of India.

In 1221, the Mongols invaded Turkmenistan. They burned Merv to the ground, destroying the magnificent architectural monuments of the Seljuks. The Mongols were brutal warriors: they massacred many of the residents of Merv and drove the survivors westward into the Kara-Kum Desert and toward the Caspian Sea. However, they did not interfere in the religious practice of their subjects, and thus Islam remained the dominant religion of the Turkmen.

Genghis Khan died in 1227, and subsequently Mongol control over Turkmenistan weakened. The Mongol leader Timur Lenk (ca. 1336–1405), who claimed to be a descendant of Genghis Khan, revived the empire for a brief period in the late 14th century, but soon afterward the Mongols retreated.

For most of the 15th through the 17th centuries, Turkmenistan was in frequent turmoil. Following the Mongols' departure, the region came under the loose control of various Muslim khans (or rulers), especially those of Khiva and Bukhara in what today is Uzbekistan. Turkmen tribes had considerable **autonomy**, however, and frequently raided the settled communities established by the khanates. Persia—now under the control of the Safavid dynasty, which itself had been founded by Turkmen from northern Iran—also was drawn into battles in the Turkmenistan region, against both the khanates and the Turkmen tribes. It was during this tumultuous period that the Turkmen people formed large tribal and kinship groups that to this day remain an important foundation of Turkmen society.

During this period, the entire area of what is now called Central Asia became known generally as Turkestan, named after the predominantly Turkic-speaking peoples who inhabited the region.

Russian Expansion

The Russian Empire, under the **czar** Peter the Great, started to take an interest in Turkmenistan and the rest of Turkestan in the early 18th century. However, after Turkmen massacred a Russian military expedition in search of trading routes in 1716, the empire's plans were delayed. The Russians stayed away for nearly a century.

During the 19th century, Turkmen tribes began seeking trade relations with the Russian empire because they needed better weapons to fight the khanates and the Persians. In spite of their offers to forge relations, the Turkmen still staged raids into southern Russia, which provoked military counterattacks. It was during this period that Russians established bases and forts in the area.

From 1863 to 1868, the Russians fought and defeated the two khanates of Bukhara and Khiva, and annexed their territory, which included western Turkmenistan. The Turkmen tribes of eastern and southern Turkmenistan, however, continued to fiercely resist Russian incursions. In 1869, Russia established the Caspian Sea port of Krasnovodsk (known today as Turkmenbashi). In 1881, General Mikhail Skobelev of Russia captured the Turkmen city of Geok-Tepe after a two-year-long struggle that ended in thousands of Turkmen casualties. Soon afterward, Ashkhabad also fell to the Russians, and the Turkmen resistance was effectively defeated.

A Russian photographer took this color picture of the Emir of Bukhara around 1900. The Russian Empire expanded to include much of Central Asia, including Turkmenistan, during the second half of the 19th century.

By 1885, all of the major Turkmen tribes had accepted Russian control. Turkmenistan became part of the territory of Transcaspia, a subdivision of Russian Turkestan. This larger province extended from the Caspian Sea on the west to the Chinese frontier in the east. In the south, Russia signed treaties with both Persia and Afghanistan to establish southern borders that are still recognized today. These borders, however, did not reflect the actual boundaries of where the Turkmen people lived, and left large numbers of Turkmen living in Persia and Afghanistan. To this day, both countries still have sizable Turkmen minorities.

The Russians soon opened a new railroad line connecting Krasnovodsk on the Caspian Sea with Ashkhabad and Merv, as well as Tashkent in modern-day Uzbekistan. The Transcaspian Railroad greatly facilitated trade and commerce, and led to the growth of new cities and towns along its route. Despite the new innovations, the native peoples did not benefit economically from Russian rule. Transcaspia was ruled by Russian military officers, many of whom were corrupt and incompetent, more interested in their own business deals than in improving the lives of the people. Turkmen culture, however, was not negatively affected. It remained distinct, and the people were free to continue practicing their nomadic way of life and the Islamic religion.

The Soviet Union

In the early 20th century, the Russian Empire found itself under internal and external pressure. Russia was large and militarily powerful, but many Russians were poor and discontented with the ruling czar, Nicholas II, and the wealthy elite who controlled the empire. The situation worsened after Russia entered World War I in 1914. Feelings of discontent spread to Russian Turkestan, and in 1916 an anti-Czarist revolt was staged throughout the region.

In March 1917, a revolt of the people forced Nicholas II to abdicate the throne. A provisional government was set up, in which Alexander Kerensky soon became the most important figure. However, Kerensky and others in the provisional government were unwilling to pull Russia out of the unpopular war. By October, a second revolution had begun, led by Vladimir Lenin and the Bolsheviks. Kerensky fled to exile, and Lenin established the world's first government based on communist principles. He also immediately withdrew Russia from World War I.

Several years of chaos and internal struggle followed, as the new Russian leaders attempted to hold on to their former imperial lands and simultaneously install a new form of government. The rebellion in Turkestan continued, but it was now directed against the Lenin government. In 1918, the Red Army of Russia captured Ashkhabad, and by the end of 1920, had secured control of most of Turkmenistan. In 1922, the government formally established the Union of Soviet Socialist Republics (U.S.S.R., or the Soviet Union), composed of Russia and the various territories it controlled. Every republic and territory now had a communist government in place.

In 1924, Turkmenistan was renamed the Turkmen Soviet Socialist Republic (or Turkmen S.S.R.). Its boundaries, as established by the Soviet Union, remain the country's boundaries today. Four other Soviet Republics also were created out of the area that had been known as Russian Turkestan: Uzbekistan, Kazakhstan, Tajikistan, and Kyrgyzstan. The newly drawn boundaries of these republics were meant to intentionally divide ethnic groups. The Soviet government in Moscow feared that if it created one large Turkic republic, the people could unite and launch a successful rebellion.

By 1929, the Soviet Union had come under the leadership of the ruthless Joseph Stalin. During the late 1920s and early 1930s, his government undertook sweeping reforms throughout the entire country. All private

Soviet leaders Vladimir Lenin and Joseph Stalin, circa 1922. Lenin (left) led the Bolshevik movement that ultimately established the Union of Soviet Socialist Republics (U.S.S.R.). Turkmenistan became one of the Soviet Republics in 1924. After Lenin's death, his deputy Stalin emerged as the leader of the U.S.S.R., and implemented policies that angered many Turkmen, such as nationalization of industrial facilities and collectivization of farms.

property was confiscated and underwent *nationalization*; farmers were forced to give up their private farms and work on government-run collective farms. Anyone who opposed this agenda was jailed or executed. Deprived of their lands, many Turkmen moved to the cities to work in state-controlled factories. By settling in the cities, many began to lose the nomadic lifestyle that was prevalent for centuries.

In addition, workers from Russia and other regions of the Soviet Union were transferred to Turkmenistan, which reduced the percentage of the republic's population that was ethnic Turkmen. Although Soviet leaders reluctantly allowed Turkmen to continue to practice Islam, they were opposed to religion. Seeking to preserve the Soviet Union as an atheist state, the government undertook measures to undermine the power of religion in daily life, and the Soviet-run schools advocated and taught atheism.

These dramatic changes aroused resistance among Turkmen. In 1927, an opposition group called Turkmen Freedom led an open rebellion that was finally crushed in 1932. Stalin retaliated by executing thousands of Turkmen. He installed new Turkmen communist leaders who were completely loyal to the Soviet Union, and also made sure that ethnic Russians were placed in control of many state institutions.

During World War II (1939–45), the invading armies of Nazi Germany destroyed much of the European regions of the Soviet Union. Many Soviet factories were moved farther east, beyond the reach of the German forces. Turkmenistan was among the republics that received these transferred factories. After the war, more factories were built in Turkmenistan, and more non-Turkmen migrated in search of jobs. Major irrigation projects, such as the Kara-Kum Canal, were undertaken in order to foster the expansion of collective farms.

By the 1950s, the Turkmen S.S.R. had become one of the most secure and stable regions of the Soviet Union. It was largely isolated from the other republics, however, and had virtually no contact with the outside world. Foreigners were rarely given permission to visit Turkmenistan, and Turkmen were rarely allowed to leave.

In 1985, Mikhail Gorbachev came to power as leader of the Soviet Union. Gorbachev recognized that the Soviet Union had become economically stagnant, and that it was no longer able to compete with the United States for world power and influence. He instituted a series of wide-ranging reforms designed to stimulate Soviet economic growth and open Soviet society to new ideas. Under Gorbachev the government encouraged limited private enterprise, and allowed opponents of communism to speak out more freely without threat of prosecution. Gorbachev also tried to create a new relationship with the United States—then led by the strongly anticommunist president Ronald Reagan—in order to ease global tensions and free up Soviet resources for other purposes.

Soviet leader Mikhail Gorbachev (right) shakes hands with U.S. President Ronald Reagan after signing a nuclear-missile treaty in 1988. During the 1980s Gorbachev attempted to reverse decades of stagnation in the U.S.S.R. by implementing policies of *Glasnost* (openness) and *Perestroika* (restructuring). Gorbachev had hoped that the reforms would strengthen the Soviet Union, but the new freedoms destroyed the system instead, as the Soviet republics declared their independence during 1990–91.

Initially, Gorbachev's reforms were slow to be introduced in Turkmenistan. The leader of the Turkmen S.S.R., Annamurad Khodzhamuradov, was a traditional communist who opposed the reforms. But many other republics embraced Gorbachev's agenda, and took the opportunity to advance it even further. By the late 1980s, the power of the Soviet Union's central government was weakening dramatically, and Gorbachev was losing control over his own reform program. One by one, various Soviet republics began declaring their ***sovereignty*** and independence, starting with the Baltic republics of Latvia, Lithuania, and Estonia.

In August 1990, the legislature of the Turkmen S.S.R. declared political and economic autonomy (the republic was not yet officially independent at this point). One year later, with the Soviet Union now on the verge of total collapse, Turkmenistan's new communist leader—Saparmurat Niyazov—called for a popular referendum on the independence issue. The people responded by voting 94 percent in favor of the measure. On October 27, 1991, Turkmenistan declared its independence, and on December 31, the Soviet Union was formally dissolved.

Independent Turkmenistan

In many ways, Turkmenistan was unprepared for independence. There had not been a strong pro-independence movement among the people of Turkmenistan as there had been in some other republics. Rather, sovereignty became a necessity because of the Soviet Union's collapse.

Saparmurat Niyazov became Turkmenistan's first president. After receiving training in Russia as an engineer, he became a member of the Communist Party of the Turkmen S.S.R., for which he held a number of important positions, including first secretary of Ashkhabad (a position similar to mayor). In 1985, Niyazov was elected first secretary of the Turkmenistan Communist Party (equivalent to president), and became regarded as a loyal ally of the Soviet leadership in Moscow.

But as the Soviet Union began to disintegrate, and as Moscow's control over its far-flung regions started to weaken, Niyazov adroitly maneuvered to become the leading voice of Turkmen independence. After the people voted for independence, Niyazov formed a new party—the Democratic Party of Turkmenistan, composed largely of former Communist Party officials. He outlawed any opposition parties, continuing the tradition of **authoritarian** government. Any politicians openly opposed to Niyazov were silenced or forced to live in exile.

In 1992, Turkmenistan's legislature adopted a new constitution that vested tremendous power in the presidency. Running unopposed, Niyazov was elected president. For the next several years, the Turkmen government focused on establishing the functions of an independent state. A new currency, the manat, was introduced in 1993, and limited economic reforms were undertaken. Niyazov actively encouraged foreign investment, especially in the oil and gas sector. For the most part, however, the economy remained highly centralized. Only in 1997 was private property finally legalized in Turkmenistan.

In 1994, a referendum was approved canceling the 1998 elections and extending Niyazov's term as president until 2002. In 1999, the Turkmen parliament voted to make Niyazov president for life; he later announced that he would voluntarily step down in 2010, when he reaches age 70.

The world generally welcomed Turkmenistan's independence, and many countries—including the United States—extended foreign aid and technical assistance to help the new Turkmen government establish itself. Before long, however, Niyazov's government came under attack from Western governments and organizations for human rights violations and for suppressing political opposition and denying freedom of speech. Niyazov attracted additional criticism for his extreme response to an attempted assassination. The president's motorcade was fired on in November 2002 as he was driving through Ashkhabad; Niyazov was

Saparmurat Niyazov was the leader of Turkmenistan's Communist Party in the late 1980s. When Turkmenistan became independent, he helped shape the government of the country and used authoritarian methods to ensure that he would not be opposed as Turkmenistan's president.

unhurt, but afterwards dozens of opposition leaders were arrested and jailed. Later, new laws were passed that further restricted individual rights and made it illegal to criticize the president.

International observers also began to accuse Niyazov of creating a "cult of personality," a phenomenon in which a country's leader is treated as an almost-divine figure. In 2001, Niyazov published a book, *Rukhnama*, which was presented as a spiritual guide for the Turkmen people. Part autobiography, part history, and part religious poetry collection, *Rukhnama* is similar to the Bible or the Qur'an, according to Niyazov. Today, the book is required reading in Turkmenistan's schools.

In 2002, Niyazov renamed the months of the year after himself and his mother, and portraits of the president appear throughout Turkmenistan. He also has adopted the title Turkmenbashi, which means "Leader of All Turkmen," and renamed several towns after himself. In June 2004, the country held an extravagant celebration to honor the 12th anniversary of Niyazov's presidency, and a new monument to him was unveiled in Ashkhabad.

Niyazov has defended these extravagant public displays by saying that it is important, after so many years of foreign rule and occupation, for the Turkmen people to develop pride in native leaders and national identity. However, most international leaders disagree with his approach. Both the European Parliament and the United Nations General Assembly have passed resolutions expressing concern about the state of human rights and the lack of political freedom in Turkmenistan.

Some people have argued that Niyazov has held on to power so firmly because he fears the rise of a radical Islamic party or movement. Niyazov has reversed the Soviet Union's policy of atheism by encouraging religious practice and recognizing Islam as an integral part of Turkmen society. His government has built several hundred new mosques since independence, including the largest mosque in all of Central Asia, and the flag of Turkmenistan incorporates Islamic symbolism. But the Niyazov government maintains strict control over religion. No private religious schools are allowed to operate, all Islamic religious officials are appointed to their positions by the government, and the constitution forbids any political activity of a religious nature. Turkmen are thus free—and even encouraged—to practice Islam, but are strictly forbidden from using religion for any political purpose. So far, this approach has enabled Turkmenistan to avoid the kind of religious extremism evident in Afghanistan, Tajikistan, Uzbekistan, Pakistan, Iran, and even in some regions of Russia, such as Chechnya.

Turkmenistan's future holds great promise, in large part due to the country's tremendous oil and gas resources. Unlike many of the former Soviet republics, Turkmenistan also benefits from having a very ***homogeneous*** population, with few signs of ethnic or religious tension. But there are definitely obstacles for the country to overcome. Before 1991, the people of Turkmenistan had virtually no experience with self-government, despite their long and eventful history as a nation. It was thus

The Akhal Teke

One of the most beautiful and majestic horses in the world is the Akhal Teke, a breed that originated in Turkmenistan. Its name derives from the name of an oasis in the Kopet-Dag Mountains, as well as the name of one of Turkmenistan's most important tribal groups.

Archaeologists have found evidence of the horse breed dating back to 2400 B.C. Because of Turkmenistan's relative isolation, the breed has remained essentially pure ever since. The Akhal Teke was the favored horse of Turkmen nomads and war-riors for centuries. Alexander the Great's favorite horse, Bucephalus, is believed to have been an Akhal Teke that he acquired on his march through Turkmenistan.

The speed and stamina of Akhal Tekes is unmatched among horses. They are capa-ble of surviving extreme heat and bitter cold, and have been known to traverse the barren Kara-Kum Desert on meager rations and little water, cover-ing as much as 70 miles (113 km) in one day. In the 1960 and 1968 Olympics they won gold medals for the Soviet Union in equestrian events. The breed's fascinating history and stunning appearance have made it treasured among horse lovers worldwide. In 1956, Soviet leader Nikita Khrushchev presented a beautiful golden-colored Akhal Teke to England's Queen Elizabeth.

not surprising that a leader such as Niyazov—who not only held the levers of power as Communist Party head, but who also enjoyed popularity as a true Turkmen—would seize and hold on to power. Although there are no free elections or political opinion polls in Turkmenistan, many analysts believe that Niyazov is genuinely well-received by the population.

Over time, international criticism and the demands and expectations of younger people in Turkmenistan will likely push the country toward a more representative form of government. However, given Turkmenistan's history, the circumstances behind its independence, and the tumultuous region in which it is situated, it is not likely that Western-style democracy will take hold in the near future.

A new mosque under construction in Ashkhabad. During the Soviet era, the practice of Islam was restricted or forbidden, but since independence hundreds of new mosques have been built in Turkmenistan.

Politics, the Economy, and Religion

Turkmenistan's politics, like the politics of all countries, has been shaped by its history and national experiences, and by the nature of its society. For around 1,300 years, the area now known as Turkmenistan has been home to Turkic peoples descending from the Oghuz tribes. But Turkmenistan has been an independent and sovereign nation for a relatively short period. For most of their history, the Turkmen have been ruled by various foreign powers and empires, from the Sassanians to the Soviets. At no point before 1991 did the Turkmen nation enjoy a democratic form of government in which the people were allowed to choose their leaders.

49

From the time when Oghuz groups first migrated to Turkmenistan, the defining features of their social and political structures were the family, the extended family, and the larger groupings of related extended families known as tribes. Tribal politics was in many ways the ideal form of government for nomadic peoples, and tribal loyalty was vital to the survival not only of the tribe, but of its individual members as well. Turkmenistan's harsh desert environment, along with the constant danger of attack, made it impossible to conceive of going it alone. If individuals were to survive, they would have to be loyal members of a larger unit.

Tribal societies throughout the world are characterized by well-defined hierarchies, centralization of authority, and usually a powerful and charismatic leader or chief. To the outsider, it may appear that the leader is all-powerful and makes all the decisions himself, but in fact, in most tribal societies the leader relies on an inner circle of advisors—often the heads of the extended families that make up the larger tribal unit. It is more likely that the leader's decisions are *consensual* rather than dictatorial. Those who openly oppose the tribal leaders' decisions often are expelled from the tribe. It is considered too dangerous to allow the tribe to split into factions. Unity is required for its survival.

Tribal societies also are communal by nature, and most property is considered to be owned by the entire tribe. The concept of personal property—which is dominant in the United States and other Western societies—is less embraced in tribal societies, a cultural trait that enabled the Turkmen to accept Soviet prohibitions on private property. It also has made it difficult for modern-day Turkmenistan to implement *privatization* of industries and encourage people to start their own enterprises.

Islam also has played an important role in the development of Turkmenistan's society and politics. For one thing, it provided a common element that all of the various tribes shared in addition to their Turkic language and culture. By joining Turkmenistan to a larger society—that of the

A portrait of a Turkmen village leader from Onaldy. Because Turkmenistan is less ethnically diverse than other former Soviet republics, it has retained many of the tribal elements of traditional Central Asian society, including the practice of having strong leaders involved in consensual decision-making.

Muslim world—Islam facilitated the introduction of new ideas and a broader global perspective into Turkmen society. Although the Islamic religion was founded and first spread by Arabs, one of the most important Islamic empires—the Seljuk—was founded by Turkmen.

Politics in Turkmenistan

Turkmenistan's current political structure reflects the family and tribal structure of Turkmen society, as well as the many historical influences that have left an imprint. Most senior government officials and bureaucrats in the Turkmen government, including President Niyazov, previously held senior positions in the administration of the Turkmen Soviet Socialist Republic when Turkmenistan was part of the Soviet Union. At the time of independence, the former Communist Party of Turkmenistan was transformed into the Democratic Party of Turkmenistan. Many leading figures in the Turkmen government, including Niyazov, also are members of the Teke tribe.

In 1992, Turkmenistan adopted a constitution declaring the country a constitutional republic. It also presented a new government that is "based on the principles of the separation of powers—legislative, executive, and judicial—which operate independently, checking and balancing one another." The constitution offered guarantees to protect the freedoms of

Turkmen carry portraits of the president and national flags past government buildings during an October 2004 parade to celebrate the 13th anniversary of the country's independence.

speech, assembly, and religion. It also vests many powers in the presidency, but limits any individual to holding office for two terms, each lasting five years.

In practice, however, the 1992 constitution has not been fully implemented. Political power in Turkmenistan is centralized in the presidency. Although there are legislative bodies and a court system, the "separation of powers" guaranteed by the constitution does not really exist. Moreover, many of the individual rights promised by the constitution have been denied or suppressed.

The President

Saparmurat Niyazov has been the leading political figure in Turkmenistan since 1985, when he was chosen first secretary of the Communist Party of Turkmenistan. He was elected president of independent Turkmenistan in 1991; facing no opposition, he received 99.5 percent of the vote. Today, he serves as chairman of the cabinet of ministers; chairman for life of the People's Council (a body of Parliament); and, as of a law passed in 2003, supreme leader of the Majlis (the other parliamentary body). Having these positions means he effectively controls the legislative functions of government as well as the executive. He also has full authority to appoint the country's judges. In 1999, the Majlis voted to exempt Niyazov from the constitutional limit of only two terms as president by making him president for life. Niyazov, however, has promised to step down by 2010. Even if he does, he undoubtedly will have a major say in determining his successor.

The Ministry of National Security and the Ministry of Internal Affairs are responsible for ensuring that the government stays in power and is not threatened by internal opposition. Both ministries are headed by people appointed by (and loyal to) Niyazov.

Despite extensive criticism of his rule from foreign governments and human rights organizations, and the existence of exiled opposition groups, there is little active opposition to Niyazov among the residents of Turkmenistan, who have never known anything other than authoritarian governments. Moreover, the strong tribal and family nature of Turkmen society means that Niyazov, as the leading figure in the large Teke tribe, enjoys social legitimacy as national leader.

In recent years there have been signs that Niyazov is attempting to moderate the personality cult surrounding his presidency. Many of the pictures of the president that adorned public buildings and government offices were removed in early 2004. Moreover, on several occasions Niyazov reminded the Turkmen people of his intention to step down as president by 2010.

Legislative Branch

The 1992 constitution established two parliamentary bodies. The **unicameral** People's Council (Halk Maslahaty) consists of 2,507 members, some of whom are elected by popular vote, some of whom are appointed by the president, and some of whom earn seats by virtue of being leaders of a particular tribal group or family clan. The council meets once a year in order to validate decisions made by the Majlis. The People's Council has its roots in an ancient tribal organization known as the Council of Elders (Aksakal Maslahaty). In traditional Turkmen tribal societies, which placed great value on the wisdom of their older members, the Aksakal Maslahaty advised the tribal leaders on their decisions.

Like the People's Council, the Majlis is a unicameral assembly. It consists of 50 members who are elected by popular vote to serve five-year terms. Every delegate to the Majlis is a member of the Democratic Party of Turkmenistan, the only legally sanctioned political party. The Majlis has supported all of President Niyazov's proposals and initiatives.

In August 2003, at President Niyazov's request, a new law was adopted that made the People's Council the supreme legislative body in

The government of Turkmenistan does not look kindly upon dissent. An example is the case of Boris Shikhmuradov, who was foreign minister in Turkmenistan's government before he became an opposition leader and accused the president of running a "primitive police state." The Niyazov government immediately accused Shikhmuradov of embezzlement and other crimes. In 2002 Shikhmuradov was arrested for allegedly taking part in an attempt to overthrow Niyazov; he was sentenced to life imprisonment.

Turkmenistan. Subsequently, the Majlis was stripped of many powers, including the power to amend the constitution. The People's Council was even granted the authority to dissolve the Majlis. President Niyazov further expanded his own power by becoming the supreme leader of the Majlis.

Political Parties

Turkmenistan's sole political party, the Democratic Party of Turkmenistan (DPT), was founded in 1991 and is chaired by President Niyazov. The DPT retains much of the organization, structure, and staff of its former incarnation as the Communist Party of Turkmenistan. The DPT claims to have 165,000 members throughout Turkmenistan.

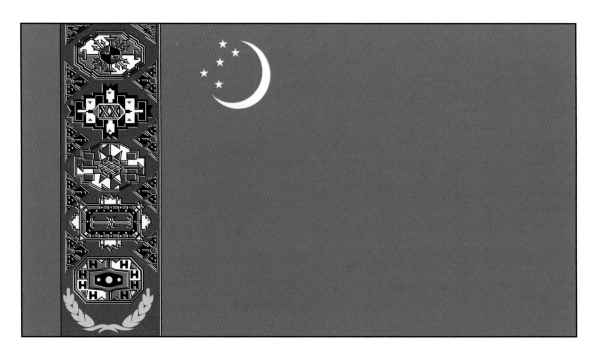

The flag of Turkmenistan has changed several times since it was adopted in 1992. The color green and the stars and crescent are traditional symbols of Islam. The red carpet medallions on the hoist side represent the nation's internationally renowned Turkmen rugs. The olive branches at the bottom were added in 1997 as a reminder of the country's neutrality.

Several political groups have attempted to register as opposition parties, but have invariably seen their registrations denied. The government has claimed that these parties offer no new policy alternatives to the DPT, or that they represent particular ethnic groups or religions and thus would be divisive (the constitution prohibits parties based on ethnic or religious identity).

Most of those Turkmen who have openly opposed Niyazov live in exile in Moscow or elsewhere in Europe. Several prominent opposition leaders, including some former high-ranking government officials, met in Vienna in June 2002 to announce the formation of the Turkmen Democratic Opposition. They accused the Niyazov government of human rights violations and authoritarianism. Other opposition groups publish newspapers or operate websites from outside of Turkmenistan. There is little evidence that any of these groups enjoys much popularity or support within Turkmenistan, and their ability to communicate to potential supporters inside the country is severely limited. Strong rivalries exist among the opposition groups and they rarely cooperate.

Judiciary

According to Turkmenistan's constitution, the judiciary is an independent branch of government responsible for upholding the constitution and applying the nation's civil and criminal laws. However, as in other areas of government, Niyazov maintains a great deal of influence over the legal system. The president appoints judges at all levels for five-year terms, which can be renewed indefinitely. The Minister of Justice, who also is appointed by the president, oversees all judges and courts.

The highest court—the Supreme Court—consists of 22 members. It only hears cases of national or constitutional importance. Just below the Supreme Courts are six **appellate courts**—one in each of Turkmenistan's five provinces and the city of Ashkhabad. Finally, there are 61 trial courts throughout the country that are the first to hear civil and criminal cases. In addition, special military courts rule on all cases concerning members of the armed services. The Supreme Economic Court rules on cases involving disputes among and between business enterprises and government agencies.

The Media

Turkmenistan's media outlets—newspapers, magazines, radio, and television stations—are controlled and financed by the government. President Niyazov appoints the heads of all media outlets, and Turkmen journalists are employees of the government. Government officials censor the newspapers and news broadcasts. As a result, Turkmenistan's media never voices any criticism of the government, its policies, or the nation's leaders.

Turkmenistan has two major newspapers—one printed in the Turkmen language and one in Russian—and five regional newspapers. The country's two television channels broadcast speeches by the president, news bulletins, and cultural programs. Sometimes Russian or Turkish entertainment programs are broadcast.

Turkmen have limited access to foreign media. Some Russian publications are available, but these are often confiscated if they contain articles critical of Turkmenistan's government. Russian television also is available, but is broadcast on a delayed basis so that unapproved material may be blocked. Wealthier Turkmen often install satellite dishes which allow them to receive uncensored television broadcasts, but they must first receive government permission. One source of outside information is Radio Free Europe/Radio Liberty, a radio station funded by the U.S. government that broadcasts in the Turkmen language from Prague in the Czech Republic.

Access to the Internet is limited by the shortage of personal computers. Moreover, the government-run telecommunications company, which is Turkmenistan's only Internet service provider, has blocked access to many foreign news sources and the Web sites of Turkmen opposition groups.

Turkmenistan's Political Future

The primary goal of Turkmenistan's government remains political stability and internal peace in a region of the world that is known for its instability and violence. In the opinion of Turkmenistan's present leaders (and many of its people as well), a strong, centralized, and authoritarian government is more likely to guarantee stability and security than a political system that is open to debate and dissent. Today, Turkmenistan is one of the most politically stable of the all the former Soviet republics, and has avoided the violence and civil wars that have plagued neighboring states such as Tajikistan and Afghanistan. It also has the lowest crime rate of any of the former Soviet republics.

If President Niyazov indeed steps down in 2010 as he has vowed to do, Turkmenistan's people may have an opportunity to begin forming a more open and representative government. The structures for such a government—a constitution, legislature, and judicial system—are in place. Whether or not a democratic system develops will depend in large part upon the aspirations of the younger generation of Turkmen, who by 2010 will be used to independence and perhaps be eager for a more direct voice in how the country is run.

Economic Overview

For most of their history, the people who inhabited Turkmenistan lived a nomadic life, herding animals from one grazing area to another. The limited rainfall and poor soil were not suitable for extensive cultivation of crops. The nomads' animals provided not only food, but also skins for making clothing and tents, and wool for making carpets, saddlebags, and blankets. Tribes living near the Caspian Sea supplemented their diets with fish. The various tribes would barter with one another, but there was no organized economy.

As the people of Turkmenistan gradually began to settle near oases and in the foothills of mountains (where mountain streams and underground *aquifers* provided water), it became possible to till the ground and grow crops. Access to water allowed for a more settled lifestyle in villages and towns, and led to the development of basic industries, such as pottery-making and textile-weaving. Influenced by the Persians, these early towns eventually developed bazaars, or organized market places, where people could trade their goods. New goods were introduced by caravans passing through Turkmenistan, as well as by invading armies.

By around 500 B.C., Turkmenistan's towns and cities had become part of a larger regional economy. But for the average person, survival was still based on herding sheep and goats, and possibly growing grains, fruits, and

The Economy of Turkmenistan

Gross Domestic Product (GDP*): $27.07 billion
GDP per capita: $5,700
Inflation: 9.5%
Natural Resources: petroleum, natural gas, coal, sulfur, salt
Agriculture (24.8% of GDP): cotton, grain, livestock
Industry (46.2% of GDP): natural gas, oil, petroleum
    products, textiles, food processing
Services (30% of GDP): government services (including
    education, health care, and the military), banking
Foreign Trade:
    Imports: $2.472 billion—machinery and equipment, food-
    stuffs
    Exports: $3.355 billion—gas, oil, cotton fiber, textiles
Currency Exchange Rate (2004): U.S. $1= 5,148
    Turkmenistani mantas

*GDP, or gross domestic product, is the total value of goods and services pro-
duced in a country annually.
All figures are 2003 estimates unless otherwise noted.
Source: CIA World Factbook, 2004.

vegetables on a small plot of land. Virtually all economic interaction took place among members of the family, clan, or tribe. This situation was to remain essentially unchanged well into the 20th century.

The Russian Empire—and later the Soviet Union—were interested in Turkmenistan primarily for strategic reasons: Turkmenistan, along with the rest of Central Asia, provided a buffer from the possessions of the British Empire to the south, and opened up the possibility of expansion toward the warm waters of the Indian Ocean and the Persian Gulf. Turkmenistan was also a supplier of raw materials—initially cotton, and later oil and natural gas. Cotton grew well in the region, and during the

Soviet era the Moscow government invested in large collective farms that grew cotton for shipment to other Soviet republics, where cotton-seed oil was extracted and the cotton fibers were used to make clothing.

Although during and after World War II some factories were moved to the republic, overall the Soviets built few manufacturing plants in Turkmenistan. It remained the poorest of the republics, and the Soviet government did very little to improve the standard of living or the welfare of the Turkmen.

Beginning in the 1970s, the Soviet Union invested large sums of money in oil and natural gas production after geologists discovered that Turkmenistan held huge energy reserves. The Soviets built pipelines to transport Turkmenistan's energy resources to the more industrialized areas of the Soviet Union. As with cotton, however, very little of the proceeds from Turkmenistan's oil and gas ever made its way back to the people. Thus, despite the ongoing discovery of new and even more extensive oil and gas reserves, life for the average Turkmen did not change dramatically.

Turkmenistan did experience some changes as part of the Soviet system: the Soviets established schools, hospitals, and other services, and invested in basic infrastructure such as roads and the Kara-Kum Canal. In addition, Turkmen benefited from the cheap, subsidized food and consumer goods provided by other Soviet republics, although the quality of goods was low and shortages were common.

When the Soviet Union collapsed at the end of 1991, many of the Soviet republics found themselves in crisis. Factories closed, entire industries disappeared, millions of workers were left unemployed, and many people lived on the verge of starvation. Turkmenistan, however, was less adversely affected. Because the Soviet authorities had never built many factories in Turkmenistan, and most of the people still relied on agriculture for a living, the economy was less disrupted than that of more industrialized republics. Moreover, many Turkmen were optimistic that with independence they finally would be able to enjoy the benefits of their country's great oil and gas wealth.

The first years of independence, however, were difficult. No longer able to rely on subsidized food and consumer goods from other Soviet republics, Turkmen witnessed a dramatic increase in prices. Oil and gas still were flowing out of the country, but all of the pipelines went through Russia and on to other former Soviet states, such as Ukraine, which were themselves in economic crisis and thus frequently unable to pay. When they did pay it was in the currency of the Russian ruble, which had become virtually worthless. Russia refused to transport Turkmenistan's oil and gas to Western European states, who would have been able to pay. Compounding these problems was the Turkmen officials' lack of training in handling the economy, which for the previous 70 years had been totally controlled by Soviet authorities in Moscow. Turkmenistan's gross domestic product (GDP)—the total value of all goods and services produced in a year—actually declined throughout most of the 1990s as the country tried to adjust to independence and seek ways to earn income from its valuable energy resources.

The economic picture started to improve by the late 1990s. In 1997, Turkmenistan opened a natural gas pipeline to Iran, avoiding Russian territory. The pipeline connected with existing Iranian pipelines that transported the gas to Iranian ports for shipment to Europe and Asia. This arrangement allowed Turkmenistan to receive prompt payment for its natural gas and lessened its dependence on Russia. During this period, cotton exports also increased as weather conditions helped produce large yields and Turkmenistan found new markets. In 1998 the country's GDP grew by 7 percent, the first increase since independence. By 2003 Turkmenistan's economy, fueled by increased oil and gas exports and rising international energy prices, was growing at an estimated annual rate of nearly 20 percent. (Although U.S. government experts provided this

Turkmenistan's Caspian Sea oil is delivered to terminals like this one in the Iranian city of Neka. From there, the oil is transferred through pipelines to refineries in Tehran and Tabriz.

estimate, they also noted that tight control over economic data by the government of Turkmenistan makes it impossible to accurately predict the growth rate.)

Turkmenistan's GDP per capita (a measure of each Turkman's average share of the country's GDP) in 2003 was around $5,700, placing Turkmenistan 106th out of the 208 economies tracked by the World Bank. The World Bank categorized Turkmenistan as a "lower middle income" nation, comparable to countries such as Brazil, China, Cuba, and Russia. Per capita income, however, is not always an accurate reflection of individual wealth or quality of life.

Turkmenistan's deputy prime minister, Yolly Gurbanmuradov (left) shakes hands with Pakistan's petroleum minister, Nouraiz Shakoor, and Afghanistan's mines and industries minister, Mehfooz Nedai, after the three ministers announced an ambitious plan to build a natural gas pipeline through the southern Afghan province of Kandahar. The proposed pipeline will carry gas from the rich oil fields at Daulatabad to the city of Multan in central Pakistan. However, unrest in Afghanistan has delayed construction of the pipeline.

Economic Reform

Upon achieving independence, Turkmenistan faced the huge task of establishing a national economy and its various structures and institutions such as a currency, banking system, tax system, and national budget. Many foreign governments and international organizations called on Turkmenistan to completely replace the communist economic system with a free market economy along the lines of those in the United States and Western Europe.

The government, however, has been reluctant to reform the Soviet-era economic structures. A few formerly state-owned enterprises have been transferred to the private sector, but the majority of companies remain government-owned. In particular, the vital gas, oil, and cotton industries remain owned and operated by the state. The prices and production levels of major agricultural products, such as wheat, are set by the government. The government also maintains Turkmenistan's currency—the manat—at a fixed exchange rate, instead of allowing market forces to determine its value. This has led to a distortion in prices and the depreciation of the manat.

Turkmenistan has attempted to attract foreign investment, but the lack of free-market reforms has discouraged investors in all but the energy sector. Even though substantial income is now earned by oil, gas, and cotton exports, the government still has been forced to borrow money from foreign governments and institutions, in part to pay for extensive subsidies. Thanks to these government subsidies, the Turkmen people receive free gas, electricity, water, and wheat. The subsidies also help to ensure the government's popularity.

Moreover, the slow rate of privatization, combined with the subsidies, has ensured that the gap between rich and poor in Turkmenistan is small. By contrast, in Russia a relatively small number of wealthy individuals control much of the economy while a large segment of the population struggles in poverty. By avoiding such extremes in wealth, the Niyazov government has reduced social tensions and class struggles.

However, because the government has failed to institute serious economic reforms, the economy of Turkmenistan is very inefficient and prone to corruption, offering few incentives to attract foreign investors or to generate entrepreneurial activity by Turkmen citizens. As long as Turkmenistan is able to sell its oil and gas, there will be little pressure on the government to make the economy more open. Government control over the economy also guarantees control over employment, prices, and personal income, and thus maintains the government's position as the most important element of Turkmen society.

Economic Sectors

Although it accounts for less than 25 percent of Turkmenistan's GDP, the agricultural sector remains the country's largest source of employment, with almost 50 percent of the population working in agriculture. The Soviet Union first encouraged cotton production in Turkmenistan, and created huge collective farms on which to grow the fiber. Today, half of Turkmenistan's irrigated land is devoted to the production of cotton. The country is one of the 15 largest producers of cotton in the world, and the world's largest producer on a per capita basis. Much of the cotton Turkmenistan produces is for export.

Despite the importance of cotton to Turkmenistan, the government has been working to diversify the agricultural sector. One particular goal is to achieve self-sufficiency in food production. Wheat and other cereal grains are being widely cultivated (Turkmenistan currently must import a large amount of wheat). Fruits and vegetables, which always have been grown on oases and in irrigated valleys, also are being grown in larger quantities. The raising of sheep, horses, camels, and other livestock is another growing component of the agricultural sector. Turkmen farms are run as farmers' cooperatives, and thus are officially no longer owned by the state. However, the government requires the cooperatives to sell their crops at prices it establishes, and all agricultural exports are managed by a state agency.

Industry accounts for about 50 percent of Turkmenistan's GDP, although it employs only around 15 percent of the population. The principal industry is oil and natural gas production; oil and gas also are the country's primary export products. In 2003, Turkmenistan produced around 210,000 barrels of oil per day (one barrel of oil contains 42 gallons), and

Cotton remains the most important crop in Turkmenistan, although in recent years the government has attempted to diversify the agriculture sector of the economy.

scientists estimate that at least 550 million barrels of oil is still under the country's soil. Some petroleum experts believe Turkmenistan may potentially hold as much as 1.7 billion barrels of oil.

Natural gas plays an even more important role in Turkmenistan's economy. Most of the natural gas reserves are located in the Amu Dar'ya river basin and along (and under) the Caspian Sea, as well as in smaller deposits in the north and east of the country. Turkmenistan produces nearly 1.7 trillion cubic feet (50 billion cubic meters) of natural gas every year, and is believed to have another 102 trillion cubic feet (2.9 trillion

Banknotes in Turkmenistan bear the image of President Niyazov.

cubic meters) in reserve, making it one of the world's most important natural gas producers. About 80 percent of the natural gas produced in Turkmenistan is exported via pipelines, with the remainder used for local consumption. Natural gas is used primarily as a fuel for heating homes, operating gas cooking ranges, and powering electric generators. Its use, especially in the United States, Europe, and other developed countries, has grown in recent decades, in part because it is a comparatively clean burning fuel that causes much less air pollution than oil or coal.

Soon after achieving independence, the government of Turkmenistan invited foreign companies to develop and expand its natural gas industry, as well as to explore for new deposits. The government's most critical goal was to construct pipelines that would allow its oil and natural gas to be shipped out of the country without going through Russia. Foreign investment and economic assistance helped construct the pipeline to Iran that opened in 1997, and today about 10 percent of Turkmenistan's natural gas is exported through Iran. But other pipeline projects have stalled because of turmoil and instability in the region, which has caused private investors to focus instead on pipeline projects in Kazakhstan and Azerbaijan. The Turkmenistan government continues to try to interest investors in a pipeline that would run south out of Turkmenistan, through Afghanistan, and toward the growing markets of India and Pakistan. Until Afghanistan establishes a much greater degree of political stability, however, Turkmenistan will have a hard time finding companies willing to invest in this project.

Turkmenistan is exploring other means of exporting its energy resources. One proposal that is being considered is the construction of electric generating plants—fueled by Turkmenistan's abundant natural gas—that will export electricity. This project would require Turkmenistan's electrical grid to be integrated with that of Iran or another neighboring country, which would then purchase the electrical power or transmit it to another foreign buyer, such as Turkey.

The Niyazov government also has sought to modernize and expand the country's oil refineries, including the large refinery at Turkmenbashi built by the Soviets. German and Japanese companies have invested $1.4 billion in the Turkmenbashi plant, which will allow it to produce such valuable oil products as lubricants, motor oil, and polymers.

In addition to oil and natural gas, Turkmenistan also produces several valuable industrial materials, including gypsum, iodine, bromine, sulfur, and salt. Other industry includes food processing, cottonseed oil, textile production, and carpet making.

Religion in Turkmenistan Before Independence

Before the fifth century B.C., the nomadic inhabitants of Turkmenistan practiced **indigenous** religions, about which very little is known today. As Persian influence and control over Turkmenistan grew, so did Persian religious trends. The most important of these was Zoroastrianism, a religion founded around 600 B.C. by a charismatic spiritual leader named Zoroaster. He preached the existence of one supreme and omnipotent deity, called Ahura Mazda, who is the creator of the world and the source of all that is good in it. But an evil power, known as Ahriman, also exists, and tempts human beings to follow the wrong path. Around A.D. 275, Zoroastrianism became the official religion of the Sassanian Empire, of which the Turkmenistan region was a part. Zoroastrian priests became powerful figures within the empire, sometimes wielding more power behind the scenes than the emperor himself.

Starting around the seventh century A.D., Turkmenistan was subject to two powerful forces: the invasion of Arab Muslims from the south, and the migration of Turkic tribes from the east. Both introduced new religious ideas to the region. The Turkic tribesmen practiced an ancient religion that believed in 17 deities. The most powerful of these, Tengri (Eternal Sky), was the creator of the universe and the father of life. His wife was the Earth, which the Turkic peoples regarded as being sacred.

Islam was introduced to the region at about the same time, and spread north into Turkmenistan from Iran. Although the Arab armies spread Islam to much of the world by force of arms, in Turkmenistan and the rest of Central Asia it was spread more through traders and **itinerant** religious mystics known as **Sufis**. The Sufis preached a very personal form of Islam, through which an individual could attain unity with Allah, or God, by practicing meditative rituals, including music and dance. Sufism was

The Five Pillars of Islam

Devout Muslims are expected to observe what are known as the five pillars of their faith:

1. *Shahada*, or profession of faith—an affirmation that "There is no god but Allah, and Muhammad is His messenger."

2. *Salat*, or daily prayer—the requirement that Muslims perform five specific prayers at certain times each day.

3. *Zakat*, or almsgiving—the responsibility of Muslims to help the poor and needy members of their community through charitable giving.

4. *Sawm*, or fasting—the duty of all Muslims to avoid eating, drinking, or certain other physical activites during daylight hours in the holy month of Ramadan, the ninth month of the Islamic lunar calendar. Ramadan is a time for Muslims to renew and strengthen their spiritual connection to Allah.

5. *Hajj*, or pilgrimage—the obligation of all Muslims to make a ritual pilgrimage to the holy city of Mecca in Saudi Arabia at least once during their lifetime, if they are physically and financially able to do so.

based more on direct personal experience with God than on scholarly religious texts and a dogmatic belief system. It also was open to incorporating local religious traditions into Islam, which made conversion of the Turkic tribes easier. Individual Turkic tribes often adopted a particular Sufi leader as their own religious guide, and upon his death members of the tribe would worship him as a saint. Because of the prominent role Sufis had in disseminating Islam, the religion developed in a much more individualistic manner in Turkmenistan and Central Asia than in the rest of the Islamic world. Turkmen followed the majority Sunni sect of Islam, and not the minority Shia sect that predominates in neighboring Iran.

Russia's annexation of Turkestan in the late 19th century represented yet another infusion of foreign culture and ideas. Russia ruled Turkestan as a colony, and maintained a strong military and cultural presence throughout the region. The main religion of the Russian Empire was the Russian Orthodox Christian Church, and Christian missionaries were sent to Turkestan to establish schools and churches. However, their efforts to convert the Muslims of Central Asia met with stiff resistance. In 1917, Muslims throughout Turkestan rose up against Russian rule in what became known as the Basmachi Rebellion.

The Soviet Union, which replaced the Russian Empire as ruler of Central Asia in the 1920s, was officially an atheist state. Soviet authorities sought to replace religious beliefs with the political philosophy of **Marxism**, the basis of communism. Muslims and Christians alike were pressured to reject their religions for this new ideology, which rejects the concepts of God and of life after death. In Turkmenistan, Soviet authorities (and their Turkmen allies) closed mosques and Islamic schools, and prohibited the teaching of Islam. Isolated within the borders of the Soviet Union, Turkmen lost contact with fellow Muslims in South Asia and the Middle East, and no longer were able to make the prescribed pilgrimage to the holy city of Mecca in Saudi Arabia.

However, the Soviet assault on religion, which was centered on the closure of mosques, had little impact on how Islam was traditionally practiced in Turkmenistan. Strict Islamic doctrine had never played a dominant role in the culture, and the people had never been particularly devout at any time in their history—as an old Turkmen saying goes, "A man starts praying only when he no longer can ride a horse."

Another factor working against the Soviet repression of Islam was the religion's adaptive nature. Unlike faiths that are based on attending regular formal services, Islam can be practiced in a variety of environments—in homes, stores, fields, or even on the sidewalk. Moreover, the particular type of individualistic Islam that had evolved in Turkmenistan made it easier for believers to practice their faith unhindered. Most people kept a tattered copy of the Qur'an hidden in their homes, and many continued to pray and follow Islamic customs and practices under Soviet rule, even if only informally. In particular, Turkmen kept the Islamic traditions and customs observed for family events such as weddings and funerals. Islam thus remained an important force in Turkmen society during the Soviet era, though in many ways more as a cultural element than a religious one.

Religion in Independent Turkmenistan

Turkmenistan's constitution calls for freedom of religion, and while nearly 90 percent of Turkmenistan's citizens consider themselves to be Muslims, the constitution does not establish Islam (or any other religion) as the official state religion. The government strictly controls Islamic institutions through the Council on Religious Affairs, a leftover from the days of Soviet rule. Muslim clerics are paid by the government, and government funds are used to build mosques. Government permission is required before any type of religious demonstration or mass meeting can be held. Through these and other measures, the government of Turkmenistan has tried to ensure that Islam does not become a political force in Turkmenistan as it has in some neighboring countries, such as Iran, Afghanistan, and Tajikistan.

At the same time, however, the government has cautiously promoted Islam as a means of strengthening Turkmen identity and signaling a clear break with the atheistic former Soviet Union. President Niyazov views Islam as a binding factor in society, and has instructed public schools to

Turkmen in hats and traditional dress kneel and pray together. Most Turkmen are Muslims, and although Islam is not the state religion, it is considered a unifying force in Turkmenistan.

include the teaching of Islamic principles in their curricula. The government has built religious schools to train clerics and ordered the construction of a number of new mosques. A few of these religious facilities have been built using donations from Saudi Arabia and other wealthy Islamic countries.

Some Muslim leaders in Turkmenistan have privately criticized the government for its strong control over religious practice. They have tried to increase the population's involvement in Islam, and some even have talked of expanding the religion's role in society and politics. These

Muslim leaders have had to operate underground, however, and are believed to have had minimal impact. There is little evidence that the people of Turkmenistan wish that religion played a greater role in politics. Such a role certainly would not be consistent with the role Islam has played throughout the country's history.

The other significant religious community in Turkmenistan is the Russian Orthodox Church. Russian Orthodox Christians make up just under 10 percent of the population, and almost all of them are ethnic Russians who relocated to Turkmenistan during the Soviet era. The government allows this community to worship freely, and there has been no evidence of conflict or tension between the Orthodox Christian and Muslim communities. Several other Christian groups have attempted to establish churches and ***proselytize*** in Turkmenistan, but the government has not looked favorably on this activity. Unlike in many Islamic countries, however, it is not a crime in Turkmenistan to convert from Islam to another religion.

To inhibit new churches from forming, the government passed a law requiring that any religious denomination in the country must prove that it has at least 500 Turkmen citizens as members; otherwise, it may not legally undertake activities in the country. In March 2004, President Niyazov lifted this requirement, although all churches must still register with the government.

Turkmenistan has a small Jewish community of around 2,000 members, centered mostly in and around Ashkhabad where there is a synagogue (a Jewish house of worship). Most Turkmen Jews are descendants of Russian Jews who moved to Turkmenistan during the Soviet era. Over 1,000 Turkmen Jews have emigrated to Israel since 1990, a country with which Turkmenistan—unlike many Muslim nations—maintains friendly relations.

Women watch as men unload sheep from a truck at a Sunday market in Ashkhabad. About 85 percent of the population of Turkmenistan is ethnic Turkmen, making it one of the most homogenous of the former Soviet republics in Central Asia.

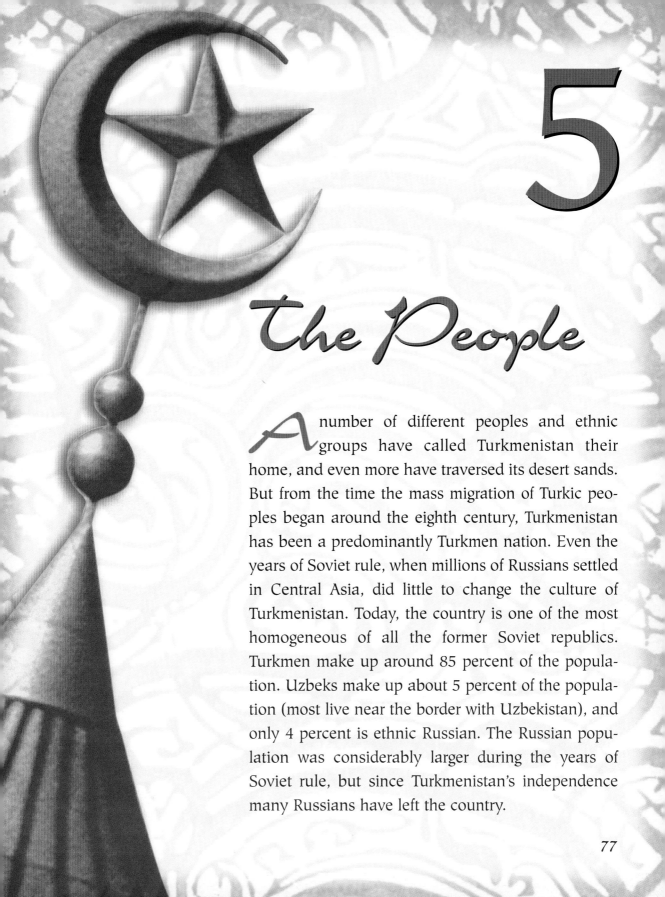

5

the People

A number of different peoples and ethnic groups have called Turkmenistan their home, and even more have traversed its desert sands. But from the time the mass migration of Turkic peoples began around the eighth century, Turkmenistan has been a predominantly Turkmen nation. Even the years of Soviet rule, when millions of Russians settled in Central Asia, did little to change the culture of Turkmenistan. Today, the country is one of the most homogeneous of all the former Soviet republics. Turkmen make up around 85 percent of the population. Uzbeks make up about 5 percent of the population (most live near the border with Uzbekistan), and only 4 percent is ethnic Russian. The Russian population was considerably larger during the years of Soviet rule, but since Turkmenistan's independence many Russians have left the country.

Turkmenistan is a relatively small country, with a population of just under 5 million, but its people share a cultural identity with millions of other Turkic peoples. The total number of the Turkic people in the world is around 130 million. The largest Turkic country is Turkey, with around 70 million people. Other countries with large Turkic populations include Uzbekistan, Kazakhstan, Kyrgyzstan, and Azerbaijan. China, Iran, and Russia also all have sizable Turkic minorities. This broader Turkic identity is a source of pride to Turkmen, and the government of President Niyazov has encouraged a deeper connection among Turkmenistan's people through the celebration of Turkic culture and history.

Languages

In 1990, Turkmen was declared the official language of Turkmenistan. It is the primary language of 72 percent of the population, and also is spoken by several million Turkmen living in neighboring countries. Russian is the primary language of 12 percent of the population. As a result of the decades of Russian and Soviet control, most Turkmen can speak, read, or at least understand Russian. About 9 percent of Turkmen also speak Uzbek.

The Turkmen language is a member of the Altaic language family, which includes Turkish, Azeri, Uzbek, Kazakh, Kyrgyz, Tatar, Mongol, and other languages spoken by the world's 130 million Turkic people. Turkmen is most closely related to Turkish and Azeri.

Like many ancient languages of nomadic peoples, Turkmen was only a spoken language until after the Muslim conquest, when Turkmen scholars began using the Arabic script to write their language. In 1929, the government introduced a new alphabet based on the modified Roman script (the script used to write English); it was similar to the alphabet that was being introduced in Turkey at the same time. In 1940, the Soviets introduced yet another script for written Turkmen—Cyrillic. Russian and certain other Slavic languages are also written in this script.

The People of Turkmenistan

Population: 4,863,169
Ethnic groups: Turkmen 85%, Uzbek 5%, Russian 4%, other 6% (2003)
Religions: Muslim, 89%; Eastern Orthodox, 9%; other or unknown, 2%
Languages: Turkmen 72%, Russian 12%, Uzbek 9%, other 7%
Age structure:
  0–14 years: 36.2%
  15–64 years: 59.7%
  65 years and over: 4.1%
Population growth rate: 1.81%
Birth rate: 27.82 births/1,000 population
Death rate: 8.82 deaths/1,000 population
Infant mortality rate: 73.13 deaths/1,000 live births
Life expectancy at birth:
  total population: 61.29 years
  males: 57.87 years
  females: 64.88 years
Total fertility rate: 3.45 children born/woman
Literacy rate: 98% (1989 estimate)

All figures are 2004 estimates unless otherwise indicated.
Source: Adapted from CIA World Factbook, 2004.

In 1996, President Niyazov decreed that Turkmen would once again be written in a modified Roman script. This decree was part of a broader strategy to solidify Turkmen as the country's dominant language and to remove vestiges of Russian influence. In 1992, a resolution was passed by the Majlis ordering all Russian geographic names to be changed to Turkmen words. In 1993, English was declared to be the official second language of Turkmenistan, although in reality Russian remains far more widely known than English.

Today, Turkmen is the official language for all legal and administrative matters, and is the language of instruction in Turkmen schools. Until independence, Russian was the language of instruction in Turkmenistan's universities, but today it is being gradually replaced in most courses by Turkmen. Most radio and television broadcasts are in Turkmen, although a few programs are in Russian as a service to the Russian-speaking minority.

The Family

For most of Turkmen history, the structure of society was based on a number of large tribes, each of which consisted of smaller clans or family groupings, which in turn were made up of extended families. For the individual, the extended family was always the most important social and economic unit, and very little contact was made with people outside of the extended family. Turkmen tribes were generally independent from one another, and even when Turkmenistan's territory was part of a larger empire the various Turkmen tribes usually maintained a degree of independence from the central authorities. Although the tribes spoke the Turkmen language and shared many cultural characteristics among each other, each also had certain characteristics that were unique, such as language dialects, styles of clothing or headgear, or certain design patterns for carpets or other decorative objects.

For nearly 70 years, Soviet leaders attempted to destroy tribal affiliations in Turkmenistan and throughout Central Asia. The Soviets wanted all citizens in their vast and sprawling empire to be loyal first and foremost to the Soviet Union and its communist ideology. They claimed to be creating a new identity that they termed "the Soviet Man." But in Turkmenistan, ancient tribal loyalties proved far too strong and resilient to succumb to Soviet policy. Today, tribal identity remains very strong among

A Turkmen woman holds her child outside their home in the village of Giami.

Turkmen, especially in rural areas. Smaller villages often are made up entirely of members of one extended family or clan. Even in urban areas such as Ashkhabad, where members of many different tribes and clans live together, individuals are almost always aware of their tribal affiliations and their family lineage.

The extended family remains a powerful force in Turkmen society. Often, grandparents, parents, married sons, and unmarried daughters all will live in the same house. In rural areas, they will all work together farming a common piece of land, or raising livestock that belongs to the family unit. This family structure has broken down somewhat in cities, in part because more people live in apartments that cannot accommodate extended families. But individuals who have relocated to larger cities still usually maintain ties with their family members in the countryside, and consider themselves part of that family.

Marriages are the most important events in Turkmen family life. In rural regions, marriages are still arranged by the two families in order to ensure that the partners belong to the same clan and that their union will serve to strengthen it. In much of Turkmenistan it is still required that the groom's family provide the bride's family with a bride-price—money or other valuables in exchange for the bride's agreement to marry the groom. Divorce is rare among Turkmen.

A newly wed bride and groom pose for a photograph in front of a statue of President Niyazov. Marriages are among the most important social events in Turkmenistan.

Many Turkmen still wear ages-old traditional dress. For men, this means baggy pants, knee high boots, a heavy silk jacket, and a large wool hat known as a *borek*. The traditional women's outfit is an ankle-length silk dress, usually red or maroon, with a kerchief or scarf over the head. Women often are adorned with beautiful silver necklaces and bracelets.

Turkmenistan has been a predominantly Muslim country for over 1,000 years, and yet women in Turkmen society have enjoyed far more freedom than women in traditional Muslim societies. Turkmen women, for example, have never been forced to wear veils (save for traditional or cultural ceremonies) or required to isolate themselves from men. In nomadic cultures such as the Turkmen, where the very survival of the family is often in question, every family member—male or female—must work. Turkmen women have always been viewed as an integral part of the family and tribal economy.

During the Soviet period, many Turkmen women—especially in the larger cities—entered the professional workforce. Soviet ideology advocated full employment rights for women, and discouraged Turkmen women from adopting the traditional role advocated by Islam. In the Turkmen Soviet Republic, women were represented in large numbers as health care workers (including physicians), educators, and employees in the service industry. Few women, however, held senior positions in the state-run enterprises, and even fewer advanced in the Communist Party hierarchy.

The Republic of Turkmenistan's 1992 constitution specifically declares that "men and women in Turkmenistan have equal rights," a position adopted by few other predominantly Muslim nations. Turkmen law provides women with the right of inheritance—also rare in traditional Islamic societies—and gives women the same marriage rights as men.

Traditional Turkmen culture has always placed a high value on the wisdom and experience of elders. No Turkmen would think of putting an elderly relative in a retirement home. In fact, the 1992 constitution states that "adult children shall be obligated to care for their parents."

Turkmen Cuisine

Turkmen cuisine reflects the nation's ancient heritage as nomadic herders. Meat dishes—made from beef, lamb, goat, and camel—are the mainstays of Turkmen cuisine. But Turkmen dishes also include grains (usually rice), beans, fruits, and dairy products. The most popular and characteristic Turkmen dish is called *plov*. It is made by frying cubes of meat (beef, lamb, goat, or camel) in a heavy pot filled with cottonseed oil, then adding carrots, onions, garlic, and perhaps other vegetables or dried fruits. When the meat and vegetables have become tender, rice and water are added. The finished dish is piled on a serving platter and eaten with flat bread called *churek*. *Plov* also can be made using only vegetables and dried fruits.

Other popular Turkmen dishes include *shashlyk* (meat kabobs), *kara-chorba* (meat soup with peppers), and *fitchi* (meat pies). Traditional non-meat dishes include herb and cheese-filled pastries, cornmeal pancakes, and porridges made with mung beans, cornmeal, and pumpkin. Camel's milk, camel's milk cream, and rich yogurt are three ingredients that are commonly used in preparing breakfast.

The most popular beverage in Turkmenistan is tea (called *chai* in Turkmen), and soft drinks are available in cities. Turkmen often gather at teahouses (known as *chaikhanas* in Turkmen) to talk and drink sweet tea. Coffee is available in hotels and some restaurants, but is too expensive for the average Turkmen. Alcoholic beverages are not forbidden in Turkmenistan, as in some Islamic countries. Turkmenistan produces wine made from grapes that grow in the foothills near Ashkhabad, but the most

In Islamic societies, serving *chai* (tea) is a sign of hospitality and friendship.

popular alcoholic beverage is vodka, which was first introduced by the Russians.

Turkmen normally eat at home. Vendors at open-air markets and street-corner stalls sell *shashlyk, fitchi,* and other foods, but most restaurants cater to foreign visitors. In the capital city of Ashkhabad, one can find restaurants serving Turkish food, Italian cuisine, pizzas, and hamburgers.

Education

One of the positive legacies of the Soviet era was the emphasis that communist leaders placed on education. At the time of independence, the literacy rate in Turkmenistan was nearly 100 percent, equivalent to that in the United States and other industrialized countries. By 1991, 65 percent of the Turkmen population aged 15 and older had completed secondary school, and 8 percent had graduated from a university or other institution of higher education. The content of the educational system during the Soviet era included Marxist ideology and propaganda, but there was also a heavy emphasis on mathematics and the sciences.

According to Turkmenistan's constitution, education is free and compulsory through the eighth grade. It is to be provided only by the state;

A group of students follow a lesson at a primary school in Ashkhabad. All children in Turkmenistan are required to go to school through the eighth grade.

religious schools are not permitted. After eighth grade, students take a comprehensive examination. Based on the results, they are directed to either secondary school or technical school, although some students terminate their education at this point and join the workforce.

After completing secondary school, students may continue their education at Turkmenistan State University in Ashkhabad, which was established in 1931; at the newer International Turkmen Turkish University, established by President Niyazov in 1994; or at one of several dozen specialty training institutions. Acceptance into one of the higher education institutions is difficult, and involves a comprehensive examination. Students who finish at the top of their classes at the universities may continue with graduate study, either at the university or at one of the Turkmen Academy of Sciences research institutes.

Turkmenistan has been in the process of reforming its educational system since achieving independence. Goals included removing much of the Soviet-era content, strengthening Turkmen identity among the country's youth, and ensuring that graduates are prepared to contribute to Turkmenistan's economic growth. One of the most important reforms was the introduction of the modified Roman script for the Turkmen language. English has been introduced as the second language, and the teaching of Russian is being phased out, although there is a dire shortage of English language teachers. Courses at universities—which until 1991 were taught in Russian—are now almost exclusively in Turkmen. The history of Turkmenistan is taught at all educational levels, and Turkmen culture and literature also have become part of the curriculum. *Rukhnama,* the book written by President Niyazov that aims to serve as a spiritual guide to the Turkmen people, is required reading for all Turkmen students.

Despite these efforts at reform, Turkmenistan's educational system faces severe challenges. Lack of adequate funding has led to a shortage of teachers, supplies, and equipment. Many schools, especially in rural areas, are in a state of disrepair. Schools in Ashkhabad are overcrowded, and students often must attend school in shifts. In an effort to remove foreign (especially Russian) influence, many non-Turkmen teachers have been removed from their jobs; however, they frequently have been the most qualified teachers. Many foreign observers of Turkmenistan's educational system have criticized the emphasis on teaching *Rukhnama* and argue that it as an effort to use education as a form of political **indoctrination**.

In another controversial move, President Niyazov decreed in June 2004 that all university degrees received outside the country since 1993 would be invalidated. This decree was intended to bolster the national university system, but it is expected to result in the dismissal of thousands of government workers and university teachers, who now will be deemed "unqualified" for their jobs because of their foreign degrees. Moreover, it places in question the future of the hundreds of Turkmen students who currently are studying at foreign schools and who had planned to return to their country.

Literature and the Arts

The written word is a relatively new development in the Turkmen language, and until the early 20th century Turkmen literature consisted primarily of poetry and epic stories—known as *dastans*—that were passed orally from generation to generation. *Dastans* are long and elaborate oral histories of a particular tribe or group, and usually entail descriptions of a hero's exploits. They are vital repositories of a tribe's history and culture.

Turkmen singers, called *bakhshi*, traveled from village to village and tribe to tribe reciting poetry and singing traditional songs, many of which were based on poems or *dastans*. Poetry was always considered the highest literary art form in Turkmen culture, and there have been many great Turkmen poets.

The most famous Turkmen poet was Fragi Makhtumkuli (1770–1840), who remains extremely popular as a symbol of Turkmen wisdom and philosophy. Some Turkmen claim that even today, Makhtumkuli's poetry is more widely read and better known than the Qur'an. His life was tragic—his marriage was an unhappy one, and his two sons died of illness at an early age—but his poetry is uplifting and hopeful.

Makhtumkuli was educated at a religious school and mastered Arabic and Persian, although his poems were all in Turkmen. He was strongly influenced by Sufis, and their mystical vision found its way into his poetry. One of his major themes is the importance of living an ethical and charitable life. In one of his poems, he wrote that giving food to a hungry person is the equivalent in God's eyes to making a pilgrimage to Mecca. Makhtumkuli also expressed his passionate desire for unity among the Turkic tribes—in many ways, he was the first to envision a unified Turkmenistan. In his poem "Exhortation in the Time of Trouble," he wrote:

> If Turkmens would only tighten the Belt of Determination
> They could drink the Red Sea in their strength,
> So let the tribes of Teke, Yomut, Goklen, Yazir, and Alili
> Unite into one proud nation.

Makhtumkuli wrote in a style that was understandable to the average person, and his pride in his Turkmen identity has helped to make him one of Turkmenistan's true national heroes. Many buildings, roads, and institutes in the country are named after him.

Turkmen music is closely connected to the nation's poetry, as many songs were based on well-known poems. The *bakhshi* who performed in villages usually accompanied themselves on the dutar, a two-stringed lute that remains the most popular musical instrument in Turkmenistan. Two other instruments commonly used in Turkmen music are the *duduk*, a long, narrow flute; and the *gidzhak*, a three- or four-stringed bowed instrument.

During the period of Russian and Soviet control, Turkmen were introduced to new musical forms, such as opera, ballet, and symphony orchestras. Today, Turkmenistan still has an active symphony orchestra, as well as opera and ballet companies. But since independence, there has been a renewed focus on traditional Turkmen music and instruments. At the Turkmen National Conservatory in Ashkhabad, students learn to perform the native music of Turkmenistan using traditional instruments.

Turkmen Carpets

When the great Italian explorer Marco Polo traveled across the Turkmenistan region on his way to China in the 13th century, he wrote in his diary, "The finest and most beautiful carpets in the world are woven here." Many people today still share Marco Polo's opinion, and carpet making remains the greatest art of the Turkmen people. It is also an ancient art form: archeologists have found evidence of carpet making in Turkmenistan from as early as the sixth century B.C.

Turkmen carpets can range in size from small prayer rugs that can be rolled up and carried under your arm (used by Muslims for their daily prayers) to huge room-sized carpets. The beauty of Turkmen carpets is in their complicated design patterns and rich colors. Each Turkmen tribe has a unique centuries-old design style or emblem used in its rugs, and carpet experts can recognize immediately the tribal affiliation of a particular rug's maker. There are five traditional geometric design styles in Turkmen carpets, each of which is depicted today on the national flag of Turkmenistan. No two Turkmen rugs are alike, and carpet making allows for individual creativity and artistic expression, an idea articulated in one popular Turkmen saying: "Roll out your carpet and we'll see what there is in your heart." Turkmen believe that a carpet conveys the weaver's dreams, hopes, joys, and sorrows.

Traditional Turkmen carpets are made from the wool of shargin sheep—a breed that is unique to Turkmenistan—which is especially soft and smooth to the touch. The rugs are colored using natural dyes made from plants, tree bark, and minerals. The principal color in most Turkmen carpets is red, ranging from bright cherry to dark burgundy. Yellow, green, and blue are used to frame and accent the rich red background.

For Turkmen nomads, carpets not only were a source of beauty and a means of artistic expression. They also served very important functions.

Turkmen craftsmen are famed for the beauty of their carpets. They are woven by hand, so a large carpet can take several years to finish. Here, a woman looks at examples in a bazaar.

Carpets made up the walls and floors of nomadic tents (known as yurts), protecting the inhabitants from the cold. Saddlebags carried valuables during long desert treks, and every Muslim Turkman carried a prayer rug on which he could comfortably kneel for his daily prayers. In the 19th century, Europeans discovered the beauty of Turkmen carpets, and they quickly became valuable collector items among wealthy Europeans.

Carpets traditionally have been woven by Turkmen women, and in rural areas of Turkmenistan today young girls still are taught from an early age how to weave and operate a loom, a skill that has been passed down from generation to generation for centuries. The Turkmen government also has established 15 carpet factories, where nearly 10,000 Turkmen work to produce their traditional carpets for the world market. In 1993, Turkmenistan opened the Turkmen National Carpet Museum in Ashkhabad, containing the largest collection of antique Turkmen textiles in the world. More than a thousand 18th- and 19th-century carpets are displayed, as well as the largest wool carpet in the world. According to the Guinness Book of World Records, this carpet, which was woven in 2001, covers over 3,229 square feet (300 square meters) and weighs 1.5 tons.

Entertainment

Life is hard in Turkmenistan, especially in rural areas, and there are limited options for entertainment. Because family and clan play such an important role, family members spend most of their leisure time with each other. Meals, particularly during holidays, are an important occasion for gathering. Music also plays an important role in Turkmen life, and village singers are popular forms of entertainment.

Cities such as Ashkhabad have bars and discos, the nicest ones located in the big hotels that cater mostly to foreigners. Horse racing is a popular sport, and there is racecourse outside of Ashkhabad. Soccer is also

Members of Turkmenistan's national soccer team, wearing green shirts, fight for the ball during a game against Saudi Arabia. Soccer is a popular sport in the country.

popular. Turkmenistan's national soccer team was formed in 1994 (before then, Turkmen players had to compete for positions on the Soviet Union's national team), and already has seen success in tournaments with other Asian teams.

Holidays and Celebrations

The biggest holiday celebration in Turkmenistan is Nowruz (New Day). Nowruz began as a pre-Islamic Persian holiday and is also celebrated today in neighboring Iran. It takes place in the spring around the time of the vernal equinox; at its roots it is a celebration to welcome the coming of spring, an important event in largely agricultural societies. Turkmen celebrate Nowruz with games, street fairs, music, and drama performances. Families gather for feasts and other holiday celebrations.

The most important Islamic month is Ramadan, the traditional annual period of fasting. During Ramadan, Muslims refrain from eating, drinking, or smoking during daylight hours. The purpose for this fast is to cleanse the body and soul, and to create empathy with those who are less fortunate. (Pregnant women, the sick, and the elderly are exempt from fasting.) Once the sun goes down, however, people are free to eat and drink again, and families gather to pray and celebrate their successful completion of a day of fasting. The last day of Ramadan is a major holiday in itself. Known as Eid al-Fitr (Festival of Breaking the Fast), it is celebrated with great feasts and boisterous parties to culminate Islam's most sacred month.

Because the Islamic calendar is lunar-based, Ramadan varies from year to year. Ramadan is not strictly enforced in Turkmenistan as it is in more rigid Muslim societies such as Iran and Saudi Arabia. For Turkmen, fasting is a personal choice. Another important Muslim holiday is Eid al-Adha (Feast of the Sacrifice), which commemorates a story told in the Qur'an about the Patriarch Abraham's willingness to obey Allah's demand that he sacrifice his son. When God saw that Abraham would obey him, he relented and told Abraham to sacrifice a sheep instead. On this holiday, Muslims traditionally slaughter a lamb or sheep and share it with their neighbors. As with Ramadan, the date of the Eid al-Adha varies from year to year.

The Orthodox Christian community in Turkmenistan celebrates Christmas, Easter, All Saints' Day, and other traditional Christian holidays.

Among Turkmenistan's official public holidays are President Niyazov's Birthday (February 18); Constitution Day (May 18); the commemoration of the 1948 earthquake (October 6); Independence Day (October 28); and Neutrality Day (December 12). Government offices are closed on these holidays, and those with a political or patriotic theme are marked by speeches and public ceremonies.

A young couple walks through a public square in Ashkhabad, the capital and largest city in Turkmenistan.

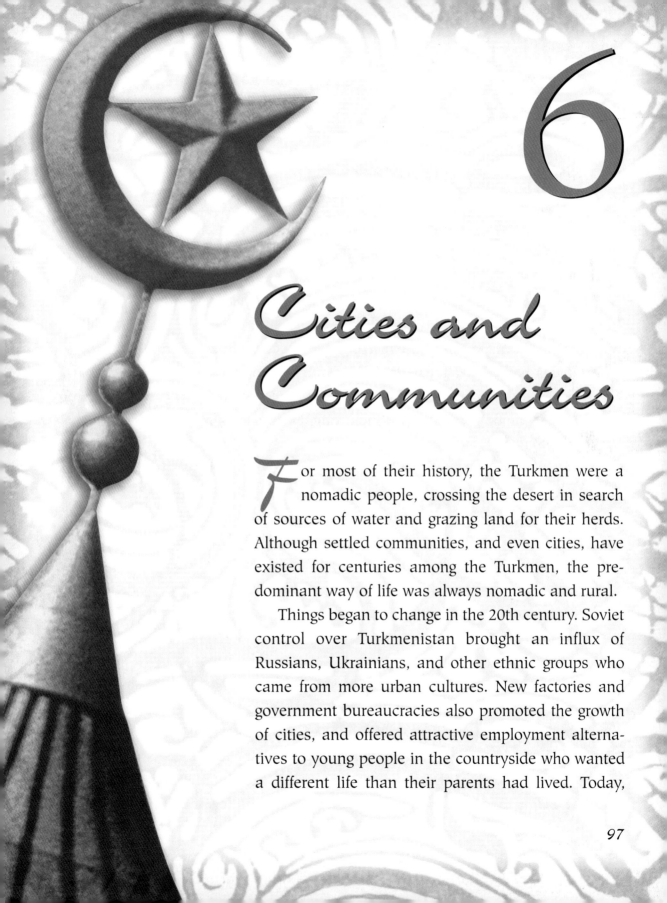

6

Cities and Communities

For most of their history, the Turkmen were a nomadic people, crossing the desert in search of sources of water and grazing land for their herds. Although settled communities, and even cities, have existed for centuries among the Turkmen, the predominant way of life was always nomadic and rural.

Things began to change in the 20th century. Soviet control over Turkmenistan brought an influx of Russians, Ukrainians, and other ethnic groups who came from more urban cultures. New factories and government bureaucracies also promoted the growth of cities, and offered attractive employment alternatives to young people in the countryside who wanted a different life than their parents had lived. Today, around 45 percent of Turkmenistan's people live in cities, and the numbers are growing. Experts estimate that by 2015, half of the country's population will be urban.

Ashkhabad

Ashkhabad is Turkmenistan's capital and largest city, with an estimated population of around 773,000 in 2004. Ashkhabad, which sits at the foot of the Kopet-Dag Mountains and at the edge of the Kara-Kum Desert, has been the location of settlements and villages for centuries. The city itself, however, was not established until 1881, when the Russians built a fort on the site, around which a town quickly grew up. In 1918, Soviet forces named the town Poltoratsk, after a Communist Party official. In 1927, after the creation of the Turkmen Soviet Socialist Republic, the city was renamed Ashkhabad, which roughly translates as "the city that was built by love."

Ashkhabad grew rapidly during the 1920s and 1930s as the Soviets established factories in the area. But in 1948, Ashkhabad suffered a massive earthquake that destroyed virtually every structure in the city and killed thousands of its residents (including President Niyazov's mother). The city was rebuilt with wide streets and buildings made of reinforced concrete to better withstand earthquakes. The completion of the Kara-Kum Canal in 1962 further contributed to the city's rebirth by providing desperately needed water.

Ashkhabad is not only the political capital of Turkmenistan. It also is the economic, cultural, and educational center of the country. Among the many factories located in the metropolitan area are those making oil drilling equipment, glass, and processed foods, as well as cotton spinning mills, silk factories, and the famous carpet-making factories. Ashkhabad is home to Turkmenistan State University, the International Turkmen Turkish University, and the Turkmen Academy of Sciences. Other cultural

Fountains surround a horse sculpture in Ashkhabad. The horse holds a special place in Turkmen culture.

and educational institutions located in Ashkhabad include the State Academy of Arts, the Institute of National Economy, the Institute of World Languages, the State Medical Institute, and the Turkmen National Conservatory of Music. The city boasts several theaters, opera and ballet companies, a symphony orchestra, and a number of museums. Since independence, Turkmenistan's cultural institutions have all focused more on preserving and promoting traditional Turkmen culture.

Very few buildings in Ashkhabad are more than 50 years old (only a handful of structures survived the 1948 earthquake), and the city has seen considerable new construction since 1991. As a result, it does not have the charm of many other Central Asian cities that boast centuries-old palaces and buildings. At first view, Ashkhabad appears to be a city of dull apartment blocks and huge government buildings. But the city also has wide, tree-lined streets, and is very orderly and clean. The center of Ashkhabad is considered to be the large Arch of Neutrality, a huge sculpture commemorating Turkmenistan's declared position of neutrality in world affairs. Nearby are the Presidential Palace, the Majlis building, and a monument to the people who died in the 1948 earthquake.

Kutluk Timur, the tallest minaret in Central Asia, reaches into the sky above Kunya Urgench. This city was once an important trade center.

Ashkhabad also has many green parks. The most famous one features a large statue of the great Turkmen poet Makhtumkuli. Every spring, Turkmen poets and writers gather in this park to recite poetry and celebrate the people's literary heritage. Ashkhabad's excellent carpet museum and history museum are fascinating repositories of Turkmen culture and important tourist attractions. In recent years, over a dozen modern hotels have been built in Ashkhabad to cater to the many foreign businesspeople and visitors who have come to Turkmenistan since 1991.

Every Sunday, Ashkhabad is the scene of one of Central Asia's most colorful and fascinating traditions: the Tolkuchka market. Hundreds of people gather on the outskirts of Ashkhabad to sell everything from camels and sheep to videocassettes and motorcycles. Vendors sell *shashlyk*, fresh fruit, and cold drinks, and musicians perform traditional Turkmen music. Inside a large walled and covered enclosure, hundreds of merchants sell silk cloth, traditional wool hats, and the world-renowned Turkmen carpets. Buyers from throughout the world haggle with the carpet merchants, trying to get the best deals on both new and antique rugs.

Ashkhabad can get extremely hot and dusty in the summer months. For a break from the heat, many residents head to the Firuza Gorge, a cool valley that meanders through the foothills of the nearby Kopet-Dag Mountains.

Turkmenabat

With 242,000 inhabitants in 2004, Turkmenabat is Turkmenistan's second-largest city. Prior to independence, it was known as Chardzhou or Charjew (some still use this name today). Turkmenabat is located along the banks of the Amu Dar'ya in the north of the country, close to the border with Uzbekistan. Like Ashkhabad, it is a relatively young city, founded in 1886 during the construction of the Transcaspian Railroad. This rail line runs through Turkmenabat on its way from the Caspian Sea to Tashkent, Uzbekistan. The city always has been an important market town for farmers, who work in the heavily agricultural outlying region. Turkmenabat also has some factories, mostly producing cotton and silk textiles.

Dashhowuz

The third-largest city in Turkmenistan, Dashhowuz (population 163,000 in 2004), was known by its Russian name—Tashauz—until 1992. Dashhowuz was founded in the late 19th century on an oasis at the far northern reaches of the Kara-Kum Desert, near what is today the border with Uzbekistan. It serves as the administrative center of the province that bears its name; a railroad hub for trains going to Uzbekistan and Russia;

and an important market town for local cotton farms. The city also has a few textile mills and food factories.

Mary

Turkmenistan's fourth-largest city, Mary, is perhaps its most fascinating. The modern city (population 129,000 in 2004), located on an oasis at the southern edges of the Kara-Kum Desert along the banks of the Murgab River, was founded in 1887. It is an important commercial center and market town for a region that produces cotton and grains, and contains leather-tanning factories as well as food and textile factories. Several large natural gas wells are located in the nearby desert. Mary's grand bazaar, a large domed structure along the banks of the river, rivals the Tolkuchka market in Ashkhabad.

But what makes Mary particularly fascinating is its ancient roots. About 18 miles (30 km) from Mary lay the ruins of the ancient city of Merv (until 1937, the city was known by this original name). As a trading center on the Silk Road, Merv was one of the most important cities of Central Asia. It was founded in the sixth century B.C. by Cyrus the Great, and was controlled at various times by Persians, Greeks, Arabs, and Mongols, among others. In the late 10th century through the 12th century, Merv was capital of the Seljuk Empire.

In 1992, the newly independent government of Turkmenistan launched the International Merv Project, in collaboration with London's famed British Museum, to conduct extensive excavations of ancient Merv. Earlier excavations had been conducted by Soviet archaeologists. The excavations have uncovered ancient walls, ramparts, fortifications, a mausoleum, and a *citadel*. Some of these structures date back to the Sassanian period. There also is archaeological evidence of the devastating destruction of Merv and the massacre of its citizens by the Mongols in 1221.

Turkmenbashi

Turkmenbashi was called Krasnovodsk by the Russians, but was renamed in honor of President Niyazov. It was founded on the shores of the Caspian Sea in 1869 by Russians, and was the Russian Empire's first outpost in Turkmenistan. With the construction of the Transcaspian Railroad in the 1880s, it became the sole port city for all of Central Asia. Cotton and other goods were shipped to Turkmenbashi where they were then shipped across the Caspian to European Russia.

Following World War II, the Soviet Union started building factories in Central Asia to replace those in Russia and the Ukraine that were destroyed by the Germans. Because Turkmenistan had a port, Soviet planners made it an important industrial center. After the discovery of oil and natural gas in Turkmenistan, the city became the terminus for pipelines, further adding to its importance.

Today, Turkmenbashi is a city of 73,000, and remains a vital port and industrial center. It also is one of the most ***cosmopolitan*** cities in Turkmenistan. City leaders claim that over 60 nationalities are represented among the population.

Iranian and Turkmen laborers work on the "dam of friendship," a joint project between the two countries in northeast Iran. At a ceremony in April 2004 to dedicate the dam, Iran's foreign minister noted that it was a symbol of the strong relationship between Iran and Turkmenistan.

7

Foreign Relations

*T*urkmenistan's foreign policy is determined by its history, its geographic location, and its economic development objectives. For nearly a century, Turkmenistan's foreign policy was made in Moscow—first by the Russian Empire and then by the Soviet Union. Along with offering economic resources, Turkmenistan and the other Central Asian republics were important to Moscow as buffers between Russia and South Asia. The Soviet Union built a number of military bases in Turkmenistan and stationed thousands of troops there. The Turkmen themselves had virtually no influence over the Soviet Union's foreign policy or how their republic was used to advance Soviet interests.

At the same time, being part of the Soviet Union offered Turkmenistan a considerable amount of protection against outside attack or interference. While life was difficult and oppressive under Soviet rule, at least Turkmenistan did not have to worry about defending its borders, protecting its resources, or negotiating treaties and trade agreements. With independence, however, Turkmenistan's new leaders found themselves in the unfamiliar position of having to formulate foreign policy objectives, create an army and border security forces, and train and deploy diplomats. Moreover, Russia—formerly the guarantor of Turkmenistan's defense—now was at odds with the former republic on a number of issues. And neighboring Central Asian republics—also now independent for the first time—were in the process of determining their own foreign policy goals, some of which conflicted with Turkmenistan's interests. Even more troubling was the fact that some of Turkmenistan's neighbors, such as Afghanistan and Tajikistan, descended into civil wars fueled in large part by Islamic radicals.

Independence also posed a new challenge for Turkmenistan's international economic relationships. When it was part of the Soviet Union, Turkmenistan shipped its oil and gas resources to other Soviet republics via Russia. In exchange, Turkmen received consumer goods, food items, and other goods produced in other parts of the Soviet Union. It was, in effect, a barter relationship between Turkmenistan and the rest of the Soviet Union in which Turkmenistan did not reap the full benefits of its valuable natural resources. With independence, however, Turkmenistan's leaders now were free to participate in the international economic system. But they quickly discovered that this new freedom posed many challenges, including how to maintain relationships with such divergent powers as Russia and Iran, and—most critically—how to transport the country's oil and gas to lucrative markets such as Western Europe and the Far East. Some experts argue that access to foreign markets is the single most important objective of Turkmenistan's foreign policy.

"Positive Neutrality"

Soon after Turkmenistan achieved independence, President Niyazov sought to address foreign policy challenges by declaring that the country's international strategy would be based on "positive neutrality" and "open doors." Positive neutrality meant that Turkmenistan would work to ensure international recognition of its independence and sovereignty, mutual non-interference among its neighbors in domestic affairs, and neutrality in external conflicts. In other words, Turkmenistan pledged to not take sides in conflicts beyond its borders. The open doors policy meant that Turkmenistan would welcome foreign investment and export trade with the world—something that was not allowed when Turkmenistan was part of the Soviet Union. In 1992, Turkmenistan joined the United Nations, and in December 1995, at Turkmenistan's request, the UN General Assembly adopted a resolution officially recognizing the country's neutrality.

Turkmenistan takes its positive neutrality policy very seriously. It is even expressed in a verse of the country's national anthem:

> My land is sacred. My flag flies in the world
> A symbol of the great neutral country

Relations with Russia and Other Former Soviet Republics

Turkmenistan's most important foreign relations are with Russia and the other former Soviet republics of Central Asia. Most of Turkmenistan's energy resources are exported via Russia, and Russia remains a source of many Turkmen imports. The two countries have signed military cooperation agreements and numerous trade and economic agreements, but disputes have arisen over how much Russia should charge in exchange for transshipment of Turkmen oil and gas to Western Europe. There is also tension over President Niyazov's efforts to reduce the Russian presence and influence in Turkmenistan. In the spring of 2004, Turkmenistan expelled a number of Russians and passed a law forbidding dual citizenship, which meant that Russians in Turkmenistan now could no longer hold citizenship in both countries. Many Russians left the country in response, and some of those who remained appealed to Russian leaders for protection.

Nevertheless, both countries continue to try to forge a positive economic and political relationship. The 2000 election of President Vladimir Putin of Russia marked a new phase in Turkmen-Russian relations. Putin came to power vowing to reestablish political stability in Russia and restore Russian influence in those areas of the world—such as Central Asia—where Moscow had formerly been dominant. On a visit to Ashkhabad in May 2000, Putin expressed interest in signing a long-term deal to buy Turkmen oil and gas. When President Niyazov reciprocated with a visit to Moscow in January 2002, Putin proposed that the gas-producing countries of Eurasia—Russia, Turkmenistan, Uzbekistan, and Kazakhstan—form a joint organization to control gas exports and prices. Putin's success in stabilizing Russia after years of political anarchy makes its relations with Turkmenistan even more critical.

Turkmenistan's relations with the other newly independent republics got off to a rocky start. From February through September 1992, Turkmenistan and Ukraine engaged in a price war over the transport of Turkmenistan's natural gas through Ukraine. At one point in the dispute, Ukraine withheld badly needed food shipments to Turkmenistan, and refused to transship 500 tons of Turkmen cotton to Turkey. These incidents—along with disagreements with Russia—have prompted Turkmenistan to seek new routes for exporting its resources.

So far, little progress has been made on this front, but the government of Turkmenistan continues to conduct discussions with Iran, Afghanistan, and Pakistan about possible pipeline projects. One ambitious, though still

Niyazov chats with Russian President Vladimir Putin (right) during a meeting in Moscow. Turkmenistan has maintained close ties with Russia, although there have been disputes over control of oil reserves and the status of ethnic Russians within Turkmenistan.

unrealized project—known as the Transcaspian Pipeline—would ship Turkmen oil and gas under the Caspian Sea to Turkey, and from there it could be shipped to Western Europe.

Turkmenistan-Uzbekistan relations have also been difficult at times. Initially, the problems were over border disputes and ethnic minorities.

When the Soviet Union divided the region into separate Soviet republics, the borders were drawn arbitrarily and with little regard for historic relationships and demography. As a result, about 250,000 Uzbeks live in Turkmenistan, and 800,000 Turkmen live in Uzbekistan. Each country is concerned about how members of its native ethnic group are treated in the other country.

After a failed assassination attempt against President Niyazov in November 2002, Turkmenistan accused Uzbek authorities of coordinating with Turkmen opposition groups and even supporting the assassination attempt. Uzbekistan's ambassador in Ashkhabad was forced to return home. But by 2004 the two countries had at least temporarily patched up their differences and were once again on friendly terms.

Relations with the United States

The United States recognized Turkmenistan's independence in February 1992. Contacts between the two nations were limited initially, but in 1993 the U.S. Congress granted Turkmenistan Most Favored Nation (MFN) trade status, an important step in expanding bilateral trade. Turkmenistan became an important partner in the U.S. Caspian Basin Energy Initiative, which sought to facilitate negotiations between private energy companies and the governments of Turkmenistan, Georgia, Azerbaijan, and Turkey to build a pipeline under the Caspian Sea and export gas from Turkmenistan to Turkey and beyond. But because of numerous disagreements among the potential partners, as well as financing problems, this project remains uncompleted.

The U.S. government, through its Agency for International Development (USAID), has provided modest economic assistance to Turkmenistan. USAID wishes to fund projects that promote economic reform in Turkmenistan, but has been rebuffed by the government. Indeed, the United States and Turkmenistan strongly disagree about the need for economic reform. The United States has publicly called for more privatization of industry, market liberalization, and fiscal reform, as well as legal and regulatory reforms that would make Turkmenistan more attractive to foreign investors. In response to Turkmenistan's refusal to consider these kinds of reforms, the U.S. government has only given modest assistance: in 2004, USAID funded $8 million for projects in Turkmenistan, primarily in the areas of human development, English language training, and professional exchange programs.

In 2002, the U.S. Peace Corps reestablished a presence in Turkmenistan. The Peace Corps, founded by former president John F. Kennedy in 1961, sends American volunteers to developing countries to offer job training and assistance. Over 50 Peace Corps volunteers in Turkmenistan teach English to Turkmen students and help provide community health care in rural areas. Perhaps more importantly, they foster feelings of goodwill toward the United States.

The United States has been a frequent critic of Turkmenistan's government over issues related to human rights, civil liberties, and political reform. In recent years, the U.S. government's annual Human Rights Report, published by the State Department, has increased its criticism of Turkmenistan and the government of President Niyazov. The 2004 report described Turkmenistan's human rights record as "poor." U.S. officials were especially critical of the repressive measures the Turkmen government took in response to the November 2002 assassination attempt against President Niyazov.

On fundamental security issues, however, the United States and Turkmenistan are in agreement. President Niyazov condemned the September 2001 terrorist attacks against the United States, and pledged his support in the war against international terrorist groups. During the U.S.-led war against Afghanistan's pro-terrorist Taliban government, Turkmenistan allowed U.S. military planes to fly over its territory and let

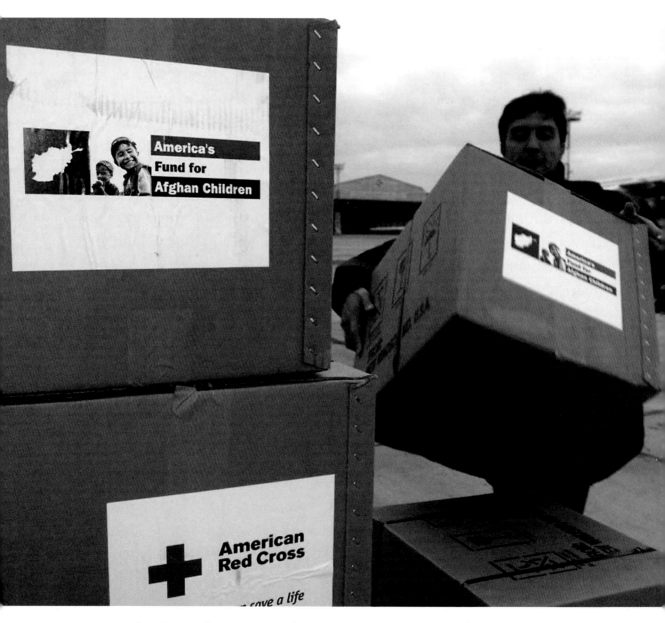

A worker in Turkmenistan piles boxes containing aid for Afghan children. The United States does not have a particularly close relationship with Turkmenistan, mainly because it has been critical of human-rights abuses by the Niyazov government. However, Turkmenistan has assisted the U.S. war against terrorists in Central Asia, and allowed humanitarian aid to pass through to Afghanistan after the U.S. invasion of that country in the fall of 2001.

humanitarian operations pass through the country. The United States provided security assistance to help secure Turkmenistan's border with Afghanistan.

While these steps were a departure from Turkmenistan's neutrality policy, President Niyazov was aware of how serious the war against terrorism was to the United States, and he shared U.S. concerns about Islamic radicalism in Afghanistan. In 2002, U.S. Secretary of Defense Donald Rumsfeld visited Turkmenistan and publicly thanked President Niyazov for his assistance in the war against terrorism. In 2004, Niyazov approved Turkmenistan's participation in a partnership program with the U.S.-led North Atlantic Treaty Organization (NATO). This plan focuses on building greater defense and political cooperation between NATO states and states of the former Soviet Union. Turkmenistan took this step in part to balance Russia's renewed ambitions for influence in Central Asia.

Relations with Iran and the Islamic World

Next to Russia and other former Soviet republics, Iran is Turkmenistan's most important foreign policy priority. This is not surprising in light of the centuries of interaction between Turkmen and Persians and the long border that the two countries share. Turkmenistan has established a generally close and friendly relationship with Iran, based primarily on joint economic cooperation but also on dozens of agreements pertaining to border security, transportation issues, and cultural exchange. In January 1994, President Niyazov traveled to Tehran, one of his first official visits to a foreign country as president. Later in 1994, the two countries reached bilateral agreements that sent Iranian specialists to Turkmenistan to aid in several projects: renovating the Turkmenbashi Oil Refinery and the Mary Cotton Processing Plant; building a gas pipeline through Iran and Europe; and constructing three major highways. In 1996, President Niyazov signed additional agreements with Iran that

Iranian President Mohammad Khatami (right) exchanges documents with Niyazov during a meeting over Caspian Sea oil. Since becoming independent, Turkmenistan and Iran have collaborated on numerous economic and security projects.

linked the two countries' electric power grids and laid out plans for construction of a jointly operated dam.

For Turkmenistan, Iran is not only a powerful neighbor with which it has a long history. It also represents the most promising conduit for Turkmen oil and gas exports that avoids Russia. In January 2004, President Niyazov called for further efforts to establish pipeline routes through Iran for Turkmen oil and gas.

Despite the close interaction with Iran, Turkmenistan has been careful to ensure that the Islamic radicalism prevalent in Iran does not reach over the border. The chance of this happening is unlikely, given that a majority of the population in Iran belong to the Shia sect of Islam, while Turkmen are overwhelmingly members of the rival Sunni sect.

Turkmenistan has maintained close ties with Turkey, whose population also consists predominantly of Turkic peoples. Because the two countries are not immediate neighbors, their interaction is limited, though Turkish firms have been very active in constructing hotels, schools, and mosques in Turkmenistan. Several thousand Turkmen students attend universities in Turkey, and Turkish television is broadcast in Turkmenistan. Turkey has agreed to purchase oil and gas from Turkmenistan if and when a Transcaspian pipeline is completed.

Turkmenistan is one of the few Muslim-majority nations that has good relations with Israel. Israeli companies are establishing business in Turkmenistan and have taken part in some of the country's largest construction projects. Each country maintains a trade mission in the other's capital to help promote bilateral trade and investment. So far, Turkmenistan's relationship with Israel has not hindered ties with Iran, Saudi Arabia, and other Islamic countries that do not recognize Israel.

Chronology

6000 B.C.	The first settled communities are established in Turkmenistan.
Sixth century B.C.	Cyrus the Great, leader of the Persian Empire, conquers what is now Turkmenistan.
Fourth century B.C.	Alexander the Great of Macedonia conquers Turkmenistan.
Seventh century A.D.	Arab armies spread the Islamic religion into Central Asia, including Turkmenistan.
800s–900s	Nomadic Oghuz Turkic tribes migrate to Turkmenistan from the east.
ca. 1000	The Seljuk Empire is founded.
13th century	Mongol armies under Genghis Khan invade Turkmenistan.
15th–17th centuries	Persians put the southern region of Turkmenistan under their rule; the khanates of Khiva and Bukhara control the northern region.
Late 19th century	Most of present-day Turkmenistan is conquered by Russia.
1918–21	The Russian civil war is waged between Bolsheviks and republicans; Turkmen rebel against Russian rule.
1922	Turkmenistan becomes part of the Soviet Union.
1925	Turkmenistan becomes a Soviet republic.
1920s and 1930s	Soviet government carries out program of agricultural collectivization and takes measures to minimize the influence of Islam.
1954	Soviets construct Kara-Kum Canal, greatly expanding Turkmenistan's arable land area.
1950s and 1960s	Oil and natural gas are discovered in Turkmenistan and the Soviet Union constructs pipelines to transport it.

Chronology

1985	Saparmurat Niyazov becomes leader of the Turkmen Communist Party.
1990	The Turkmen Republic's legislature declares economic and political autonomy from the Soviet Union.
1991	After a public referendum, Niyazov declares Turkmenistan an independent country.
1992	Turkmenistan adopts a new constitution that establishes a strong presidency; Niyazov is elected president in direct popular vote.
1994	Referendum passes that cancels the 1998 presidential election and extends Niyazov's term until 2002.
1998	Turkmenistan opens a new natural gas pipeline to Iran.
1999	Parliament appoint Niyazov president for life.
2000	Niyazov announces that he will voluntarily step down by 2010.
2002	Niyazov survives assassination attempt; more than 40 opposition leaders are arrested in a crackdown against dissent.
2003	In August, a new law is adopted making the People's Council the supreme legislative body in Turkmenistan; Parliament passes law that forbids dual citizenship.
2004	A number of Russians lose citizenship and are expelled from the country; in June, all university degrees received outside the country since 1993 are invalidated.

aquifer—an underground source of water that can be tapped for wells.

appellate courts—courts that hear cases on appeal.

atheistic—not believing in God.

authoritarian—a form of government in which one or a few powerful leaders make all decisions for a society.

autonomy—freedom of action.

bishopric—in the Christian Church, an important city or region in which a bishop is resident.

caliph—the spiritual and political ruler of the Muslim world.

citadel—a fort or fortress.

consensual—mutual agreement by all parties involved.

cosmopolitan—worldly and sophisticated.

czar—the title used by the ruler of imperial Russia.

equidistant—equally far from two or more places.

homogeneous—of the same or a similar kind of nature.

inclusive—broad in orientation or scope.

indigenous—originating in an area or environment.

indoctrination—the instruction of students or others on a particular point of view or ideology.

irrigation—a system of supplying water to agricultural land that otherwise is dry.

itinerant—traveling from place to place to perform work.

Marxism—the philosophy entailing the economic and political theories of Karl Marx, who argued for a socialist and classless society.

monotheistic—belief in only one God.

nationalization—the process in which a government takes control of privately owned property or businesses.

nuclear families—family units composed of immediate family members (parents and children).

oasis (pl. oases)—spring-fed areas in the middle of a desert where water is plentiful and plant life grows.

Glossary

prehistoric—the time before recorded history.

privatization—the process in which state-owned enterprises are sold to private individuals or groups.

proselytize—to actively try and convert others to your religion or beliefs.

referendum—a political process in which a decision is made by direct vote of the people.

sovereignty—freedom from external control.

Sufis—followers of a mystical branch of Islam.

terminus—the end or final destination.

unicameral—a legislature that has only one elected body.

Bonavia, Judy, et al. *The Silk Road*. Sheung Wan, Hong Kong: Odyssey Publications, 2004.

Edgar, Adrienne Lynn. *Tribal Nation: The Making of Soviet Turkmenistan*. Princeton, N.J.: Princeton University Press, 2004.

Harvey, Janet. *Traditional Textiles of Central Asia*. New York: Thames and Hudson, 1996.

Kleveman, Lutz. *The New Great Game: Blood and Oil in Central Asia*. New York: Atlantic Monthly Press, 2003.

Maslow, Jonathan. *Sacred Horses: The Memoirs of a Turkmen Cowboy*. New York: Random House, 1994.

Roy, Olivier. *The New Central Asia: The Creation of Nations*. New York: New York University Press, 2000.

Soucek, Svat. *A History of Inner Asia*. New York: Cambridge University Press, 2000.

Sumner, Christina, with Heleanor Feltham. *Beyond the Silk Road: Arts of Central Asia*. Haymarket, Australia: Powerhouse Publishing, 1999.

Internet Resources

http://www.turkmens.com/Turkmenistan.html

This comprehensive site includes information and many pictures depicting the natural and cultural life of Turkmenistan.

http://www.ayan-travel.com

This is the Web site of a travel agent who specializes in Turkmenistan. It also contains excellent photographs and information.

http://www.turkmenistanembassy.org/

The Web site of the Embassy of Turkmenistan offers extensive and up-to-date information about the country.

http://www.usemb-ashgabat.usia.co.at/

The home page of the U.S. Embassy in Ashkhabad is a good resource for learning about U.S.-Turkmenistan relations.

http://www.eurasianet.org

Turkmenistan is one of several countries covered in this comprehensive site about Central Asia.

http://www.chaihana.com/

A site run by former Peace Corps volunteers in Turkmenistan, it has excellent firsthand accounts of living and working in Turkmenistan.

Numbers in **bold italic** refer to captions.

Index

Picture Credits

The **FOREIGN POLICY RESEARCH INSTITUTE (FPRI)** served as editorial consultants for the GROWTH AND INFLUENCE OF ISLAM IN THE NATIONS OF ASIA AND CENTRAL ASIA series. FPRI is one of the nation's oldest "think tanks." The Institute's Middle East Program focuses on Gulf security, monitors the Arab-Israeli peace process, and sponsors an annual conference for teachers on the Middle East, plus periodic briefings on key developments in the region.

Among the FPRI's trustees is a former Secretary of State and a former Secretary of the Navy (and among the FPRI's former trustees and interns, two current Undersecretaries of Defense), not to mention two university presidents emeritus, a foundation president, and several active or retired corporate CEOs.

The scholars of FPRI include a former aide to three U.S. Secretaries of State, a Pulitzer Prize–winning historian, a former president of Swarthmore College and a Bancroft Prize–winning historian, and two former staff members of the National Security Council. And the FPRI counts among its extended network of scholars—especially its Inter-University Study Groups—representatives of diverse disciplines, including political science, history, economics, law, management, religion, sociology, and psychology.

DR. HARVEY SICHERMAN is president and director of the Foreign Policy Research Institute in Philadelphia, Pennsylvania. He has extensive experience in writing, research, and analysis of U.S. foreign and national security policy, both in government and out. He served as Special Assistant to Secretary of State Alexander M. Haig Jr. and as a member of the Policy Planning Staff of Secretary of State James A. Baker III. Dr. Sicherman was also a consultant to Secretary of the Navy John F. Lehman Jr. (1982–1987) and Secretary of State George Shultz (1988).

A graduate of the University of Scranton (B.S., History, 1966), Dr. Sicherman earned his Ph.D. at the University of Pennsylvania (Political Science, 1971), where he received a Salvatori Fellowship. He is author or editor of numerous books and articles, including *America the Vulnerable: Our Military Problems and How to Fix Them* (FPRI, 2002) and *Palestinian Autonomy, Self-Government and Peace* (Westview Press, 1993). He edits *Peacefacts*, an FPRI bulletin that monitors the Arab-Israeli peace process.

WILLIAM MARK HABEEB is a professor and international affairs consultant in Washington, D.C. He specializes in Middle East politics and conflict resolution, and has written widely on such topics as international negotiation, the politics and culture of North African states, and the Arab-Israeli conflict. He received his Ph.D. in international relations from the Johns Hopkins University School of Advanced International Studies.